CAMPAIGN
AND
ELECTION
REFORM

A Reference Handbook

Other Titles in ABC-CLIO's
Contemporary
World Issues
Series

Books in the Contemporary World Issues series address vital issues in today's society such as terrorism, sexual harassment, homelessness, AIDS, gambling, animal rights, and air pollution. Written by professional writers, scholars, and nonacademic experts, these books are authoritative, clearly written, up-to-date, and objective. They provide a good starting point for research by high school and college students, scholars, and general readers as well as by legislators, businesspeople, activists, and others.

Each book, carefully organized and easy to use, contains an overview of the subject, a detailed chronology, biographical sketches, facts and data and/or documents and other primary-source material, a directory of organizations and agencies, annotated lists of print and nonprint resources, a glossary, and an index.

Readers of books in the Contemporary World Issues series will find the information they need in order to better understand the social, political, environmental, and economic issues facing the world today.

CAMPAIGN
AND
ELECTION
REFORM

A Reference Handbook

Glenn H. Utter
and
Ruth Ann Strickland

**CONTEMPORARY
WORLD ISSUES**

ABC-CLIO

Santa Barbara, California
Denver, Colorado
Oxford, England

Library of Congress Cataloging-in-Publication Data

Utter, Glenn H.
   Campaign and election reform : a reference handbook / Glenn H. Utter and Ruth Ann Strickland.
      p.   cm.—(Contemporary world issues)
   Includes bibliographical references and index.
   1. Elections—United States.   2. Election law—United States.
3. Electioneering—United States.   4. Campaign funds—United States.
5. Political participation—United States.   I. Strickland, Ruth
Ann.   II. Title.   III. Series.
JK1976.U88   1997
324.7'0973—dc21   97-37960
                                                               CIP

ISBN 0-87436-862-6

02   01   00   99   98   97   10   9   8   7   6   5   4   3   2   1

ABC-CLIO, Inc.
130 Cremona Drive, P.O. Box 1911
Santa Barbara, California 93116-1911

This book is printed on acid-free paper ∞.

Typesetting by Letra Libre

Manufactured in the United States of America

Contents

Preface

Citizens have often reacted with a certain level of cynicism to campaigns and elections. H. L. Mencken, the noted curmudgeon of U.S. journalism, once compared a national campaign to "the best circus ever heard of, with a mass baptism and a couple of hangings thrown in," an event better even than war. And George Bernard Shaw commented that an election is "a moral horror," a battle without blood, and a mud bath for all those involved in it. Despite such evaluations, voting has come to signify the very essence of democracy. This is true in part because the term "democracy" is now used primarily to refer to representative democracy.

When the United States first became a nation, many prominent Americans still regarded democracy with suspicion. Political parties, a major ingredient in the development of representative democracy, had not yet been invented. According to the newly adopted national constitution, U.S. senators were to be selected by state legislatures and the president was to be chosen by a group of individuals, called the electoral college, who were appointed by state legislatures. Only members of the House of Representatives were to be elected by the citizens, according to electoral rules determined by the respective states. From that inauspicious beginning, the history of campaigns and elections is an account of various reforms intended to provide for more honest and fair electoral procedures and to extend the right to vote. Various measures, such as the elimination of property qualifications for voting, granting women the right to vote, introducing the secret ballot, guaranteeing voting rights to minorities, and providing for the regulation of campaign practices, have significantly altered the campaign and election process.

At times "reforms," rather than expanding the franchise, established significant restrictions. Most obviously, the election laws introduced in southern states following Reconstruction severely limited the voting rights of minorities. Stringent registration requirements introduced in the late nineteenth century and intended to limit vote fraud undoubtedly discouraged many Americans from voting. Since passage of the Voting Rights Act in 1965 and the Federal Election Campaign Act in 1974, much greater attention has been given to facilitating voting. However, despite the many recent reforms, there has been a gradual decline in voter turnout over the last three decades. Troubled by this trend, reformers have recommended their favored explanations and solutions. For instance, in the early 1990s Frances Fox Piven and Richard Cloward campaigned vigorously for voter registration reform, claiming that overly strict registration laws prevented many Americans, especially the less well-to-do, from participating in the electoral process. They argued that the National Voter Registration Act, which went into effect in January 1995, would significantly increase voter participation. However, the disappointing turnout rate in the 1996 presidential election did not support their optimism.

Various measures, such as election-day registration, voting assistance for the disabled, and early voting, have contributed to a fairer campaign and election process but are responsible primarily for making the voting procedure more convenient for those who already are inclined to participate. Nearly 50 percent of eligible citizens remain aloof from electoral politics. In a continuing effort to deal with this situation, recent proposals call for an alteration in electoral mechanics. For instance, rather than employing the single-member district plurality system, some argue that a variation of proportional representation, such as cumulative voting, should be introduced. Such alternatives would give citizens a greater sense of the importance of their vote and would grant minority group members greater opportunity to be elected to office. However, a proportional system, which would also increase the influence of minor parties, has not gained much support from Democratic and Republican party leaders.

Campaign finance is one of the most difficult reform issues to resolve. Campaign finance laws so far have been ineffective in controlling the use of money in politics. While some point to the corrupting influence of money and the need for stricter regulations, others argue that the constitutional right to free speech includes the right to use one's resources freely to affect the political process. In contrast to proposals further limiting the amount individuals may contribute to political campaigns, some recommend that limits on donations and spending should be greatly eased or even eliminated and that at the same time strong disclosure legislation should be enacted that would allow citizens to gain information about the sources of candidates' campaign funding.

Clearly, reform proposals are generally guided by considerations of political advantage. The rules and regulations governing campaigns and elections are seldom neutral. Whether intentionally or not, they almost inevitably advantage some political interests and disadvantage others. However, while admitting that political reform is itself a part of the political process, we believe that any treatment of campaign and election reform must be guided ultimately by considerations of fairness and a clear understanding of democratic principles.

Many people contributed to the various phases of this project. We wish to thank James Vanderleeuw, who made significant contributions to the early stages. We also wish to thank those who provided valuable information and advice. They include Douglas Amy, Kathleen Barber, Richard Cloward, Chandler Davidson, Richard Engstrom, Stanley Halpin, Omar Jabara, Laughlin McDonald, Mark Petracca, Richard Pildes, Frances Fox Piven, and Edward Still. While acknowledging their assistance, the authors take final responsibility for any errors.

Introduction

Throughout the history of the United States many changes in the electoral system have been classified as campaign and election reforms. However, what represents reform to one person amounts to antidemocratic reaction to someone else, and what some consider an advancement in the right to vote, others believe only provides greater opportunities for fraud. Just what constitutes reform? The term might qualify as an essentially contested concept, for there has often been fundamental disagreement over the reform status of specific measures. For instance, the introduction of voter registration undoubtedly decreased the amount of vote fraud, but it also discouraged many eligible Americans from voting. We will touch on many changes that could be termed reforms from at least some ideological perspective. Among such changes we include measures that extend the right to vote, enhance the integrity of the electoral process by limiting the opportunity for fraud, increase the convenience of registration and voting procedures for the average voter, improve the efficient operation of the election system, help ensure that elections reflect the choices of the electorate, and eliminate biases in favor of or against specific individuals or groups. We will touch on many changes, both large and small, that have been proposed or instituted since the early years of the nation.

Suffrage Expansion

The most basic reform involves the expansion of the right to vote. The history of voting in the United States is a history of suffrage expansion. When delegates from 12 of the 13 states met in Philadelphia in the summer of 1787 to write a new constitution, voting rights in the states generally were restricted to white males who owned property. The new constitution said little about voting other than providing for the popular election of members of the House of Representatives. Voting qualifications were left to the individual states because regulations varied widely among them and the delegates thought it prudent not to attempt a resolution of the differences.

In the first half of the nineteenth century property qualifications steadily disappeared in all of the states, except for certain elections dealing, for instance, with tax issues. Following the Civil War, ratification of the Thirteenth, Fourteenth, and Fifteenth Amendments constituted a constitutional revolution in which the federal government received significantly greater powers to ensure the rights of citizens in the several states. The Fifteenth Amendment specifically guaranteed the right to vote to former slaves. The national Constitution notwithstanding, southern states were able to deny voting rights to African Americans during the later years of the nineteenth century and the first decades of the twentieth by instituting what many southern whites considered voter registration "reforms." Such strategies as the literacy test, "good character" requirements that disfranchised those convicted of certain crimes, the grandfather clause that exempted many whites from voter registration requirements, and intimidation virtually eliminated minority voting in southern states.

At the same time black men were being denied the right to vote, women were crusading for the franchise. To a certain extent the women's rights movement in the United States grew out of the antislavery cause. Elizabeth Cady Stanton, the wife of an abolitionist leader, organized the first women's rights convention in Seneca Falls, New York, in 1848. During the Civil War Stanton and Susan B. Anthony established the Women's National Loyal League in order to lobby for what became the Thirteenth Amendment, which abolished slavery. Following the Civil War many in the women's rights movement expected that women would be granted the franchise along with black men. However, the more cautious supporters of black suffrage believed that combining their goal with the push for woman suffrage would jeopardize both causes. In 1869 rival woman suffrage organizations were established: the more radical National Woman Suffrage Association, based in New York, which called for immediate nationwide enfranchisement of women, and the more conservative American Woman Suffrage Association, headquartered in Boston, which was more willing to accept the precedence of black suffrage. The two organizations combined in 1890 to form the National American Woman Suffrage Association. The fight for woman suffrage continued for over 50 years before final victory was achieved in 1920 with ratification of the Nineteenth Amendment. There were successes along the way, especially in western states, but they were few as the frustrating struggle dragged on year after year. In 1904, two years before her death, Anthony made her final appearance before a Senate committee considering a woman suffrage amendment. She reminded the senators that she was the only surviving member of a group that 35 years before had appealed to Congress for the franchise.[1] The early advocates did not live to see the end result of their efforts, but they had prepared the way for a new generation that made the final push for woman suffrage.

The United States traveled a tortuous road of reform to remedy the injustices that denied the franchise to minorities. The white primary, which prohibited blacks from voting in the Democratic primary, was declared unconstitutional by the Supreme Court in 1944 (*Smith v. Allwright*). However, southern states resorted to other methods of discrimination to discourage minority voting. The Civil Rights Act of 1957, the first civil rights legislation since 1875, authorized the U.S. attorney general to file suits in federal district court to gain injunctions against violations of the Fifteenth Amendment.[2] This act failed to bring about significant reforms. The Attorney General's Office filed only four suits in the three years following the act's passage.[3] Attempting to remedy some of the weaknesses of the 1957 legislation, Congress passed another civil rights act in 1960. Although the new act authorized federal district court judges to appoint federal referees to replace state election officials and required local election administrators to store voting records for 22 months after an election, it ultimately had little more effect than its predecessor. By 1965 only 35.5 percent of eligible African Americans were registered to vote in the South, compared to 73.4 percent of eligible whites.[4] In 1964 Congress had passed a significant new civil rights act. Although it focused primarily on questions of public accommodation, school funding, and employment, one section placed limitations on the use of literacy tests.

This legislation was soon followed by the Voting Rights Act of 1965 (VRA). Section 2 reinforced the Fifteenth Amendment, prohibiting any voting qualifications, standards, or procedures that denied or abridged the right to vote because of race or color. The act bolstered the attorney general's suit-filing authority, but most important, it authorized the Justice Department to circumvent the judiciary in southern states to intervene in the interest of blacks who had been denied the right to vote. In certain jurisdictions, the literacy test was suspended for five years and voting regulations were to remain unaltered unless the attorney general or the District Court of the District of Columbia approved any application to change the voting system. The act provided for federal registration examiners and election observers to ensure that voting procedures would remain fair and nondiscriminatory. In just two years the proportion of eligible blacks registered to vote increased significantly, to over 52 percent. In no state targeted by the act were fewer than 50 percent of eligible blacks registered.[5] The VRA demonstrated how effective reform legislation can be in bringing about increased voter participation if it targets a specific problem.

The 1970 revisions to the legislation continued the strict provisions of the 1965 act. Literacy tests were suspended in all states for an additional five years. In 1975 Congress extended the act once more and expanded its provisions to cover language minorities. Election administrations were required to provide bilingual election materials if 5 percent of the jurisdiction's voting-age population constituted a single language minority and if the illiteracy rate in that group exceeded the national rate. Literacy tests were eliminated rather than simply suspended.

Since passage of the Voting Rights Act of 1965, which effectively ensured the right of minorities to register and vote, concern gradually shifted to questions of the effectiveness of the franchise. For instance, at-large elections came under attack for their tendency to deny minority candidates representation on governing bodies. Originally a progressive reform measure, at-large elections were geared to encourage participation in citywide policy concerns rather than parochial interests. But one result of such elections was the inability of minority groups to gain sufficient support citywide to elect favored candidates. After 1965 a number of dilution methods, such as the introduction of at-large elections and the annexation of areas with large white populations, were used to ensure majority white voting strength. Gerrymandered districts also guaranteed victories for white candidates.[6] The preclearance provisions of the VRA helped to stem the tide of proposals to alter voting systems. In *Allen v. State Board of Elections* (1969) the Supreme Court identified vote dilution as an unallowable limitation on the right to vote and hence subject to the preclearance provisions of the VRA. In addition, the "results test," added as part of the 1982 amendments to the VRA, stipulated that regardless of motivation, changes in election laws that cause dilution of minority vote strength are invalid.[7]

Electoral Mechanics

Although the number of minority elected officials in the South has increased dramatically in recent years—from less than 100 before passage of the VRA to over 3,000 by 1994[8]—many have contended that an even greater number of minority officials should be elected to public office. Representatives in the United States are generally elected through the single-member district plurality system, which is generally considered to favor the major parties and the dominant group in the community. One way of expanding minority representation is to construct districts that include sufficient minority residents to increase significantly the probability of electing minority candidates. The Justice Department's efforts to increase minority representation in Congress met a severe obstacle when the Supreme Court limited the ability of states to redistrict for this purpose. Remanding North Carolina's redistricting plan, which had created an oddly shaped congressional district, members of the Court in *Shaw v. Reno* expressed concern about the formation of districts that segregate, or "balkanize," citizens by race.

In order to obviate the problem of districts that have met with judicial disapproval, advocates of greater minority representation have suggested alternatives to the single-member district system. Cumulative voting is one such plan. Instead of voting for one candidate to fill a single legislative seat, citizens are responsible for electing several representatives. In a multimember district, each voter has as many votes as there are seats to be filled. If there are seven seats, the voter can cast all votes for one candidate, one each for seven candidates, or any other combination. A minority group may concentrate votes on one candidate in order to increase its chance of gaining representation. While this plan can be called semiproportional, many recommend the introduction of a more direct proportional representation (PR) system. In one version of PR, the list system, seats are allocated to political parties according to the proportion of popular votes they received. In another type of PR, preferential voting is employed. Assuming there are, for example, five seats to be filled and several more candidates than seats, each voter ranks his or her most preferred candidates from first to fifth choice. Any candidate receiving a certain minimum percentage of first-preference votes is declared a winner. If all seats are not filled after the first tally, the candidate with the fewest votes is eliminated and the second choices on those ballots are transferred to the remaining candidates. This procedure, called the single transferable vote, is continued until all seats are filled. Joseph Zimmerman suggests that if enough representatives are elected (at least five) in a multimember district, the single transferable vote can provide greater opportunities for women and minorities to gain office.[9]

These varied methods of electing representatives indicate how important electoral mechanics are to the outcome of elections. Alternatives to the single-member district system can achieve the same objectives as redrawing district lines to favor minority groups, a procedure the courts have found objectionable. However, although some states have experimented with these alternative voting systems and recently several local jurisdictions have introduced variants of these methods, the two major parties may find them far too threatening to the two-party system, for not only minority group members but also minority political parties could benefit from alternatives to the single-member district plurality system.

Term Limits

Another issue of electoral reform, term limits, has occupied the attention of many political activists in recent years. By 1996, 21 states had adopted some form of term limits for state legislators.[10] They vary from Maine's stringent requirement that incumbents step down three years after term limit adoption to the 12-year cap in Louisiana, Nevada, Oklahoma, and Utah.[11] The appeal of term limits results in part from the success that incumbents have experienced in gaining reelection and in part from the perception of a disaffected public that long-term politicians cannot be trusted. Although many Republicans have supported term limits, a Republican-controlled Congress since 1995 has failed so far to pass a term limit proposal. Although Congress has not acted, at least 15 states have approved initiatives to limit the length of service of their members of Congress. Some argue that such limits will not survive judicial scrutiny.[12] Prohibiting the names of incumbents from appearing on the ballot, as nine states now do, might be considered discrimination against a particular class of people—incumbent congressmen. Others contend that term limits, interpreted as an instrument for encouraging rotation in office rather than a qualification for public service, can meet constitutional requirements. According to Mark Petracca, rotation represents a fundamental part of republican government and the rights of citizenship.[13] On the other hand, opponents argue for prudence, claiming that a state with term limits imposed on its congressional delegation faces decreased political influence at the national level.[14] The entire nation might suffer from a constitutionally established national term limit provision because, as opponents of such a restriction argue, a less professional legislature translates into even greater dominance by professional staff and special interests.

Vote Fraud

In order for democratic elections to acquire sufficient legitimacy, voters must be assured that the electoral process has been justly administered and their votes honestly counted. Reformers have attempted to control vote fraud in its various forms. During the early years of the nation, voting was conducted simply by electors registering their preferences orally. Subsequently, political parties and candidates printed their own ballots, distinguishing them by color or special symbol. Voters were provided the ballot of the preferred party. Because voters could not prevent others from discovering how they voted, these systems often resulted in intimidation and violence. The introduction of the secret, or Australian, ballot (so called because it was used first in Australia before being adopted in the United States), eliminated much of the opportunity either to threaten or to promise rewards to voters.

Unscrupulous politicians introduced various vote fraud techniques, such as repeat voting and casting an already prepared ballot (called the Tasmanian dodge). Should the opportunity arise, corrupt election officials could deface ballots cast for opposition candidates, correct favorable but spoiled ballots, substitute premarked ballots, stuff ballot boxes with additional ballots, or simply misreport vote totals.[15] In order to discourage fraud, various actions are specifically prohibited under federal statute (18 U.S.C. 241 and 242), including preventing a qualified citizen from casting a ballot, stuffing ballot boxes, impersonating a qualified voter, altering ballots, registering voters illegally, fraudulently casting absentee ballots, and voting more than once in the same election.[16] Federal statutes forbid any act that can broadly be construed as vote buying, such as offering payment for voting or registering to vote. In 1980 the Election Crimes Branch (ECB) of the Public Integrity Section of the U.S. Department of Justice's Criminal Division was established.[17] The ECB focuses on prosecuting criminal violations of federal election law. Such criminal offenses include stuffing ballot boxes, intimidating voters, destroying ballots, falsifying voter registrations, impersonating voters, paying citizens to vote, and falsifying election returns. The ECB prosecutes some 150 criminal cases each year.[18]

Although some doubt the honesty of mechanical and electronic voting systems, the introduction of the voting machine represented a significant reform because the fraudulent practices associated with the printed ballot could be effectively controlled. The mechanical lever machine, which could count votes automatically, eliminated the need for individual paper ballots. In addition, election reform laws in the states that required at least one poll watcher from each of the major political parties certainly discouraged the more blatant forms of fraud.

The introduction of computer technology represented the opportunity to cast and count ballots even more quickly and accurately. Computer-tabulated voting in most cases requires the production of machine-readable ballots that allow officials to maintain a paper trail to document security at the various stages—from production and storage prior to use, to accounting for unvoted and spoiled ballots, and finally storage of voted ballots in anticipation of any challenge to the vote outcome.[19] By 1992 nearly two-thirds of the electorate cast ballots that were counted electronically.[20] Although many saw this innovation as a major improvement over previous procedures, others remained unconvinced that electronic counting represented progress; instead, they held that new systems provided opportunities for vote fraud on a grand scale. Questions have arisen about the potential for fraud in computer counting of ballots. Howard Strauss, a computer scientist at Princeton University, has been quoted as saying that computerized election security is "not a door without locks, it's a house without doors."[21] Some fear that a small group of individuals could gain, or already have gained, access to the computer programs employed to tally votes, manipulating the results for a favored candidate in a sufficiently large number of election jurisdictions to alter the election results. As computerized vote counting becomes more centralized, concerns continue to be raised about such possibilities as computer operator misconduct, remote entry into the computerized counting process, inputting of false data, sabotage for political reasons, and simple malicious mischief that could have dire consequences for the legitimacy of the election process.[22] William Kimberling has noted that traditional safeguards against fraud—the decentralization of election administration, the system of checks whereby the two major political parties monitor each other's electoral behavior, and public accountability made possible by a paper trail—are all weakened by the major advantage of computer systems: the achievement of a highly centralized procedure for the swift counting of large numbers of ballots.[23] Potentially even more controversial are direct recording electronic voting machines (DREs), which, because they record votes electronically, leave no paper trail at all. Though some believe that DREs resolve the problems of ballot accountability, others argue that they open new vistas for vote fraud.

James Condit, Jr., head of Cincinnatus News Service, claims that the computerized vote tallying of Voter News Service, located in New York City, may have denied Pat Buchanan a 1996 Arizona Republican primary victory. Condit points to other possible examples of vote fraud via computer high jinks and urges a return to the paper ballot that precinct workers count by hand after the polls close on election day.[24] But others emphasize that the traditional voting and counting procedure itself proved notoriously inaccurate and allowed many opportunities for fraud.

Poll workers, who often worked a 12-hour day, were expected to count quickly and accurately a large number of ballots by hand. Rather than returning to this system, reforms will probably focus on tightening computer security. Nonetheless, without some paper trail, election officials must find some valid way to assure voters that their ballots have been honestly recorded and counted. Otherwise questions can easily be raised about the honesty of elections.

The Electoral College

The electoral college has come under severe criticism and is a favorite focus for reform proposals. Critics argue that the system for electing the president represents an eighteenth-century device that fails to meet the needs of a modern governing system. During an era in which democratic principles prevail, the United States still allows the most powerful political official in the world to be selected via the creaking machinery of the electoral college. Not since 1804, when the Twelfth Amendment provided for separate ballots for president and vice president, has the presidential election system been formally modified, although informal modifications have occurred. The Constitution does not specify the way in which a state's electors shall be chosen, but by 1836 all states except one had adopted selection by popular vote. Although today 538 electors choose the president, these individuals are determined by the voters in each state who cast their ballots for presidential candidates. Each state has a number of electors equal to its representation in Congress (House and Senate). The winner-take-all tradition also developed, whereby all of a state's electoral votes go to the candidate winning the most popular votes. Today only two states—Maine and Nebraska—allow for electoral vote distribution according to popular vote distribution within the state.

Those advocating reform note that the electors chosen through popular vote have no constitutional obligation to cast their votes for the candidate they pledged themselves to support. Occasionally a "faithless" elector casts a vote for a candidate other than the one to whom he or she is pledged. This action could lead to a constitutional crisis if only a handful of electoral votes separate the two major candidates. In order to win the presidency, a candidate must receive a majority of the electoral votes.

Should no candidate receive a majority (a situation that could occur if more than two candidates receive electoral votes), then the House of Representatives is to select the next president from among the top three electoral vote recipients. However, in the House, each state may cast just one vote. Therefore states with small populations, such as Arizona, New Mexico, and Montana, would have as much say in the election of the president as do large states such as California, Texas, and New York. Such a system contradicts the fundamental democratic principle of one person, one vote, for a citizen in California would have a small fraction of the influence in the selection of the president that a resident of Arizona would have. Perhaps the most serious charge against the electoral college is that the popular vote winner might not win in the electoral college. The only undisputed example of this happening is the election of 1888, when Benjamin Harrison won a majority of the electoral college vote even though the incumbent, Grover Cleveland, received more popular votes. Those critical of the electoral college argue that the system has not changed in any way that would prevent such an event from occurring again. The minority candidate in the popular vote may be elected if he or she wins narrowly in large states but loses in smaller states by larger vote margins. Given the greater contemporary commitment to democracy, such an event would represent a significant threat to the legitimacy of the political process.

These and other criticisms of the electoral college have led to several reform proposals. To counter the faithless elector problem, an "automatic plan" could be established. Rather than choosing a group of individuals to elect the president, the popular vote in each state would be translated immediately into electoral votes. Another possible reform involves instituting the procedure used by Maine: Electoral votes would be allocated by vote outcomes in each congressional district rather than statewide. A state's two additional electoral votes (corresponding to its two senators) could be awarded to the statewide popular vote winner. This plan would assure a more accurate translation of popular votes into electoral votes. A more sweeping reform would completely scrap the electoral college and introduce direct popular election. Given the perception that the present electoral system is outmoded and undemocratic, this alternative is the most likely successor to the electoral college.

Those who defend the present system focus their arguments on the weaknesses of direct popular election. Compared to popular election, the electoral college more likely assures that the winning candidate will receive a broad geographical distribution of support. A popular vote proportion greater than a bare majority in any state adds nothing to a candidate's electoral college votes; candidates must win in several states in order to accumulate the necessary majority of electoral votes. Further, the present system augments the position of minorities, who may have greater influence over the vote outcome in individual states than in the nation as a whole. Finally, many admit that the electoral college in its winner-take-all form encourages the continuation of the two-party system and hence reinforces the stability of the political process.[25] Direct popular election could encourage several candidates to enter the race, possibly dividing the vote broadly among them and thereby considerably complicating what at first appeared to be a very simple electoral process. A minimum percentage of the vote required for election (possibly 40 percent) would need to be established, as would provision for a runoff election in case no candidate won on the first ballot. The complications of direct popular election have led to yet another reform proposal. Called the national bonus plan, this procedure maintains the electoral college but calls for adding 102 "bonus" electoral votes, to be awarded to the popular vote winner. The popular vote winner would thus be assured of receiving a majority in the electoral college. With one candidate being virtually guaranteed a majority, the embarrassment of presidential selection by the House of Representatives would also be eliminated. If combined with the automatic plan, the national bonus plan would resolve all the above mentioned criticisms of the electoral college. A chief virtue of the bonus plan is that it would resolve the difficulties of the electoral college while maintaining its advantages and avoiding possible unexpected consequences of more radical reform.

Low Voter Turnout

Low voter turnout in the United States is a difficult problem for those concerned with election reform. Despite the Voting Rights Act of 1965 and other legislation intended to ensure the right to vote for all eligible Americans, the rate of turnout in national elections steadily declined in the three decades following the 1960 presidential election. Curtis Gans notes that there are two discrete problems: low voter turnout and declining turnout over the last three decades.[26] Declining voter turnout has been associated with such possible causes as diminished feelings of political efficacy, weakened political party identification among citizens, and less dependence on newspapers as the prime source of political news.[27] Reformers such as Frances Fox Piven and Richard Cloward have focused attention on institutional barriers to higher voter turnout.[28] Piven and Cloward were major supporters of legislation that would facilitate voter registration. Noting that the single best predictor of voting is whether a person is registered, they reasoned that the higher the proportion of adult Americans who are registered, the greater will be the turnout rate. Low turnout results from the continued presence of registration and voting regulations that discourage potential voters from exercising the franchise.

In 1993 Congress passed the National Voter Registration Act (NVRA), which requires states to offer the opportunity for citizens to register at driver's license offices and other agencies, including offices where individuals apply for Aid to Families with Dependent Children, food stamps, Medicaid, and disability services.[29] The legislation also requires all states to institute a system of mail-in registration. Piven and Cloward anticipated major reforms in political party platforms as registration rates across race, income, and age became more equalized and turnout rates increased. They expected the registration rolls to swell by 40 million from January 1995, when the act took effect, to the 1998 midterm elections. However, the aggregate turnout figures for the 1996 presidential election do not bear out their optimism. Although a large percentage of registrants do vote, this inclination may not apply as readily to those who previously have not taken an active part in politics but now find themselves registered to vote. As Jerry Calvert and Jack Gilchrist suggest, voter turnout may not increase among traditional nonvoters who have disproportionately low incomes, who are unemployed, who are members of a minority group, or who are young.[30] Members of these groups, who have historically low voter turnout rates, will not necessarily demonstrate increased voting levels simply because they have registered to vote.

Calvert and Gilchrist cite evidence that registration deadlines less than thirty days before the election and election-day registration are strongly associated with higher voter turnout levels. In contrast, they cite evidence that in states that have instituted postcard registration, turnout actually declined, and that of ten states that enacted motor-voter registration prior to the national legislation, eight experienced declining voter turnout averaging nearly 6 percent.[31] In Minnesota, which adopted same-day registration in 1974, any eligible citizen may register and vote on election day after presenting a driver's license or other valid identification. Since enacted, nearly 20 percent of Minnesota's voters have registered on election day.[32] However, this reform appears to offer added incentive for those already predisposed to vote and does not significantly increase the turnout rates among those not so inclined. According to Gans, the solution to low voter turnout, and especially declining turnout, lies with a series of variables not directly related to election regulations. He lays the blame for declining voter turnout on such things as inadequate civic training for youth, the lack of a sense of civic virtue, the declining importance of political parties in mobilizing voters, and vituperative campaign tactics that alienate voters.[33]

The reform recommended to deal with low voter turnout varies with the explanation offered for low levels of voting in the United States. Kimberling summarizes ten such explanations.[34] Those who focus on the need for greater learning recommend voter education programs, whereas those who identify apathy as a major cause of low voter turnout support motivational campaigns. Others point to the strong relationship between voting and participation in other community affairs. Another explanation emphasizes an individual's stage of life, noting that strong interest in public affairs often develops only as individuals mature. A constitutional approach focuses on the basic structure of government, arguing that centralized parliamentary systems experience greater voter turnout than the American system because they offer simpler vote choices and the more disciplined political parties in these systems provide stronger incentives for citizens to vote. An administrative approach identifies regulations that discourage registration and voting, and a closely related explanation holds that Americans often lack the necessary information about registering and voting. The assimilation perspective associates voting with the degree to which a group has been integrated into the mainstream of American political culture; those failing to participate have not yet entered the course of political life. Class struggle theory attributes low voter turnout to the conscious efforts of the upper classes to discourage participation by the poor. Finally, critical realignment theory suggests that turnout rates tend to vary over time, depending upon the level of competition between the political parties and the stakes involved. Some of these approaches to turnout offer very specific reforms; the administrative perspective, for example, counsels modification of election laws to encourage greater registration and voting rates. Others, such as the stage-of-life viewpoint, offer few obvious solutions to the problem. None of the approaches does very well by itself in explaining declining voter turnout over the last three decades.

Early Voting

Another reform measure designed to encourage voting participation is "early voting," a procedure that allows citizens to vote in person during extended hours on weekdays and weekends for a period before election day. Unlike absentee voting, a person need not apply to vote early, and ballots cast early do not differ from those cast on election day and cannot be challenged individually, as can absentee ballots. Texas, the first state to establish early voting, began its program gradually. In 1987 the state legislature passed a measure eliminating the requirement that individuals voting absentee must state a reason for so doing. In 1989 the state legislature enacted legislation that required the most populous counties to offer extended voting hours for the final week of absentee voting. In 1991 the legislature took the final step toward early voting, allowing any eligible voter to cast an early ballot during a designated period prior to election day. In Texas early voting begins 20 days before the election and ends on the fourth day before the election.[35] While critics of early voting argue that the program increases the costs of campaigns and elections and provides greater opportunities for fraud and voter intimidation, supporters believe that the program gives more discretion to voters, thus encouraging higher levels of turnout. Regardless of the criticisms, voters, who can avoid long lines and cast their ballots more conveniently, have found early voting appealing. In some areas, from 20 to 50 percent of voters have taken advantage of the chance to vote early. A possible consequence of early voting may be an alteration in campaign strategy. With a large proportion of voters going to the polls before election day, candidates may find it necessary to shift campaign spending away from the last few days before the election in order to appeal to early voters. The program's effects on overall turnout is uncertain. As with election-day registration, early voting probably represents a convenience for those already inclined to vote but does not act as a significant spur to those less inclined to enter the political process.

Simplifying Election Forms

States have begun to simplify election forms as another measure intended to encourage registration and voting. Existing materials are often verbose, formal, and filled with bureaucratic and legal jargon. A study sponsored by the U.S. Department of Education estimated that 90 million Americans might find it difficult to read and understand printed information that appears on official forms such as those distributed by election officials.[36] In order to make election forms less forbidding, Mike Fox recommends various word substitutions to increase clarity. For instance, use "so" rather than "accordingly"; "you/your" instead of the impersonal "applicant/applicant's"; "here is" rather than "attached herewith is"; "quickly" rather than "expeditiously"; "give up" rather than "forfeit"; and "asked" rather than "propounded." In addition, Fox recommends that election materials provide only the information necessary for the voter to comply with election procedures. Forms can also include clear definitions of key words with which voters should be familiar, such as "absentee voter," "eligible voter," "precinct," and "ballot." Any extraneous content adds to the probability of misunderstandings and failure to read and complete the forms. Fox suggests that election officials test revised forms with focus groups to determine the level of readability and comprehensibility.[37] Although a minor reform, document revision might well have a positive effect on voter registration and election participation.

Voting and the Disabled

As with many other areas of activity, individuals with disabilities have received increased consideration in recent years with regard to the accessibility of polling places. An estimated 49 million Americans have disabilities, including impairment to vision, mobility, communication, and dexterity, that require special provision to ensure that they have access to the electoral process. The Voting Accessibility for the Handicapped Act of 1984 was the first federal attempt to ensure accessible voting facilities. Because certain features of the polling place that present no difficulties for the average voter may represent serious obstacles to the handicapped, election officials are required to take steps to ensure that the handicapped can exercise their right to vote. The Americans with Disabilities Act (ADA) of 1990 expanded the responsibility of election officials to provide accessible registration offices and polling places.[38] In addition, amendments to the Voting Rights Act of 1965 specify that voters needing assistance due to blindness, disability, or inability to read or write may receive assistance if they wish.[39] The 1993 National Voter Registration Act, which provides for registration by mail and at various public agencies, also mandates registration at "any office in the State that provides State funded programs primarily engaged in providing services to persons with disabilities."[40] ADA guidelines mandate appropriate automobile accessibility, passenger loading zones, public transportation stops, temporary ramps, and wheelchair accessibility to polling places and booths. Election officials and poll workers should be sensitive not only to the existence of physical barriers but also to the special needs of voters with disabilities, especially those with impaired communication. Those with poor vision might need better lighting, large type, or assistance in reading the ballot; those with impaired mobility cannot travel long distances from the street to the polling place within the building and may require seats while voting; and those with limited dexterity may require such special help as levered doorknobs and appropriate ballot-marking devices.[41] With such a large proportion of the population experiencing some form of disability, recent measures to increase physical accessibility to the polling place represent significant election reforms.

All-Mail-Ballot Elections

Some states have introduced all-mail-ballot elections, in which official ballots are mailed to all registered voters, typically two or three weeks prior to the deadline set for their return. Usually such elections have involved referenda and nonpartisan candidates.[42] Sixteen states (Alaska, California, Colorado, Florida, Kansas, Minnesota, Missouri, Montana, Nebraska, Nevada, New Mexico, New York, North Dakota, Oregon, Utah, and Washington) have adopted some variation of the mail-ballot election. Surveys of election officials in those states indicate that one perceived advantage of such elections is increased voter participation. Although fraud, including the possibility of bribery and intimidation, could be a major concern, election officials tend to regard mail-ballot elections as being just as free from fraud as polling place and absentee ballot voting. To avoid fraud, signature verification becomes especially important. The first all-mail-ballot election occurred in Monterey, California, on a ballot measure for a flood control district with approximately 45,000 eligible voters.[43] Although postage costs can be high, this expense apparently compares favorably to the costs of establishing polling places and hiring and training poll workers and all the other expenses associated with traditional elections. Although experience with all-mail-ballot elections has so far been limited, this interesting innovation represents a reform whose popularity might spread and possibly significantly increase voter turnout, especially in local referenda and nonpartisan elections. However, increased turnout may have resulted from the novelty of the voting procedure and any positive effect on turnout so far observed might subside. Nonetheless, other benefits of the all-mail-ballot election, such as cost effectiveness and convenience, may lead to its continued use and to adoption by additional jurisdictions.

In December 1995 Oregon held the first all-mail-ballot party primaries and in January 1996 conducted the first all-mail-ballot election to fill a U.S. Senate seat following the resignation of Senator Robert Packwood.[44] The election was conducted efficiently and apparently at reduced costs. The Oregon experience has encouraged officials in other states to consider mail voting. In Texas, Comptroller John Sharp asked the 1997 state legislature to consider the introduction of all-mail balloting in elections to vote on proposed amendments to the state constitution. Texas already allows those older than 65 and the disabled to vote by mail. Critics argue that the use of all-mail ballots in a state considerably larger than Oregon would open the door to extensive vote fraud opportunities. Texas, with five times as many registered voters as Oregon, could face unforeseen administrative difficulties in statewide mailed balloting.

Voting Assistance Programs

Concern that every eligible citizen, regardless of circumstance, have the opportunity to cast a ballot in an election led to passage of the 1955 Federal Voting Assistance Act. This legislation established the Federal Voting Assistance Program (FVAP), located in the Office of the Secretary of Defense. The original intent of the legislation was to assist members of the armed forces to register and vote in their home jurisdictions.[45] The responsibilities of the program specified in the original act were expanded in 1968 and 1975 by the Overseas Citizens Voting Rights Act and in 1986 by the Uniformed and Overseas Citizens Absentee Voting Act. The program now assists not only members of the armed forces and their families but also those in the merchant marine and any U.S. citizen who is living abroad. Citizens may register and vote if they meet voter requirements in the last place they lived before moving to another country. The program assists those residing overseas in communicating with local election officials and works with those officials to promote more efficient absentee registration and voting procedures. The office's publication, *Voting Assistance Guide,* provides prospective overseas voters with registration and absentee voting information regarding the procedures of individual states. The office also distributes materials that encourage U.S. citizens to register and vote and has cooperated with the Advertising Council and the National Association of Secretaries of State in a national media campaign to encourage voting. The FVAP prescribes to the states an official postcard form (Federal Post Card Application) that facilitates overseas registration and voting. The active role that the FVAP plays in facilitating and encouraging voting may serve as a model for a more generalized reform program that encourages Americans' participation in the electoral process.

Public Employees

Public employees have often been the focus of campaign and election reform. They have traditionally been pressured to donate a portion of their salaries to a political party or candidate as a condition for continued employment. The Political Activities Act, or Hatch Act, passed in 1939, prohibited employees of the federal government from contributing to political parties or candidates. Under the 1993 amendments to the act, federal government employees may participate in political activities such as signing petitions for candidates or ballot issues, assisting in partisan and nonpartisan voter registration drives, and serving as poll workers in a partisan or nonpartisan election. However, federal employees may not run for public office in partisan elections, wear political buttons while on the job, receive political contributions, or engage in partisan political activity involving anyone who interacts with the employee's government agency.[46] Members of the armed forces are also prohibited by statute from campaigning for a candidate or issue or from soliciting contributions from others while on active duty.[47] The reforms initiated by the Hatch Act have been effective in protecting federal employees from pressures to make campaign contributions. Although the 1993 provisions eased restrictions somewhat, the act's restrictions remain largely intact. Despite criticisms that the Hatch Act denies federal employees the right to participate in the democratic process, the Supreme Court upheld the legislation, ruling in 1947 (*United Public Workers v. Mitchell*) that a person may be removed from employment for taking part in political management or political campaigns. In 1973 the Supreme Court ruled that the country's best interest required a system of federal service dependent on merit rather than on political support. The reforms instituted by the Hatch Act will continue to be examined, but the legislation undoubtedly has improved the conditions of federal employment and helped to establish a system of public employee hiring based on merit, not political loyalty.

Legislative Apportionment and Gerrymandering

The gerrymander has been a focus of political controversy throughout American history. Drawing district lines to benefit a political party or faction predates the term "gerrymander," which was coined in 1811 when Governor Elbridge Gerry of Massachusetts was associated with an attempt by the Democratic-Republican party to gain an advantage in state legislative elections. Redistricting inevitably involves conscious decisions about just where district boundaries will be drawn. The problem is as real today, even with the assistance of computer programs, as it was in the nineteenth century. Malapportionment, a closely related issue, involves the failure to redraw district lines according to shifts in population. In a landmark decision (*Baker v. Carr*, 1962), the Supreme Court ruled that federal courts have jurisdiction in cases concerning apportionment of legislative districts because malapportionment may deny equal protection of the law provided for in the Fourteenth Amendment. This case led to several other challenges to state and local government districting policies. In *Gray v. Sanders* (1963) the Court ruled that each person's vote must have equal weight in primary elections for U.S. senators and state executive officers. In yet another significant decision (*Reynolds v. Sims*, 1964), the Court ruled that seats in both houses of a state legislature must be apportioned on the basis of population. Like the U.S. Congress, state legislatures often contained two chambers: one that was apportioned according to population and a second that provided equal representation to geographical areas. Ruling that the dual system of representation at the national level resulted from the special constitutional arrangements of federalism, the Court denied the validity of providing for representation in state legislatures for geographical areas rather than people. In 1964 the Supreme Court ruled in *Wesberry v. Sanders* that state legislative and congressional districts must be drawn in such a way as to assure approximately equal population in each district. Another case before the Court (*Avery v. Midland County*, 1968) involved the huge population inequalities that had developed in local jurisdictions. One commissioner precinct in Midland County, Texas, which included the city of Midland, contained 97 percent of the residents of the county while the other three precincts shared the remaining 3 percent. The Supreme Court applied the rule that representative districts must be of approximately equal size. Today any representative body that derives its members from districts must abide by the equal population rule.

Campaign Advertising and the Mass Media

The strong focus in recent decades on television campaign advertising has raised concerns about the costs of campaigning and the altered character of election campaigns. Campaign ads have become professionally produced equivalents to product advertising, often lasting no longer than 30 seconds. A study of the 1988 presidential campaign discovered that fewer than 13 percent of television ads lasted more than 60 seconds.[48] Many media researchers have concluded that such brief messages cannot adequately present positions on national issues. Darrell West has discussed several possible measures to reform media campaign practices.[49] If, as some researchers have concluded, ads contribute little to citizen knowledge, campaigns could be shortened considerably, thus supposedly decreasing the requirements for media advertising. Because the decline of political parties has been identified as one reason for the increased use of media advertising, some suggest that strengthening parties may help to limit media influence. With parties having greater impact on voting behavior, the ephemeral influences of advertising would play a smaller role in citizens' vote choices. However, the popularity of past reforms, such as the use of primaries to nominate candidates, that have weakened party organization may limit the extent to which parties may be revitalized. In addition, voters may be unwilling to offer their loyalty to parties, given the general trend toward declining party identification. A more direct strategy for controlling media advertising involves structuring the format for ads. One proposal would require candidates to appear in any advertisement that refers to the opponent. Another would mandate stricter regulations about identifying the sponsors of media ads, and yet another would require candidates to appear in ads at least 50 percent of the time.[50] But there is little evidence that requiring candidates to appear in ads would reduce negative advertising.

West recommends an oversight strategy dependent upon the willingness of journalists to monitor campaign ads and evaluate them for truthfulness. Despite the possibility that journalists might be criticized for cynicism and could come under attack by the candidates, who may wish to blame the messenger rather than the message, West believes that they can improve the political process by encouraging candidates to focus on substantive issues. For West's idea to work effectively the possibility of journalistic exposure must act as a deterrent to false, misleading, or extremely negative ads. In recent elections the news media have begun to evaluate candidates' television spots, pointing to inaccuracies and exaggerations. The effectiveness of the "watchdog" role can only be determined by monitoring future campaign advertising for possible decreases in rates of misleading or negative statements.

Nontraditional Voters

Issues have been raised about the registration of "nontraditional" voters, including college students living away from home and individuals who lack a traditional address (for example, the "homeless"). Voter registration for college-age citizens is a major concern. In the 1994 congressional elections the turnout rate for the youngest voters was only 20 percent, the lowest of any age group. Elfi Blum-Page observes that roughly half the states use a "no-gain, no-lose" policy whereby students do not lose residency in their home state by attending school elsewhere, nor do they gain residency in the state where they are presently living.[51] In order to ensure effective franchise for students, it has been suggested that students be given the opportunity to vote in their college communities. However, concerns have been raised about potential election fraud or the prospect that students may out-vote residents in college towns. In many states, due to reforms in election law and litigation, students have increasingly been able to register and vote in the location they prefer.

The Urban Institute has estimated that there are as many as 600,000 homeless people in the United States, many of whom are eligible voters except for the lack of a permanent address. Should a homeless person be denied the right to vote for what may amount to economic reasons? Denying the vote to the homeless might be justified as the price of protecting the electoral process against vote fraud. The argument has also been made that the right to vote should be limited to those with a genuine stake in the community, and permanent residence serves as a principal criterion for community membership.[52] However, Margaret Sims suggests that a nontraditional address does not necessarily indicate lack of commitment to the community.[53] As a result of a campaign by the National Coalition for the Homeless, plus provisions of the NVRA and court rulings that permanent address requirements disfranchise the homeless as a class and violate the equal protection clause of the Fourteenth Amendment, many states have enacted legislation and revised voter registration regulations to accommodate homeless citizens. The NVRA's requirement for registration programs at public offices serving those on public assistance may be a major way of registering the homeless.

In March 1996 an interesting piece of reform legislation was introduced in the U.S. House of Representatives. Titled the Voting Rights of Former Offenders Act, the measure was designed to limit or eliminate provisions that deny the franchise to convicted felons.[54] Data from 1995 indicate that approximately 5.3 million people are in federal, state, or local jails, on probation, or on parole. This number represents 2.8 percent of the adult population.[55] The District of Columbia and 45 states disfranchise convicted felons for varied lengths of time, and 32 states provide for disfranchisement during probation or parole.[56] Those advocating a change in disfranchisement policy argue that it violates the Fourteenth Amendment's equal protection clause, the Fifteenth Amendment's prohibition against denying the right to vote based on "previous condition of servitude," and the Eighth Amendment's constraint on cruel and unusual punishment. These arguments have so far been unpersuasive, for no federal court has ruled unconstitutional any state laws that disfranchise felons. The proposed reform legislation is a measure that, given present popular sentiment, has little chance of becoming law.

Campaign Finance and the Federal Election Campaign Act

Several common arguments have been made in favor of campaign finance reforms that would further limit contributions and expenditures:[57] First, private campaign contributions violate the principle of suffrage equality because those able to contribute more resources have a greater opportunity to have their voices heard in the political process. Second, private contributions distort the election process by causing the wrong people to be candidates—that is, those who have attracted campaign contributions but not necessarily wide popular support. Third, money may lead to the corruption of public officials because they are likely to base their decisions on the urgings of campaign contributors. Fourth, a type of carpetbagging may occur when individuals contribute to candidates in districts throughout the nation, a practice that raises questions about whether legislators truly represent their constituents. Fifth, a private system of campaign finance is said to consume far too much of a candidate's time and energy. A system of public financing would allow candidates more opportunity to confront the issues in a public forum. Sixth, large amounts of money in campaigns may reduce the quality of debate by allowing candidates to focus their campaigns on the expensive medium of television, where brief presentations avoid genuine discussion of issues. Finally, the candidate with the most funds can take an anticompetitive advantage in the campaign.

In 1972 Congress passed the Federal Election Campaign Act to regulate donations to U.S. House and Senate campaigns, including primaries, and to provide for regulation of corporate and individual participation in federal election campaigns. A reaction to heavy campaign spending and the potential influence of personal wealth on the electoral process, the new legislation replaced previous federal corrupt practices acts. Following the Watergate revelations, which included charges of illegal activities during the 1972 presidential campaign, Congress enacted the Federal Election Campaign Act of 1974. This act provided for public funding of presidential elections and partial funding of presidential primaries and caucuses through a system of matching payments supported by funds to be provided by a voluntary checkoff on income tax returns. Among other provisions, the legislation held individuals to a maximum $1,000 contribution to a candidate and a total of $25,000 in donations to political campaigns in any election year. Interest groups and political committees were limited to a contribution of $5,000 to a candidate in a primary or general election. The act also created the Federal Election Commission (FEC), an independent regulatory agency assigned the responsibility of administering federal campaign finance laws, including provisions for the public funding of presidential elections, regulation of contributions and expenditures to candidates for federal office, and reception of campaign finance disclosure reports from political committees.[58]

Many reformers have concluded that the operation of the FEC has been a major disappointment. Congress has not provided the agency with sufficient appropriations to handle its large workload, and the commission lacks an investigative staff sufficiently knowledgeable to conduct investigations of financial reports. The requirement setting the number of commissioners at six (three Democrats and three Republicans) has resulted in tie votes and hence stalemate and inaction. In 1979 Congress denied the FEC the authority to conduct random audits of congressional campaigns, further weakening the agency's ability to deter violations of campaign finance regulations. Because a chairman can serve for only one year, the FEC lacks the leadership potential a permanent chairman could provide. Violators of campaign election laws have little to fear from the FEC, for the lengthy investigation procedures often force delays, and civil penalties may not exceed $5,000 or the amount of the contested contribution, whichever is greater. The commission once levied fines of $190,000,[59] but such a large amount is uncommon. Although creation of the FEC was part of a major attempt to reform the campaign finance system, serious limitations on the operation of the FEC have led to recommendations for additional reform. Many proposals focus on the question of soft money contributions, which have gone virtually uncontrolled and unreported under present legislation. The recommendations range from forbidding national party committees from using soft money to finance federal campaign activities to prohibiting nationally organized soft money fund-raising campaigns.

Given the large role played by political action committees (PACs) in the funding of campaigns, reformers have recommended that corporate, union, or trade association PACs be eliminated, or at least that their contribution limits be reduced. Some have recommended that the practice of bundling, which involves the collection of contributions from several individuals to be passed on to a candidate, be prohibited. Another reform proposal calls for spending limits on U.S. House and Senate campaigns. Public financing of congressional elections has gained some support as a means of limiting the potential dangers of special interest funding of campaigns. Although public financing could provide an opportunity to candidates who otherwise lack financial resources, opponents of the proposal contend that public financing would actually limit the ability of challengers to raise the money needed to compete effectively against incumbents.

Other proposals call for granting the FEC authority to conduct random audits and to inspect a candidate's campaign contributions and receipts if there is evidence of a violation.[60] Though some individuals focus on strengthening the FEC, others doubt the potential effectiveness of the commission, and still others express concern about granting a government agency significant new powers at a time when government downsizing and deregulation have become popular objectives. Larry Sabato and Glenn Simpson recommend reforms that emphasize more stringent disclosure with increased penalties for noncompliance, a proposal they call "deregulation plus."[61] They note that, unlike attempts to limit contributions and expenditures, disclosure legislation has fared well in legal challenges. They also recommend that each state establish stringent disclosure laws and penalties that will serve as genuine deterrents to misconduct. Kathleen Sullivan also supports the elimination of contribution and spending limits along with a vigorous system of disclosure, arguing that an increased supply of money would mean less influence for any individual contributor and that disclosure rules would allow voters to retaliate against those accepting large donations from questionable sources.[62] To counteract somewhat the advantage of incumbents, Sabato and Simpson suggest the creation of discounts on mail and media time for challengers.

Efforts to reform various aspects of the campaign and election process will certainly continue. The furor over campaign finance improprieties following the 1996 presidential election has given new urgency to campaign finance reform and the revamping of other aspects of the campaign and election process. Revelations of illegal contributions surfaced regularly, with the Democratic and Republican parties exchanging charges of misconduct. Reports that 938 people, among them several hundred contributors to Democratic party campaign coffers, were President Clinton's overnight guests at the White House disturbed many Washington insiders and aides to former presidents, who saw the practice as an unprecedented misuse of a government office to raise campaign funds.[63] If partisan infighting subsides sufficiently, Congress will undoubtedly institute another round of campaign finance reform. The prospects for success will depend on the willingness of Congress to grant the FEC or another agency the authority and resources to enforce any new regulations and on Congress's ability to circumvent any threat to free speech that catches the eye of the courts.

Notes

1. Alma Lutz, *Susan B. Anthony: Rebel, Crusader, Humanitarian* (Boston: Beacon Press, 1959), p. 298.

2. Bernard Grofman, Lisa Handley, and Richard G. Niemi, *Minority Representation and the Quest for Voting Equality* (Cambridge: Cambridge University Press, 1992), p. 13.

3. Ibid.

4. Ibid., p. 20.

5. Ibid.

6. Richard L. Engstrom, "The Voting Rights Act: Disfranchisement, Dilution, and Alternative Election Systems," *PS: Political Science and Politics* 27 (December 1994), 685.

7. Ibid., 687.

8. Ibid.

9. Joseph F. Zimmerman, "Alternative Voting Systems for Representative Democracy," *PS: Political Science and Politics* 27 (December 1994), 675.

10. Anita Chadha and Robert A. Bernstein, "Why Incumbents Are Treated So Harshly: Term Limits for State Legislators," *American Politics Quarterly* 24 (July 1996), 363.

11. Ibid.

12. Patrick J. Fett and Daniel E. Ponder, "Congressional Term Limits, State Legislative Term Limits, and Congressional Turnover: A Theory of Change," *PS: Political Science and Politics* 26 (June 1993), 212.

13. Mark P. Petracca, "A New Defense of State-Imposed Congressional Term Limits," *PS: Political Science and Politics* 26 (December 1993), 703.

14. Fett and Ponder, "Congressional Term Limits, State Legislative Term Limits, and Congressional Turnover," 215.

15. George C. S. Benson, *Political Corruption in America* (Lexington, MA: Lexington Books, 1978), p. 173.

16. William Kimberling and Peggy Sims, *Federal Election Law 96: A Summary of Federal Laws Pertaining to Registration, Voting, and Public Employee Participation* (Washington, DC: Office of Election Administration, 1996), p. 18.

17. Craig Donsanto, "The Election Crimes Branch," *Journal of Election Administration* 16 (Summer 1989), 20.

18. Ibid., 20–21.

19. Marie Garber, *Innovations in Election Administration 10: Ballot Security and Accountability* (Washington, DC: National Clearinghouse on Election Administration, 1995), pp. 7–15.

20. Ibid., p. 3.

21. Quoted in James J. Condit, Jr., "A House without Doors: Vote Fraud in America," *Chronicles* (November 1996), 15.

22. William Kimberling, "Secure against What? An Approach to Computer Security," *Journal of Election Administration* 13 (Winter 1986), 12.

23. Ibid., 11.

24. Condit, "A House without Doors," 17. See also James M. Collier and Kenneth F. Collier, *Votescam: The Stealing of America* (New York: Victoria House, 1996) for an extensive account of alleged vote fraud in recent elections.

25. William Kimberling, "Electing the President: The Genius of the Electoral College," *Journal of Election Administration* 15 (Autumn 1988), 19–20.

26. Curtis Gans, "Voter Participation Revisited," *Journal of Election Administration* 16 (Summer 1989), 9.

27. Ibid., 10.

28. Frances Fox Piven and Richard A. Cloward, "Northern Bourbons: A Preliminary Report on the National Voter Registration Act," *PS: Political Science and Politics* 29 (March 1996), 39–42.

29. Ibid., 39.

30. Jerry W. Calvert and Jack Gilchrist, "Suppose They Held an Election and Almost Everybody Came!" *PS: Political Science and Politics* 26 (December 1993), 696.

31. Ibid., 697.

32. Ibid.

33. Gans, "Voter Participation Revisited," 10.

34. William Kimberling, "Voting for President: Participation in America," *Journal of Election Administration* 15 (Autumn 1988), 23–26.

35. Margaret Rosenfield, *Innovations in Election Administration 9: Early Voting* (Washington, DC: National Clearinghouse on Election Administration, 1994), p. 7.

36. Mike Fox, *Innovations in Election Administration 13: Simplifying Election Forms and Materials* (Washington, DC: Office of Election Administration, 1996), p. 1.

37. Ibid., p. 37.

38. Paradigm Design Group/Paralyzed Veterans of America, *Innovations in Election Administration 15: Ensuring the Accessibility of the Election Process* (Washington, DC: Federal Election Commission, 1996), p. 1.

39. Ibid., p. 5.

40. Ibid., p. 7.

41. Ibid., p. 36.

42. Margaret Rosenfield, *Innovations in Election Administration 11: All-Mail-Ballot Elections* (Washington, DC: National Clearinghouse on Election Administration, 1995), p. 1.

43. Ibid.

44. See Priscilla L. Southwell and Justin Burchett, "Survey of Vote-by-Mail Senate Election in the State of Oregon," *PS: Political Science and Politics* 30 (March 1997), 53–57 for an overview of this election and voter reaction to vote-by-mail.

45. Henry Valentino, "The Federal Voting Assistance Program," *Journal of Election Administration* 16 (Summer 1989), 28.

46. Kimberling and Sims, *Federal Election Law 96,* p. 25.

47. Ibid., p. 30.

48. Darrell M. West, "Reforming Campaign Ads," *PS: Political Science and Politics* 25 (March 1992), 76.

49. Ibid.

50. Ibid., 75.

51. Elfi Blum-Page, "The Effects of Residency on Student Voting Rights," *Journal of Election Administration* 17 (1996), 24. See also Kenneth Eshleman, *Where Should Students Vote?* (Lanham, MD: University Press of America, 1989).

52. Margaret Sims, "Voter Registration for the Homeless," *Journal of Election Administration* 17 (1996), 6.

53. Ibid., 15.

54. Brian J. Hancock, "The Voting Rights of Convicted Felons," *Journal of Election Administration* 17 (1996), 39.

55. Ibid.

56. Ibid., 35.

57. The reasons for campaign finance reform presented here are derived from a presentation by Kathleen Sullivan, "Political Money and Freedom of Speech," University of California at Davis, February 13, 1997.

58. Meredith Whiting, E. Patrick McGuire, Catherine Morrison, and Jessica Shelly, *Campaign Finance Reform* (New York: The Conference Board, 1990), p. 14.

59. Ibid.

60. Ibid., p. 17.

61. Larry J. Sabato and Glenn R. Simpson, *Dirty Little Secrets: The Persistence of Corruption in American Politics* (New York: Times Books, 1996), p. 330.

62. Kathleen Sullivan, "Political Money and Freedom of Speech."

63. Dan Balz and Lou Cannon, "Under Clinton, Old Practices on a New Scale," *Washington Post National Weekly Edition* 14 (March 10, 1997), 8–9.

Chronology 2

This chapter tracks the significant progress that has been made throughout American history to extend the right to vote to all adult citizens and to improve the electoral system and its representativeness. This progress has not been even, however. We have included events that decidedly represent steps backward for voting rights. For instance, during the last decades of the nineteenth century, while states outside the South were generally expanding voting rights, southern states were instituting provisions to restrict African Americans' access to the ballot box. We have also indicated periods in the history of campaigns and elections during which fraud and corruption played a notable role. The chronology of campaign and election reform is by no means complete, for reform measures continue to be urged, including increased assurance of ballot integrity, better regulation of campaign contributions and spending, and the enhancement of citizen representation through the establishment of alternative voting systems.

1787   The delegates at the Constitutional Convention in Philadel-

1787
(cont.)

phia, altering the basis for representation set out in the Articles of Confederation, establish a popularly elected branch of the national legislature that will represent people and not just states. The delegates decide to leave voting qualifications to the states because such qualifications vary considerably from state to state. The convention thereby avoids the potential controversy of attempting to establish uniform standards.

Delegates do not agree on the method of electing the president until the closing days of the convention. The president will be elected by states, with each state possessing as many electors as it has representatives and senators in Congress. Each elector will be granted two votes for president; the candidate who receives the most votes, assuming that he has received a majority of the votes, will be elected president, and the candidate with the second-highest number of electoral votes will be elected vice president. It is assumed that state legislatures will choose the electors, who will then cast their two ballots for president.

1791

Vermont enters the Union with a liberal constitution that allows for full male suffrage.

1792

Kentucky enters the Union with a constitution as liberal as Vermont's, indicating that the push toward universal suffrage extends beyond any localized movement.

New Hampshire eliminates a taxpaying requirement for the right to vote, as it had previously abandoned property ownership as a qualification.

1796

President George Washington establishes the two-term tradition by refusing to be considered for a third term as president.

Under the original provisions of the electoral college, in which the candidate with the highest number of electoral votes is elected president and the candidate with the second highest total is elected vice president, John Adams and Thomas Jefferson, leaders of rival political factions, become president and vice president respectively. The election results provide an initial indication that the electoral college requires revision.

1798   A Federalist-controlled Congress passes the short-lived Alien and Sedition Laws. One section of the Sedition Law makes speaking or writing against the president or Congress a misdemeanor punishable by a fine or imprisonment. If allowed to continue, these laws could restrict the operation of free elections.

1800   Thomas Jefferson and Aaron Burr receive the same number of electoral votes. The framers of the Constitution, when establishing the method of electing the president, did not foresee the development of political parties. The Democratic-Republican party leadership have designated Jefferson the party's presidential candidate and Burr the vice presidential candidate. However, electors who support this party cannot distinguish between a vote for president and a vote for vice president. Therefore the two candidates receive the same number of ballots for president.

1801   Due to the electoral college tie, the House of Representatives, after 35 ballots, elects Thomas Jefferson the next president. Aaron Burr becomes the vice president.

1803   Ohio joins the Union with a minimal property ownership qualification for voting: In order for a person to qualify as a voter, the state's constitution requires payment of a county tax or work on the public highway.

1804   Due to the dilemma raised by the outcome of the 1800 election, the Twelfth Amendment, which alters the method of electing the president, is ratified.

1804 (cont.)	Electors will now cast distinct ballots for president and vice president, thus avoiding the circumstance, made highly probable by the development of political parties, in which two candidates receive the same number of electoral votes or in which candidates of opposing political parties are chosen to serve as president and vice president.
1809	Maryland eliminates property ownership and tax payment as voter qualifications but also limits voting to white males who are U.S. citizens and establishes a one-year state residency requirement.
1810	Louisiana eliminates property qualifications for voting and instead establishes residency requirements of six months in the election district and two years in the territory.
1812	The new state of Louisiana requires tax payment in order to vote. Alternatively, a person may vote if he has purchased land from the national government.
	The term "gerrymandering"—the redrawing of election district boundaries so as to advantage one party or group and disadvantage others—is coined. When the Massachusetts legislature creates an oddly shaped district with the grudging acquiescence of Governor Elbridge Gerry, Elkanah Tinsdale draws a cartoon of the district with the shape of a salamander superimposed over it, calling the district a "gerrymander." The term soon becomes a part of the American political vocabulary.
1816	Indiana, in its constitution, allows white male citizens to vote who have lived in the state one year and who have not committed "infamous crimes."
1818	Illinois establishes a residency requirement of just six months for voters.
1819	Maine enters the Union with a constitution that grants the vote to free blacks and Indians.

Connecticut adopts a new constitution that includes as voter qualifications minimal property holdings, one year of military service, or payment of a state tax and "good moral character."

1820   A constitutional convention in Massachusetts amends the state constitution to eliminate any property qualification for voting.

1824   With five candidates running for the presidency, no presidential hopeful receives the necessary majority of the electoral vote in the November balloting. Four individuals win electoral votes: Andrew Jackson (99 electoral votes), John Quincy Adams (84 electoral votes), Henry Clay (37 electoral votes), and William H. Crawford (41 electoral votes).

1825   After considerable deal making, the House of Representatives on February 9 elects John Quincy Adams president of the United States, even though Jackson led in both popular and electoral votes. With each state having one vote, Adams is elected by a majority of one state (13 votes for Adams, 7 for Jackson, and 4 for Crawford). The Jackson backers believe they have been cheated out of the presidency.

1826   Residents of New York in a referendum reject a tax payment qualification in the state's constitution, thus eliminating any property or taxpaying requirements for voting.

1828   Backers of John Quincy Adams and Andrew Jackson introduce questionable tactics into the presidential campaign. For instance, Adams, who used his own funds to purchase a billiard table for the White House, is accused of purchasing gaming tables with public money, and Jackson's opponents recount stories of his supposed premarital relations with Mrs. Jackson.

1829   James Madison, a delegate at the Virginia constitutional convention, supports tax payment as a re-

1829 *(cont.)*	placement for property ownership as a suffrage qualification.
1831	The Anti-Masonic party becomes the first political party to nominate a presidential candidate by the convention method. This minor party does not last, but the convention replaces the unpopular congressional caucus as the accepted method for nominating presidential candidates.
	Delaware's new constitution continues restrictive voting qualifications with a requirement that voters pay a state or county tax.
1832	The Democratic party for the first time uses the convention method of nomination, selecting a vice presidential candidate to run with Jackson, who is the party's obvious presidential nominee.
	With vote buying a common practice, the price of an uncommitted vote in a New York City election is estimated to be five dollars.
1834	Tennessee adopts a new constitution in which all property qualifications are eliminated.
1835	Michigan enters the Union with universal white male suffrage.
1836	Arkansas enters the Union without a property qualification for voting. A white male citizen may vote after satisfying a six-month residency requirement in the state.
1839	The Whig party introduces into the Senate the first bill designed to regulate campaign finance. Under its provisions, no federal employees shall provide any funds for the election of national or state political officials. The measure fails.
1840	The Whigs win the presidency from incumbent Democratic president Martin Van Buren by nominat-

ing the war hero of Tippecanoe fame, William Henry Harrison, with John Tyler as his vice presidential running mate. The Whigs have no platform, avoid issues, and appeal to the emotions of the voters. The jingle "Tippecanoe and Tyler too" becomes part of American political folklore.

Demands for woman suffrage arise at a London meeting of the World Anti-Slavery Convention.

1841   The intransigence of the Rhode Island legislature against political reform leads Thomas Wilson Dorr to call a constitutional convention without the state legislature's authorization. The convention writes a new constitution that provides for universal manhood suffrage. The new constitution is ratified by the voters.

1842   Thomas Dorr is elected governor of Rhode Island under the new liberal constitution, but the old government, with the support of President John Tyler, arrests Dorr. All political factions of Rhode Island, frightened by Dorr's Rebellion, agree to a new constitutional convention that grants suffrage to all native-born male citizens.

1844   New Jersey's new state constitution eliminates property qualifications for voting.

In New York City, 55,000 votes are cast on election day, although the total number of eligible voters is estimated to be 41,000, thus indicating extensive vote fraud.

1845   Congress determines a uniform date on which all states will choose presidential electors. They shall be chosen "on the Tuesday next after the first Monday in November, in every fourth year."

1848   Wisconsin enters the Union with a constitution that allows those aliens to vote who state they intend to become U.S. citizens.

1848 *(cont.)*	Some of the women who attended the World Anti-Slavery Convention in London in 1840 organize a meeting in Seneca Falls, New York, to call for woman suffrage. Women at the meeting also call for equal rights in education, business, the professions, and politics and equal rights under the law.
1851	With little political opposition, Ohio drops its tax-paying requirement for voting.
1855	Connecticut ratifies a constitutional amendment that includes the ability to read the state constitution or statutes as a requirement for voting.
1856	North Carolina becomes the last state to eliminate a property qualification for voting but replaces it with a taxpaying requirement. In its party platform, the American ("Know-Nothing") party, which enjoys the support of the nativist movement, criticizes Wisconsin for allowing aliens to vote. The party calls for suffrage rights to be limited to citizens and demands stricter naturalization laws. Religion becomes an issue in the dirty politics of the presidential campaign. The Know-Nothings accuse Republican candidate John C. Frémont, an Episcopalian, of Catholic sympathies. Such pamphlets as *Frémont's Romanism Established* and *The Romanish Intrigue: Frémont a Catholic* are circulated among the electorate.
1857	In Massachusetts, a constitutional amendment is approved that specifies the ability to read the state constitution and write one's own name as eligibility requirements for voters.
1859	Oregon enters the Union under a constitution that allows aliens to vote after one year of residence and a declaration of intention to become a U.S. citizen.

1863   Massachusetts eliminates a taxpaying requirement for voting.

1867   On January 7 Congress passes a bill that grants blacks the right to vote in the District of Columbia. Congress subsequently overrides President Andrew Johnson's veto of the legislation.

On January 10 Congress enacts legislation granting the right to vote to blacks in the territories.

On March 2 Congress passes the Military Reconstruction Act, which provides for the governance of the former Confederate states and their reentrance into the Union. Former slaves must be given the right to vote in elections to select delegates for constitutional conventions, and the new constitutions must guarantee them suffrage rights. The law also requires these states to ratify the Fourteenth Amendment, which declares in part that "no State shall make or enforce any law which shall abridge the privileges or immunities of citizens of the United States."

On March 23 Congress enacts legislation that specifies the criteria for voter registration in the southern states to determine who can vote in elections to select delegates to constitutional conventions. Blacks are enfranchised under this legislation.

Congress passes the Naval Appropriations Act, which includes a provision prohibiting any officer or government employee from asking a Navy yard workman to contribute funds for political purposes. A workman shall not be discharged for expressing political views.

1868   North Carolina eliminates a taxpaying requirement for voter registration.

With the assistance of federal troops, over 700,000 blacks in southern states have been registered to vote.

1869   The National Woman Suffrage Association is estab-
        lished to further the fight for the right of women to
        vote. Elizabeth Cady Stanton becomes the president
        and Susan B. Anthony the vice president.
            The American Woman Suffrage Association is
        formed later in the year, led by Lucy Stone. Unlike
        the National Association, whose leaders focus on a
        national policy, this more conservative organization
        prefers to follow a state-by-state strategy in win-
        ning the right to vote.

        The territorial legislature of Wyoming extends the
        franchise to women.

        It is estimated that 25,000 to 30,000 votes in a New
        York City election are the result of repeat voters, il-
        legal registration, and noncitizen participation in
        the election.

1870   The Fifteenth Amendment gains ratification, declar-
        ing that "the right of citizens of the United States to
        vote shall not be denied or abridged by the United
        States or by any State on account of race, color, or
        previous condition of servitude." Despite this
        amendment, black citizens find it increasingly diffi-
        cult to exercise the right to vote.
            Congress passes the Enforcement Act, which
        specifies criminal penalties for anyone who violates
        the constitutional right to vote.

        The Mormon-dominated territorial legislature of
        Utah decides in favor of woman suffrage.

        Blacks in Kansas who have been denied suffrage
        bring suit in the courts (*Anthony v. Halderman*) but
        lose on the technicality that they failed to indicate
        residence of at least 30 days in their ward.

1871   The Force Act establishes an enforcement mecha-
        nism to protect the right to vote that involves the
        appointment of federal officers to oversee elections.

A federal court in South Carolina (*United States v. Crosby*) refuses to punish those who employed intimidation to prevent a black man from going to the polls. Because the intimidation occurred on the black man's premises, the court rules the national Constitution and federal legislation does not apply.

1872   Susan B. Anthony, an avid supporter of woman suffrage, votes in the presidential election. She is arrested two weeks later and found guilty of violating a federal law against illegal voting. Anthony refuses to pay a modest fine, but the judge does not require her imprisonment, thus preventing her from appealing to the Supreme Court on a writ of habeas corpus. Nationally sanctioned woman suffrage is not achieved for nearly 50 years.

Congress enacts a provision requiring a secret ballot for electing members to the U.S. House of Representatives.

1874   A court in Kentucky (*United States v. Reese*) establishes a very narrow interpretation of the Fifteenth Amendment that makes it extremely difficult to demonstrate race as the motive for denying suffrage.

Congress establishes a uniform date for electing members of the U.S. House of Representatives, which in presidential election years coincides with the date for electing presidential electors: "the Tuesday next after the first Monday in November, in every even numbered year."

1876   Democratic presidential candidate Samuel Tilden receives more popular votes and is the apparent electoral vote winner over Rutherford B. Hayes, but Republican strategists take advantage of conflicting returns from three southern states to challenge the results.

The U.S. Supreme Court in *United States v. Reese* and *United States v. Cruikshank* quashes indictments under the Enforcement Act of 1870 and the Force

1876
(cont.)

Act of 1871, claiming that the federal government has exceeded its authority. By its decisions, the Court has seriously weakened crucial sections of the legislation intended to protect the voting rights of blacks.

Colorado enters the Union with a constitution that allows women to vote in school elections and includes a provision allowing for a woman suffrage referendum.

1877

An electoral commission is established by Congress in January to resolve the conflicting electoral vote returns in the 1876 presidential election. Composed of 15 persons (five senators, five representatives, and five Supreme Court justices), the commission decides the winner of the disputed 1876 presidential election along strict party lines. The eight Republicans overrule the seven Democrats and grant all contested electoral votes to Hayes, thus giving the Republican candidate a one-vote victory. Tempers run high, but violence is avoided. For a generation resentful Democrats will consider the election to have been stolen by the Republicans.

In the Compromise of 1877, southern Democrats agree to accept the electoral commission decision in return for the withdrawal of federal troops from the South and a relaxation of the federal guarantee of voting rights. The compromise results in the increasing exclusion of southern blacks from the electorate.

The new Georgia constitution requires that all taxes be paid before a person may vote.

1881

A federal court in Indiana rules that no violation of national law has occurred in denying a citizen, white or black, the right to vote in a state election. Federal involvement becomes legitimate only if the motive for such denial is race, which is a charge very difficult to establish.

1882   South Carolina enacts the so-called Eight Box Law, which creates eight categories of election with eight separate ballot boxes. The measure is intended to disfranchise illiterate blacks.

1883   Congress passes the Pendleton (Civil Service Reform) Act. Among its provisions, the act states that no public employee may be obligated to contribute to a political fund and that no public employee may be removed from office for failing to do so.

1887   In response to the disputed 1876 presidential election, Congress passes the Electoral Count Act, which establishes a means for dealing with the possible situation in which conflicting state authorities certify differing sets of electors. If such a controversy arises, Congress, voting as two separate houses, will decide which set of electors to accept. Should Congress fail to resolve the issue, the electors certified by the state governor will be accepted.

Congress passes the Edmunds-Tucker Act, which outlaws the Mormon practice of plural marriage. The act also disfranchises women in the Utah Territory.

1888   Two states, Kentucky and Massachusetts, adopt the Australian ballot. This reform provides for a uniform ballot printed at public expense, thus providing for secret voting under official supervision.

Benjamin Harrison wins a majority of the electoral college votes and gains the presidency even though his Democratic opponent, incumbent president Grover Cleveland, received just over 110,000 more popular votes nationwide.

1889   Seven more states adopt the Australian ballot.

Montana enters the Union with a constitution that allows women to vote in school elections and women who pay taxes to vote on tax issues. North Dakota, South Dakota, and Washington enter the

1889 *(cont.)*	Union, each allowing women to vote in school elections.
1890	The American and National Woman Suffrage Associations merge, creating the National American Woman Suffrage Association. Elizabeth Cady Stanton is elected president and Susan B. Anthony vice president.
	Six states and territories adopt the secret, or Australian, ballot.
	The new Mississippi constitution includes provisions intended to disfranchise blacks. The constitution requires payment of a two-dollar poll tax and, after 1892, the ability to read or understand the constitution as criteria for granting suffrage.
	Wyoming enters the Union with a constitution that grants full suffrage rights to women, thus becoming the first state, except for New Jersey for a brief period in the eighteenth century, to allow women the right to participate in all elections.
1891	Eighteen states and territories adopt the Australian ballot.
1892	In *Sproule v. Fredericks* the Mississippi constitution of 1890 survives the charge that by denying the franchise to blacks the state has violated the provisions for reentering the Union after the Civil War. The Court rules that those provisions lapsed as soon as Mississippi reentered the Union, and in any event no case has been made that the constitution in fact discriminates on the basis of race.
1893	The Arkansas constitution is amended to require payment of a poll tax as a qualification for voting.
	With passage of a referendum, Colorado becomes the second state to grant women full suffrage rights.

1894 Local "good government" organizations send delegates to the initial meeting of the National Municipal League, which is the first national organization concerned with municipal reform. Major concerns among delegates at this meeting are the streamlining of city government and the elimination of political machines.

    Congress repeals sections of the 1870 Enforcement Act and the 1871 Force Act.

1895 In addition to a literacy test, the South Carolina constitutional convention establishes a grandfather clause that states that until 1898 any person who could vote in 1867, his descendants, or any naturalized citizen is exempt from the literacy requirement. This provision is intended to disfranchise blacks while allowing illiterate whites to vote. The literacy qualification requires the ability to complete the registration applications without error.

1896 Idaho amends its state constitution to grant the full franchise to women.

    Utah enters the Union with a constitution that restores full suffrage rights to women, rights that were rescinded by the 1887 Edmunds-Tucker Act.

1897 Delaware eliminates a taxpaying requirement for voting.

1898 A constitutional convention in Louisiana follows South Carolina's lead by establishing strict literacy tests that include a loophole for those who were qualified to vote in 1867, their descendants, and naturalized citizens—the so-called grandfather clause.

1899 Members of the National Municipal Reform League reach agreement on a model city charter that calls for the replacement of ward electoral systems by at-large electoral systems, the institution of nonpartisan

1899
(cont.)

elections, the holding of municipal elections at times different from those established for federal and state elections, and the elimination of larger bicameral city councils in favor of smaller unicameral councils. The goal of these reforms is to eliminate the power of political machines by altering election outcomes.

1901

Alabama follows the lead of Mississippi, South Carolina, and Louisiana in denying suffrage to blacks. After providing exemptions to assure the franchise for whites, the new constitutional provisions dictate that after 1903 only those who can read and write any part of the constitution and who have been gainfully employed the preceding year may register to vote. Property ownership may substitute for the literacy test. Those found guilty of various petty crimes may also be denied suffrage.

1902

Virginia adopts suffrage provisions similar to those enacted the previous year in Alabama, a major objective of which is to disfranchise blacks.

1903

Provisions of the Alabama constitution claimed to be discriminatory against blacks are upheld in *Giles v. Harris.*

1904

In the face of burgeoning campaign donations from businesses, Perry Belmont, head of the National Publicity Law Association, leads the way for reform, urging Congress to enact legislation that limits political contributions from corporations.

In *Giles v. Teasley* the U.S. Supreme Court again denies the attempts of blacks to disallow disfranchisement methods established under southern state constitutions.

1907

In response to allegations of heavy corporate funding for his 1904 presidential campaign, Theodore Roosevelt proposes that candidates for federal office disclose campaign finances and be prohibited from receiving corporate contributions. Roosevelt also makes a proposal for public funding of federal elections.

Congress passes the Tillman Act, which prohibits candidates for federal office from receiving corporate contributions.

1910   Congress passes the Federal Campaign Disclosure Law, which is the first federal legislation designed to require candidates for federal office to disclose campaign financing sources.

An Adams County, Ohio, judge convicts 1,679 individuals of vote selling. This number represents more than one-quarter of all voters in the county.

1911   Congress sets the number of members of the U.S. House of Representatives at 435 and calls for reapportionment of congressional districts every ten years.

1912   Arizona enters the Union with a constitution that grants full suffrage rights to women.

1913   The Seventeenth Amendment to the U.S. Constitution is ratified, providing for the popular election of U.S. senators.

The Illinois legislature grants women the right to vote for presidential electors.

1914   Congress establishes the time for electing senators, setting it to coincide with elections to the House of Representatives.

1915   In *Guinn v. United States,* a decision that ultimately does little to assure minority voting rights, the U.S. Supreme Court declares Oklahoma's grandfather clause unconstitutional.

1917   The New York State constitution is amended to grant full suffrage rights to women.

1920   The Nineteenth Amendment to the U.S. Constitution is ratified, guaranteeing to women the right to vote in federal and state elections.

After the final ratification of the Nineteenth Amendment, leaders of the National American Woman Suffrage Association organize the League of Women Voters. The new organization's initial objective is to encourage women to make informed use of their newly won right to vote.

1921   The U.S. Supreme Court in *Newberry v. United States* rules that congressional regulation of campaign financing does not extend to party primaries. Therefore, candidates in primaries cannot be required to disclose sources of campaign contributions and may engage in unlimited campaign spending. This undercuts congressional regulation of campaign financing by allowing large campaign contributors undue influence over election outcomes through their financial participation in the party nomination process.

1925   Due in part to revelation of such embarrassing incidents as the Teapot Dome scandal and corruption in Warren G. Harding's campaign of 1920, Congress passes the Federal Corrupt Practices Act, which requires congressional candidates to disclose campaign receipts and expenditures. This ineffective legislation excludes primaries from its regulations and applies only to expenditures made with the candidate's "knowledge and consent."

1935   In *Grovey v. Townsend* the U.S. Supreme Court finds the white primary constitutional.

1937   In *Breedlove v. Suttles* the U.S. Supreme Court upholds the constitutionality of the poll tax.

1939   The Hatch, or Political Activities, Act prohibits political parties from soliciting contributions and other support from federal employees. Federal employees are prohibited from taking part in such political activities as running for public office, campaigning for or against candidates, raising funds for candidates, circulating petitions, or organizing political rallies. The legislation bans campaign contributions by federal contractors.

1940   Franklin Roosevelt breaks the two-term tradition and is elected president for an unprecedented third term.

1941   The U.S. Supreme Court in *United States v. Classic* rejects its earlier position in *Newberry v. United States* and asserts that Congress has the authority to regulate campaign finances in party primaries. Although Congress can now regulate the nomination process, it will not do so until 1971.

Congress passes the Smith-Connally Act, which for the duration of World War II prohibits candidates for federal office from receiving financial contributions from labor unions.

1942   The Servicemen's Voting Act facilitates registration and voting by those actively engaged in the armed forces on military bases and overseas.

1943   The idea of term limits is raised in Congress but receives little support.

The Congress of Industrial Organizations creates the first political action committee.

1944   The U.S. Supreme Court in *Smith v. Allwright* declares the white primary unconstitutional. The Democratic party in southern states may no longer exclude African Americans from participation in the party nomination process. The Democratic party's domination in these states means that the party nominee is virtually assured victory in the general election, and thus the exclusion of African Americans from the Democratic primary considerably di-

1944 (cont.)	minishes the ability of African Americans to affect election outcomes. By striking down the white primary, the Supreme Court helps to ensure meaningful African American electoral involvement.
1946	In *Colegrove v. Green* the U.S. Supreme Court holds that malapportionment of legislative districts is a political question to be decided through the political process, not by the courts.
1947	Congress passes the Taft-Hartley Act, which makes permanent the prohibition on the receipt of financial contributions from labor unions by candidates for federal office.
	Senator W. Lee O'Daniel of Texas proposes term limitations for members of Congress, but the measure is soundly defeated.
1948	Election fraud is suspected when future president Lyndon B. Johnson wins a U.S. Senate seat from Texas. A precinct worker in Duval County who is friendly to Johnson discovers 203 additional ballots, all but one of which has been cast for Johnson, giving the Democratic candidate an 87-vote victory.
1951	The Twenty-second Amendment to the U.S. Constitution is ratified, prohibiting anyone from holding the office of president for more than two full terms and limiting to a total of ten years the time that office may be held by any one individual.
1955	The Federal Voting Assistance Act provides assistance to members of the armed forces in registering and voting. The Federal Voting Assistance Program is created in the Department of Defense and is charged with carrying out provisions of the act.
1957	Congress passes the first civil rights bill since the 1870s. Weak in its enforcement provisions, the law relies on litigation to protect citizens against discrimination in registration and voting procedures.

1959   In *Lassiter v. Northampton County Board of Elections* the U.S. Supreme Court upholds the constitutionality of the literacy test.

1960   Congress passes a civil rights act that requires the retention of original registration and voting records for 22 months following an election so that they will be available should questions or challenges arise. The legislation authorizes a federal district judge to appoint federal officials to replace state registrars of voters if a pattern of discrimination is discovered.

In *Gomillion v. Lightfoot* the U.S. Supreme Court rules that racial gerrymandering in Tuskegee, Alabama, violates the Fifteenth Amendment guarantee of minority voting rights.

Voter registration rates of African Americans in the South is still less than half that of whites.

1961   The Twenty-third Amendment to the U.S. Constitution is ratified, under which the District of Columbia will be treated as a state for purposes of electing a president. The district shall have electoral votes equal to the number it would have if it were a state, but no more than the least populous state.

President John F. Kennedy makes campaign financing a priority issue by establishing a bipartisan commission to study campaign costs.

1962   Overturning the 1946 *Colegrove v. Green* decision, the U.S. Supreme Court in *Baker v. Carr* rules that federal courts have jurisdiction over questions concerning apportionment for state legislative districts and declares that malapportionment can be so unfair as to deprive a person of equal protection under the law as provided by the Fourteenth Amendment to the U.S. Constitution.

1964   The Twenty-fourth Amendment to the U.S. Constitution is ratified, prohibiting the use of the poll tax

1964 (cont.)	as a condition for voting in any federal election, thereby outlawing a procedure long used by state legislatures to limit the right to vote.

The U.S. Supreme Court in *Reynolds v. Sims* rules that state legislative districts must be apportioned as equally as possible according to population, based on the principle of "one man, one vote."

The U.S. Supreme Court in *Wesberry v. Sanders* applies the principle of apportionment on the basis of "one man, one vote" to congressional districts.

Congress passes the Civil Rights Act, which, although not primarily aimed at protecting voting rights, does place limitations on the use of literacy tests as a criterion for voter registration.

1965	Congress passes the Voting Rights Act, which finally provides for effective enforcement of the Fourteenth and Fifteenth Amendments. This landmark legislation suspends the use of the literacy test as a prerequisite for voting. Under this act any form of discrimination that is meant to prevent African Americans from registering to vote and from voting is prohibited. Several states and jurisdictions within states come under special coverage and must submit plans to the U.S. Justice Department for its approval before redistricting can occur. Important results of this legislation are that African American voter registration substantially increases, especially in southern states, and electoral arrangements that diminish African American voting strength, such as the at-large election, are challenged in federal court. The Justice Department is granted the authority to bypass the judiciary in southern states in order to assist disfranchised African Americans.

1966	The U.S. Supreme Court in *Harper v. Virginia State Board of Elections* declares unconstitutional the use of the poll tax as a condition for voting in state elec-

tions, thereby outlawing a procedure long-used by state legislatures to limit the right to vote.

Congress passes the Long Act, which provides federal subsidies to political parties to be used in presidential elections. Although this act is signed into law by President Lyndon Johnson, it is never implemented; in 1967 Congress will vote to make the act inoperative. This act, however, is the precursor of the public financing of presidential elections provided for in the Federal Election Campaign Act amendments of 1974.

1967   The Twenty-fifth Amendment to the U.S. Constitution is ratified, providing for the transition of power from president to vice president when a sitting president is unable to fulfill the duties of the office. The amendment includes detailed provisions for the suspension and resumption by the president of his duties. In addition, it specifies that on the resignation or death of a sitting president, the vice president will immediately assume the duties of the office and that if the office of vice president becomes vacant the president will nominate a new vice president who will then be approved by a majority vote in both houses of Congress.

The proportion of African Americans registered to vote in the southern states covered by the special provisions of the 1965 Voting Rights Act now exceeds 50 percent.

Congress requires that the single-member district system be used by states in elections to the U.S. House of Representatives. Each state is required to create as many congressional districts as it has members in the House, with one member elected from each district.

1968   The Overseas Citizens Voting Rights Act expands the responsibilities of the Federal Voting Assistance Program.

1969   The U.S. House of Representatives approves an amendment to the U.S. Constitution establishing the direct election of president and vice president. A majority of the popular vote would be required for election, and in the event that no presidential ticket were to receive a popular vote majority, a runoff would be held between the top two vote getters. The U.S. Senate fails to act on this proposal.

Maine alters its method of selecting presidential electors. Two are to be chosen by statewide popular vote and the remainder by vote in each congressional district.

In *Allen v. State Board of Elections* the U.S. Supreme Court rules that vote dilution methods such as gerrymandering can adversely affect the right to vote.

1970   Congress amends the Voting Rights Act to prohibit residency requirements for voting that exceed 30 days and to extend the right to vote to those 18, 19, and 20 years of age. However, the constitutionality of extending the franchise by an act of Congress instead of through constitutional amendment is in question.

The U.S. Supreme Court rules in *Oregon v. Mitchell* that Congress does not possess the authority to set the voting age for state elections.

1971   The Twenty-sixth Amendment to the U.S. Constitution is ratified, guaranteeing to those 18, 19, and 20 years of age the right to vote in federal and state elections.

Congress passes the Federal Election Campaign Act, which replaces the Federal Corrupt Practices Act of 1925. The new legislation sets limits on candidates' spending on communications media, establishes limits on financial contributions to candidates, and requires both disclosure of financial contributions made by political action committees and disclosure by candidates of contributors.

Congress passes the Revenue Act, which provides for public funding of presidential campaigns.

1973   The U.S. Supreme Court in *U.S. Civil Service Commission v. National Association of Letter Carriers* upholds provisions of the Hatch Act prohibiting federal employees from engaging in partisan political activity.

1974   As a result of investigations leading to and following Richard Nixon's resignation, substantial illegalities in campaign funding for his 1972 presidential reelection campaign are discovered. The revelations provide the impetus for amendments to the Federal Election Campaign Act that initiate public funding of presidential campaigns. Congress establishes spending limits for presidential and congressional candidates and for national political parties that pertain to party primary, general, and runoff elections. The act also sets contribution limits for individuals, political action committees, and political parties and provides for voluntary public financing of presidential elections. The Federal Election Commission is established to implement these provisions by enforcing financial contribution and expenditure disclosure requirements.

The U.S. Supreme Court in *Richardson v. Ramirez* upholds the right of states to disfranchise convicted felons.

1975   Congress amends the Voting Rights Act to include language minorities, particularly Hispanic Americans, in addition to racial or ethnic minorities as groups that warrant special protection. Literacy tests are permanently eliminated as a condition for voter registration.

President Gerald Ford, Speaker of the House Carl Albert, and Senate President Pro Tempore James Eastland appoint the first two members to the Federal Election Commission.

1975
(*cont.*)

Louisiana adopts the bipartisan primary, in which all candidates for the same office appear on the same ballot. If no candidate wins a majority of votes cast, a runoff election is held between the top two vote getters. This electoral arrangement is designed to help ensure Democratic control of the state.

The Overseas Citizens Voting Rights Act, originally passed in 1968, is expanded.

1976

The U.S. Supreme Court in *Buckley v. Valeo* upholds limits on contributions to congressional office seekers but rules candidate spending limits an unjustified infringement on free expression. The Supreme Court declares unconstitutional the method by which Federal Election Commission members are appointed.

Congress amends the Federal Election Campaign Act to reflect the Supreme Court's decision in *Buckley v. Valeo* and to allow for expenditures by political action committees on behalf of candidates. The act modifies contribution limits established in 1974, requires political action committees to keep accurate records, and changes the method by which members of the Federal Election Commission are chosen. The president will appoint commissioners to six-year staggered terms, with senatorial consent.

The Democratic party moves away from the winner-take-all system of delegate selection in presidential primaries by adopting a system of proportional delegate selection. This is meant to further "democratize" the nomination process.

The nation witnesses the first publicly funded presidential campaign.

1977

A Monterey, California, flood control district, with approximately 45,000 voters, conducts the first all-mail-ballot election.

1979   Congress amends the Federal Election Campaign Act to ease contribution and expenditure disclosure requirements, establishing the distinction between "hard" and "soft" money. Voter registration efforts and "get out the vote" campaigns for presidential candidates are made exempt from contribution and expenditure limits. Congress also restricts the Federal Election Commission's discretion in enforcement, denying the commission the authority to conduct random audits of a candidate's campaign expenditures.

     The U.S. Senate rejects a proposed constitutional amendment to elect the president and vice president by popular vote.

1982   Congress amends the Voting Rights Act, adding the "results test," which outlaws any electoral arrangement that has the effect of weakening minority group voting strength. This replaces the previous "intent" test used by federal courts whereby specific electoral districting schemes are outlawed if discriminatory intent can be shown.

     The Democratic National Committee (DNC) chair, concerned with the rising cost of the presidential nomination process, appoints a commission headed by Governor James B. Hunt of North Carolina to study the process. The Hunt Commission recommends shortening the presidential nomination process and setting aside a portion of delegate positions at the national nominating convention to be filled with elected officials and party leaders. The DNC accepts the commission's recommendations.

1984   The Democratic party introduces "Super Tuesday" into its presidential nomination process, whereby a series of mostly southern states hold their presidential primaries on the same day. The purpose is to shorten the nomination process and to increase the nomination chances of moderate and conservative Democratic contenders.

1984 (cont.)	The Voting Accessibility for the Elderly and Handicapped Act requires states to provide polling places that are accessible to elderly and handicapped voters.
1986	The U.S. Supreme Court in *Thornburg v. Gingles* rules that the "effects" provision of the 1982 Voting Rights Act amendment requires that state legislatures avoid discriminatory results in drawing legislative districts. Some observers interpret this decision to mean that states must act to maximize minority representation, although just how far states can go in creating legislative districts that provide for the election of minority candidates is in question.

The Uniformed and Overseas Citizens Absentee Voting Act combines and replaces the 1955 Federal Voting Assistance Act and the 1975 Overseas Citizens Voting Rights Act. The act is administered by the Federal Voting Assistance Program in the Pentagon. Members of the uniformed services and the merchant marine, along with their spouses and dependents, and civilian U.S. citizens living abroad are guaranteed the right to register and vote in elections for federal office. The law provides for a Federal Post Card Application for registering and absentee voting and establishes a federal write-in, or "blank," ballot for those located in remote areas. It can be obtained from U.S. embassies, consulates, or military bases.

1988	In Wisconsin and Minnesota, which instituted election-day registration in 1976, voter turnout nonetheless falls below the 1972 level. Turnout also declines in Texas, despite the introduction of a liberalized absentee voting program.
1990	Congress passes the Americans with Disabilities Act (ADA), which expands the responsibilities of state and local election officials in guaranteeing accessibility for all, regardless of physical disabilities, to registration and polling places.

1991   Senator Hank Brown of Colorado fails to have an amendment included in the Senate campaign finance reform bill that would have established term limits.

            Texas becomes the first state to institute a system of early voting.

1992   Nearly 67 percent of voting-age African Americans in the South are now registered to vote, compared to 68 percent outside the South. These figures indicate the success of the Voting Rights Act.

            It is estimated that in this year's election two-thirds of the electorate will use a ballot that is electronically read and counted.

1993   The U.S. Supreme Court in *Shaw v. Reno* addresses the question of the extent to which states can proceed in creating legislative districts to ensure the election of minority candidates. The Court finds that any legislative districting done for obvious racial purposes that results in bizarrely shaped districts possibly violates the Fourteenth Amendment's equal protection clause, even when the purpose is to ensure the election of minority candidates. The decision is seen as a limitation on the single-member district system to provide a remedy for vote dilution.

            The National Voter Registration Act requires states to offer citizens the opportunity to register or renew their registration when receiving or renewing driver's licenses; when applying for assistance from Aid to Families with Dependent Children (AFDC), for assistance from Special Supplemental Food Program for Women, Infants, and Children (WIC), or for disability benefits; and at armed forces recruitment offices. The legislation also requires all states to institute mail-in registration. Among other provisions of the legislation, states are required to accept the national voter registration form specified by the

1993
(cont.)

Federal Election Commission and to refrain from removing individuals from the registration rolls for failure to vote or for changing address within the registrar's jurisdiction.

Under amendments to the Hatch Act, federal government employees may run for office in a nonpartisan election, sign petitions for the ballot, assist in voter registration drives, serve as a poll worker, and serve as a poll watcher for a candidate or political party. Among the act's continued prohibitions are running for office in a partisan election and taking part in partisan political activities while working.

1994

As the result of state elections in 1994, there are now laws in 20 states that limit the congressional term of service. The constitutionality of such state provisions, however, is in question.

The Arkansas Supreme Court rules unconstitutional state-imposed congressional term limits.

1995

The National Voter Registration Act takes effect in January.

The U.S. Supreme Court decides in *U.S. Term Limits v. Thornton* that term limits imposed by states on their representatives in the U.S. Congress are unconstitutional. The ruling is based on the qualifications clauses of the U.S. Constitution (Article I, Sections 2 and 3). The decision does not affect any term limits that states have imposed on their own state legislators.

The U.S. House of Representatives rejects a proposed constitutional amendment to impose a 12-year lifetime limit on congressional service in both the House and the Senate. The House also rejects modifications to the amendment to allow states to place term limits on congressional officeholders. The Senate Judiciary Committee recommends that the full Senate consider a 12-year congressional term limit.

President Bill Clinton and Speaker of the House Newt Gingrich agree to establish a bipartisan commission to deal with the problems of the electoral system.

1996   One year after President Clinton and Speaker Gingrich pledged to work for election reform, no action has been taken to form a commission.

Oregon becomes the first state to hold a congressional election by an all-mail ballot. The election is held in January to fill the unexpired term of Senator Robert Packwood, who resigned in disgrace.

1997   In February members of the House of Representatives vote on 11 different versions of term limit proposals, rejecting each one. Supporters of term limits disagree on whether the limit should be set at 6, 8, or 12 years.

Revelations surface about campaign fund-raising for the 1996 election, including allegations that President Bill Clinton offered overnight stays in the White House to Democratic campaign contributors and that Vice President Al Gore made phone solicitations from the White House for campaign funds. Additional claims, including charges that foreign governments contributed campaign money, lead to congressional hearings on campaign finance and allegations of wrongdoing.

Biographical Sketches 3

The individuals selected for this chapter include both those presently active in some aspect of campaign and electoral reform and those from past generations who played a role in the improvement of election procedures. Each has made significant contributions to election reform, including such areas as campaign contributions and expenditures, alternative voting systems, woman suffrage, political corruption and vote fraud, voter turnout, election procedures and administration, and voting rights.

Herbert E. Alexander (1927–)

Herbert Alexander has been referred to as "Mr. Campaign Finance" in recognition of his expert knowledge of the use of money in politics and for his grasp of campaign reform issues. He has studied patterns of campaign donations and spending for four decades in his position as executive director of the Citizens' Research Foundation, a position he assumed in 1958. When Alexander moved to the University of Southern California in 1978 the foundation moved with him. Every four years Alexander examines the financial records of political campaigns made available by the Federal Election Commission. He also interviews many campaign workers to complete his analysis of money in local, state, and federal elections.

Alexander received his Ph.D. from Yale University in 1958. In 1961 President John F. Kennedy appointed him the executive director of the President's Commission on Campaign Costs. The president asked this bipartisan group to recommend methods of financing presidential election campaigns. In April 1962 the commission submitted its report, which contained a broad plan for reforming campaign financing. The report included recommendations for federal legislation as well as possible measures that state governments could take to reform campaign financing. Specific proposals for reform involved improved disclosure policies, limitations on donations, tax incentives, more effective deterrence of corrupt practices, and improvements in political broadcasting. Alexander went on to serve as a consultant to the president, the Treasury Department, and Congress with regard to early drafts of legislation. Once Congress passed the Federal Election Campaign Act in 1971 Alexander became a full-time consultant to the comptroller general, assisting in the establishment of the Office of Federal Elections at the General Accounting Office. Alexander served as a consultant to the Senate Select Committee on Presidential Campaign Activities from 1973 to 1974, the New Jersey Election Law Enforcement Commission from 1973 to 1978, the New York State Board of Elections from 1974 to 1976, and the Illinois State Board of Elections and the governor of Rhode Island in 1987. He continued his role as a consultant in 1989 when he provided assistance to the New York City Campaign Finance Board. In 1990 Alexander served on the Senate Campaign Finance Reform Panel.

Alexander has published a number of studies dealing with campaign finance. He coauthored *Financing the 1992 Election,* published in 1995. This publication, the ninth in a series addressing campaign finance, examines funding of the presidential and congressional elections, investigates the activities of political action committees, and analyzes the possibilities for electoral reform. Alexander's *Financing Politics: Money, Elections, and Political Reform,* published in 1992, provides a historical overview of campaign finance, explores the various aspects of contemporary campaign finance on the national and state levels, and appraises reform efforts. Alexander does not object primarily to the amounts of money being spent on political campaigns, noting that candidates must spend money in order to reach the public, but he does advocate disclosure of campaign donations and expenditures.

Douglas J. Amy (1951–)

Douglas Amy is a major advocate of election reform and proportional representation systems. Born in the state of Washington, Amy graduated summa cum laude from the University of Washington, where he also earned his masters degree in political science. He received his Ph.D. in political science from the University of Massachusetts at Amherst in 1981. He served as a visiting assistant professor at Oberlin College before moving to the Department of Politics at Mount Holyoke College in 1981 where he presently serves as a full professor.

Since 1987 Amy's main research interest has been alternative electoral systems and the prospects for election reform in the United States. In 1993 he published *Real Choices/New Voices: The Case for Proportional Representation Elections in the United States.* This was the first book in the past 50 years to argue for abandoning what Amy considers a deeply flawed single-member district election system and replacing it with proportional representation (PR) elections. Amy argues that PR elections would ensure fair and accurate representation for all parties, help to eliminate gerrymandering, encourage the election of more women to office, increase voter turnout, encourage the creation of a multiparty system that would give Americans more choices at the polls, and help to ensure fair representation for racial and ethnic minorities without creating special districts for them. The publication of this book has helped to stimulate the current growing public interest in alternative electoral systems.

Since publication of *Real Choices/New Voices* Amy has spent a good deal of his time promoting this political reform, writing numerous articles, papers, and op-ed pieces about proportional representation and the need for election reform. In addition he has given many speeches and talks on this topic to various civic and professional groups around the country and has been interviewed on C-SPAN and a number of public and commercial radio stations.

Amy has also been active in several organizations that have promoted PR as an important electoral reform. He has served for many years on the advisory board of the Center for Voting and Democracy in Washington, D.C., a nonprofit organization dedicated to educating the American public about alternative electoral systems. He has also been an officer in the Fair Ballot Alliance of Massachusetts, a statewide organization promoting a switch to PR elections. In an effort to make information about proportional representation and election reform more readily available to the public, Amy created in 1996 a World Wide Web site with information about proportional representation. Called the Proportional Representation Library, the site contains beginning readings on PR, in-depth articles by scholars and activists, an extensive bibliography of readings, and a guide to other PR-related Web sites.

Susan Brownell Anthony (1820–1906)

Susan B. Anthony played a major role in the fight for woman suffrage during the second half of the nineteenth century. Anthony's involvement in the temperance movement led her to the realization that women could affect policy only if they had full citizenship rights, including the right to vote. Beginning in 1865 she initiated an effort to have the rights of women protected under the Fourteenth and Fifteenth Amendments, along with those of former slaves. Her appeals fell on deaf ears, however, even among former male allies in the abolitionist movement. Anthony's fight for woman suffrage reached a crucial stage in 1871, when she was persuaded that the Fourteenth Amendment could be used in the fight for the right to vote. She decided to test this interpretation by attempting to vote in the November 1872 election. Anthony and a few other women in Rochester, New York, succeeded in registering and voting. Having attended the Republican National Convention earlier that year, where she received at least the glimmer of hope that the Republican party favored rights for women, Anthony campaigned for the Republican party and voted a straight Republican ticket in the election. No flood of women followed her example, however. Within two weeks a deputy federal marshal arrested her for violating a federal law originally intended to prevent former southern rebels from voting. At the conclusion of the trial the presiding judge read his decision from a document, which he had already written before the closing arguments, stating that the right or privilege of voting originates in the state, not the national, constitution. Therefore, because state law forbade women to vote, the only course to take was to direct the jury to find the defendant guilty. Anthony was fined $100 and the costs of prosecution, an assessment she declared she would not pay. She was denied the opportunity of taking her case to the national arena when the judge stated that he would not require her imprisonment pending payment of the fine, thus blocking an appeal to the Supreme Court on a writ of habeas corpus.

After this event, which could have been of far greater historical significance for women had the case reached the federal courts, Anthony spent the remaining 34 years of her life engaged in a campaign for suffrage that produced few clear victories. Her major objective was to see a woman suffrage amendment added to the national constitution, and in her pursuit of that goal she continued to lecture throughout the nation on behalf of the rights of women. Although Anthony favored a national rather than a state-by-state strategy, she campaigned in specific states and territories that showed promise of extending the franchise to women. In May 1877 she traveled to Colorado, only to see a suffrage measure defeated. She saw Wyoming in 1890 and Utah in 1896 admitted to the Union with constitutions granting suffrage rights to women. Both were territories in which she and Elizabeth Cady Stanton had lectured in 1871. Colorado and Idaho also granted the franchise to women, but campaigns in other states failed.

Anthony remained active in women's rights organizations, serving as president of the National American Woman Suffrage Association from 1892, when Elizabeth Cady Stanton retired from the office, until 1900, when she had reached the age of 80. Anthony remained active in the last years of her life, continuing to attend meetings of the association. In 1904 she spoke for the last time before a Senate committee, advocating, with no perceptible results, a constitutional amendment guaranteeing woman suffrage. In November 1905 she had the opportunity to speak with President Theodore Roosevelt but failed to elicit a commitment from him to support woman suffrage. Anthony, frail and ill, attended her last convention in Baltimore in January 1906, less than two months before her death.

Kathleen L. Barber (1924–)

Kathleen Barber's distinguished career as a political scientist has been supplemented by active political involvement in the Cleveland, Ohio, area and by a deep concern for political reform. Her long experience culminated in the publication in 1995 of *Propor-*

tional Representation and Election Reform in Ohio, the first book-length study to investigate the effects of proportional representation on municipal government.

Barber received a B.A. from Wellesley College in 1944 and an M.A. in 1965 and Ph.D. in 1968 from Case Western Reserve University. She taught at John Carroll University in Cleveland from 1968 until her retirement in 1989, serving as chair of the Political Science Department from 1977 to 1985. A lifelong political activist, she has served in a number of political positions, including membership on the Shaker Heights, Ohio, City Council from 1973 to 1979 and as vice mayor in 1979. She also served on the Shaker Heights Charter Commission in 1985 and 1986. Barber has been active in the Ohio Democratic party, serving as a member of the Cuyahoga County Democratic Party Executive Committee from 1978 to 1980 and the Democratic Party State Executive Committee from 1980 to 1982. She twice served as a delegate to the Democratic National Convention. Among more recent community activities, Barber has been chair of the Citizens Committee for County Government Reform, appointed by the Cuyahoga County commissioners. Barber's long career as an educator, researcher, and political activist has won her such recognition as the Outstanding Educator Award from John Carroll University in 1972, admission to the Ohio Women's Hall of Fame in 1986, and the Citizens League Research Institute Civic Leadership Award in 1993.

Many of Barber's writings in political science and law journals are directly relevant to current public policy questions, such as municipal housing code enforcement, Occupational Safety and Health Administration inspections and the right to privacy, the challenge of coping with radioactive spills, and equal rights for women. She has also published articles on Ohio judicial elections and reapportionment in Ohio and Michigan. She presented results of her study of proportional representation in Cleveland at the American Political Science Association convention in 1988 and chaired a panel on proportional representation at the organization's 1991 meeting.

Her book on proportional representation presents case studies of five Ohio cities (Ashtabula, Cincinnati, Cleveland, Hamilton, and Toledo) that elected council members by proportional representation voting systems from 1915 to 1960. Barber discovered that when proportional representation systems were used, independents, African Americans, and ethnic minorities succeeded in winning representation on city councils in areas where previously they had been excluded from holding seats. These results contributed to making the proportional representation system controversial, even though her findings indicate that the feared increase in political conflict and instability did not occur. Barber's study takes on added significance now that increased attention is being given to alternative electoral systems in the wake of federal court disapproval of the creation of majority-minority districts. The continuing underrepresentation of political and racial minorities is leading political activists in many states to propose the adoption of new systems for electing representatives. Barber's study should provide guidance for those considering changes in election law at the state and local levels.

Perry Belmont (1851–1947)

Six-term member of the U.S. House of Representatives, minister to Spain, and Democratic party activist, Perry Belmont played a major role in early attempts to regulate campaign finance. He was born in New York City, the son of August Belmont, an international banker, and graduated from Harvard College, where he distinguished himself in political economy and history. Belmont attended the University of Berlin and received a bachelor of laws degree from Columbia University. After practicing law for five years he was elected to Congress, where he became active in foreign policy, serving as chairman of the Committee on Foreign Affairs in the 48th and 49th Congresses. In 1888 he left the House to become the minister to Spain but resigned in 1889 over disagreements with Secretary of State James G. Blaine. In 1894 Democratic party members attempted to nominate Belmont for the governorship of New York, but he declined. A firm believer in the democratic process, Belmont remained active in party politics. He became a delegate to five Democratic National Conventions.

Disturbed by the large role of private money in politics, Belmont began a push in 1905 for legislation to require the publicizing of campaign contributions. He founded the National Publicity Law Organization, which pressured political parties to make public statements of campaign expenditures. Belmont's efforts led to success in 1910 when Congress passed the Federal Publicity Law, which required candidates and parties to make public at the time of the election the sources and amounts of contributions to campaign funds. Belmont continued lobbying for finance reform, and the following year Congress amended the law to cover publication of primary campaign expenses as well.

Belmont's interest in campaign finance continued. In 1925 Congress passed the Federal Corrupt Practices Act, the first of a series of acts that ultimately proved unsuccessful in controlling the size of contributions and expenditures in political campaigns. The legislation limited individual contributions to $5,000 for a congressional candidate and $10,000 for a senatorial candidate. Dissatisfied with congressional performance, Belmont published *The Return to Secret Party Funds,* in which he related the continuing problems of money and politics. In 1926 he published *The Survival of the Democratic Principle,* a book that outlined the development of democratic values, examined federalism, and investigated U.S. tariff policies. Another publication, *Political Equality, Religious Toleration, from Roger Williams to Jefferson,* was a plea against bigotry in the 1928 campaign when Al Smith, a Roman Catholic, became the Democratic presidential candidate. Belmont's interest in foreign policy also continued. A foe of isolationism, he published *National Isolation and Illusion* (1925), in which he attempted to demonstrate the nation's interdependence with Europe.

James Coolidge Carter (1827–1905)

James C. Carter was a founder of the National Municipal League, an organization that campaigned for government and election reform in the late nineteenth and early twentieth centuries. He is a model of the highly principled professional of the late nineteenth century who saw a vital need to reform the political process. Born in Lancaster, Massachusetts, Carter graduated from Harvard College in 1850. He studied at Dane Law School at Harvard and in 1853 began a law practice in New York City. He remained with the firm of Davies and Scudder for the remainder of his life. His devotion to legal work was so intense that early in his career he became physically exhausted and was forced to leave the law practice for at least a year. However, overall he had a very successful legal career, being elected president of the American Bar Association (1894–1895) and being chosen five times as president of the New York City Bar, an organization he founded. Carter's reputation as a highly gifted legal mind became well established.

Carter's involvement in the Tweed Ring cases, in which party boss William Tweed and his associates were tried for theft of government funds, first led to his interest in municipal reform. In 1875 Governor Samuel Tilden appointed Carter to a commission to develop a plan for municipal administration for cities in the state of New York, a task that further developed his enthusiasm for reform. Carter became the first president of the National Municipal League in 1894 and served until 1903. This organization supported municipal reform and to that end constructed a model city charter. The organization backed the at-large electoral process that was intended to emphasize the overall good of the municipality rather than the selfish interests of smaller groups that the old ward system had encouraged. The league recommended holding municipal elections at different times from state and national elections, thus discouraging national or state political issues from intervening in local government. Powerful political machines such as Tammany Hall in New York City were also a target of league reform efforts.

An avid supporter of the common law, Carter published an article in 1883 opposing a proposal to codify common law in New York State. In 1888 the New York governor appointed him to serve as a member of the constitutional commission. In 1892 President Benjamin Harrison appointed Carter a counsel, along with two others, to present U.S. claims before the Bering Sea tribunal. He made an address in Paris in February 1893 that is considered the zenith of his legal career. However, Carter is best known for his contributions to political reforms that became major influences on the American political process in the twentieth century.

Carrie Clinton Lane Chapman Catt (1859–1947)

What had been denied to Susan B. Anthony and Elizabeth Cady Stanton during their lifetimes, Carrie Chapman Catt saw come to fruition. Due in no small part to her leadership efforts, the woman suffrage amendment was finally ratified in 1920. An intelligent and aspiring young woman, she graduated from Iowa State College in 1877. Intending to attend law school, she instead became a high school principal and then in 1883 the superintendent of the Mason City, Iowa, school system. She left this position in 1885 to marry Leo Chapman and began working as an assistant editor on Chapman's newspaper. In 1886 her husband died while on a trip to California. The extreme hardships she faced as a young widow gave her the resolution to enter the cause of women's rights. She became actively involved in the Iowa Suffrage Association and in 1890 attended the first meeting of the National American Woman Suffrage Association (NAWSA). Susan B. Anthony, the association's president, quickly recognized her organizational talents and recruited her for participation in state suffrage campaigns, as well as for appearances before congressional committees considering a national suffrage amendment.

In June 1891 Carrie Clinton Lane Chapman married George W. Catt, a civil engineer who supported her devotion to the suffrage movement. She was able to continue her reform activities and in 1900 became president of the NAWSA upon Anthony's retirement. In her four years in this position, she advocated a number of election reforms, including the direct primary and the initiative and referendum. When her husband died in 1905 she inherited sufficient resources to allow her to devote her energies to the women's rights cause. The long battle for suffrage rights gradually bore fruit. In 1908 Catt participated in the formation of the New York Woman Suffrage party and directed a campaign for the franchise in that state that finally succeeded in 1917. In 1915 she returned to the presidency of the NAWSA, and through her leadership a major effort began at both the national and state levels. Catt was a major factor in persuading President Woodrow Wilson to throw his support behind a national amendment for woman suffrage. A proposed amendment first passed the House of Representatives in January 1918, but the Senate did not approve an amendment until June 1919. With Tennessee's ratification in August 1920 the necessary three-fourths of state legislatures had approved the amendment, and woman suffrage became a reality. In order to assist women in exercising their newly won right, Catt pushed for the establishment of the League of Women Voters. After 1920 Catt became active in efforts to establish an international peace system but remained devoted to preserving the integrity of the women's movement. She quickly responded to those critics who tried to portray the woman suffrage movement as radical or communistic. She collaborated with others in producing *Victory: How Women Won It*, a detailed account of the battle for woman suffrage. In 1940 at the age of 81 Catt participated in the Woman's Centennial Congress. She addressed the meeting, urging greater involvement by women in public affairs. Highly respected, Catt established a model of participation in nontraditional roles, including electoral politics, for coming generations of women.

Richard A. Cloward (1931–)

Richard Cloward, in cooperation with Frances Fox Piven, his associate at the Human Service Employees Registration and Voter Education Campaign (Human SERVE), has worked for over a decade to persuade government to institute programs to increase voter turnout. Cloward holds that government has not only the negative responsibility of not preventing people from registering to vote but also the positive duty to assure that eligible persons become voter registrants. Cofounder, treasurer, and executive director of Human SERVE, Cloward has worked for the adoption of legislation that would allow people to register to vote when they apply for welfare, food stamps, Medicaid, unemployment benefits, and driver's licenses. Cloward's efforts as director of Human SERVE proved successful in 1993 with the passage of the National Voter Registration Act, the so-called motor-voter bill, which President Clinton signed on May 20 of that year. Cloward believes that the motor-voter bill is an important step toward the complete enfranchisement of low-income and minority groups and is hopeful that as a result of this legislation 95 percent of eligible Americans will become registered to vote.

Cloward received his Ph.D. in sociology from Columbia University in 1958 and has taught at the Columbia University School of Social Work since 1954. He has published numerous articles and books on such topics as delinquency and gangs, the functions of the public welfare system, poor people's movements, and the fate of the welfare system during President Ronald Reagan's administration. In 1988 Cloward, in cooperation with Frances Fox Piven, published *Why Americans Don't Vote,* a book that attributed low voter turnout not to the causes identified in the widely accepted explanations that focus on characteristics of citizens, such as apathy and alienation, but instead to laws that fail to sufficiently encourage Americans to register and vote.

Cloward has gained recognition for his efforts to expand voter registration. In 1986 the Eugene V. Debs Foundation awarded him the Bryant Spann Memorial Prize. The prize, which recognizes publications that demonstrate "social vision and commitment to social justice," was given for a two-part article, coauthored with Frances Fox Piven, on voter registration, "Trying to Break Down the Barriers" and "How to Get Out the Vote in 1988," which appeared in the November 2 and 23, 1985, issues of *The Nation*. In 1994 the National Association of Secretaries of State awarded Cloward the Jim Waltermire Award in recognition of his contributions as cofounder and executive director of Human SERVE to the increase of voter participation. In 1996 the Tides Foundation awarded Cloward the Jane Bagley Lehman Award for Excellence in Public Advocacy in recognition of his efforts to expand citizen participation in voting.

James J. Condit, Jr. (1953–)

Jim Condit heads Citizens for a Fair Vote Count, a Cincinnati-based organization that campaigns against the use of computer-counted ballots and mechanical voting machines. He argues that these methods invite extensive vote fraud because they lack a paper trail that can be used to verify election results. Fearful of a small elite group manipulating election returns, Condit attacks the practice of counting ballots away from public scrutiny, employing technologically sophisticated methods unfamiliar to most citizens. He supports the reintroduction of the traditional paper ballot that is hand counted by local election workers in each voting precinct the night of the election, with the results being posted at polling places for all to see.

Born in Cincinnati, Ohio, Condit became politically active while still a teenager. As a high school senior he helped to form an antiabortion group. In 1972 he was chosen as an alternative delegate at the Republican National Convention, where he testified at the platform hearings in favor of an antiabortion plank. Condit received his B.A. from Xavier University in 1974 with a major in Latin and a minor in Greek. He continued to work in the antiabortion movement and participated in John Birch Society education programs.

Condit's deep concern about the verifiability of election results began in 1979. He had founded the Cincinnatus Political Action Committee that year, presenting himself and five others as a "pro-life" slate of candidates in a local election. The evening of the election a computer breakdown during the vote count suddenly seemed to reverse the fortunes of the young antiestablishment candidates. Frustrated over an unexpectedly poor showing, Condit's organization two years later filed suit against the Hamilton County, Ohio, Board of Elections to challenge computerized elections in the Cincinnati area. In 1985 the Condit organization received a favorable ruling, which stated that no adequate safeguard existed to prevent unauthorized programming of the county computer, leaving the door open to election rigging. However, the judge refused to take any remedial action. Two years later an appeals court overruled the judge's original decision.

Undaunted, Condit continued to document cases of vote fraud in American elections. On the scene in Iowa during the 1996 Republican caucuses, he gathered evidence that election fraud had denied Patrick Buchanan 13 percent of his vote total. The major target for his allegations was Voter News Service, a polling organization for the major television networks. Condit told his story of vote fraud on over 750 radio stations between March and November 1996. In August 1996 the Cincinnatus Political Action Committee broadcast over 50 political ads on radio and cable television challenging vote counts that Condit claimed had transformed Robert Dole from a weak candidate to the landslide victor in the Republican primaries. The commercials suggested that had ballots been counted by hand rather than by computer, Pat Buchanan could have been the Republican presidential nominee. In November 1996 Condit summarized his fears about computer voting fraud in an article that appeared in *Chronicles,* a conservative magazine published by the Rockford Institute.

In 1997 Condit renewed his campaign to reestablish the paper ballot. He favors outlawing computer and mechanical vote-counting methods, which he considers vulnerable to undetectable alterations, whether intentional or not. Possible doubts about the practicality of a return to hand-counted paper ballots notwithstanding, Condit has raised serious questions about ballot security and the verifiability of election results.

Richard Henry Dana III (1851–1931)

Like his father before him, Richard Dana committed himself to reforming the American political process. He hoped to achieve this reform through the introduction of the Australian, or secret, ballot and the establishment of a civil service system. He was born in Cambridge, Massachusetts, to an aristocratic Episcopalian family that believed in active public service. He graduated from Harvard College in 1874 and was admitted to the bar after graduating from Harvard Law School in 1877. The nature of American politics in the late nineteenth century disturbed Dana. Rather than encouraging service and honest discussion of the public good, the structure of the political process placed far too much emphasis on party loyalty and the self-interested pursuit of patronage. Dana focused on the way votes were cast as a major cause of political corruption. Before 1889 oral voting was the norm, and this system encouraged misconduct by political parties, which strove to maintain discipline among their supporters.

Dana called for the introduction of the Australian ballot, the system that Great Britain had been using since 1872. He drafted the legislation that would institute closed voting in Massachusetts. When the state legislature passed the measure, Dana participated in a campaign of voter education to prepare the electorate for the 1889 election, the first one in Massachusetts in which the secret ballot was employed. The secret ballot caught on quickly, and by 1892, 38 states had adopted measures introducing closed voting. In backing the secret ballot Dana intended to separate the citizen from the influence of professional party organizations. However, a change in the ballot procedure, although eliminating some corrupt practices, did not have the broader effect of altering what Dana considered the evils of the two-party system. In 1884 for the only time in his life Dana ran for public office. He lost the mayoral contest in Cambridge partially because he lacked the support of his own Republican party organization, which objected to his independent politics.

Dana continued to press for civil service reform, an issue closely related to campaign and electoral reform, and in 1884 he wrote the Massachusetts Civil Service Reform Act. From 1889 to 1892 Dana edited the *Civil Service Reform Record* and from 1913 to 1923 he served as president of the National Civil Service Reform League. Although a strong advocate of election reform, Dana opposed woman suffrage, claiming that it would create serious conflict between men and women that would endanger social stability.

Chandler Davidson (1936–)

Chandler Davidson is well known for his research on minority voting rights. He received a B.A. from the University of Texas at Austin, where he majored in English and philosophy. He was elected to Phi Beta Kappa and after graduation spent a year at the

University of Poitiers in France as a Fulbright scholar. Davidson then received a Woodrow Wilson fellowship to pursue graduate study and obtained his Ph.D. from Princeton University in 1969. His dissertation topic dealt with the politics of African Americans in Houston, Texas. Since 1966 he has taught at Rice University in Houston, where he was chair of the Department of Sociology during the 1980s and is presently chair once again.

In his first book, *Biracial Politics* (1972), Davidson focused on the rise of black politics in the South beginning in the 1950s. His second, an edited collection of essays titled *Minority Vote Dilution* (1984), was cited as an authoritative source in several legal opinions, including the 1986 U.S. Supreme Court opinion in *Thornburg v. Gingles*, a leading case on minority vote dilution. His book *Race and Class in Texas Politics* was published in 1990. Between 1987 and 1994 Davidson and Bernard Grofman, a political scientist at the University of California, Irvine, organized a research project focusing on the Voting Rights Act, funded by the National Science Foundation and the Rockefeller Foundation. This collaboration led to the publication of *Controversies in Minority Voting: The Voting Rights Act in Perspective* (1992), an edited collection of papers on the Voting Rights Act. Davidson and Grofman published a second edited volume, *Quiet Revolution in the South: The Impact of the Voting Rights Act, 1965–1990* (1994), which contained the results of empirical studies by 27 scholars and voting-rights lawyers that trace the impact of the Voting Rights Act. Both books have been cited by the U.S. Supreme Court in voting rights opinions. In 1993 the Gustavus Myers Center for the Study of Human Rights chose *Controversies in Minority Voting* as their Outstanding Book on Human Rights in the United States, and in 1994 the American Political Science Association awarded *Quiet Revolution in the South* the Richard Fenno Prize as the best book published on legislative studies.

As a result of his scholarship on voting rights, Davidson has appeared on numerous panels at meetings of historical, political science, and sociology associations. He has worked as a consultant or appeared as an expert witness in over 30 lawsuits involving voting rights and other civil rights matters. In 1976 he was the plaintiffs' chief expert in the case that eventually resulted in Houston's present method for electing council members. Davidson testified before the U.S. Senate Judiciary Committee in 1981 on the proposed amendment to Section 2 of the Voting Rights Act, which established a "totality of circumstances" test to determine violations of voting rights. He also gave testimony before the Subcommittee on Civil Rights of the U.S. House Judiciary Committee in 1994. Davidson has worked as a consultant to the U.S. Department of Justice in voting cases in the South, including cases in Mobile, Alabama, and Selma, Alabama, and has conducted research for the State of Texas in *Vera v. Richards*, a congressional redistricting case growing out of the redistricting process in the 1990s.

Richard L. Engstrom (1946–)

Richard Engstrom has conducted extensive investigations of electoral reform. Research professor of political science at the University of New Orleans, Engstrom has written widely on various topics related to elections. He received his B.A. from Hope College in Michigan in 1968 and his M.A. in 1969 and Ph.D. in 1971 from the University of Kentucky. Engstrom joined the political science faculty at the University of New Orleans upon graduation and has remained there throughout his career. He served as department chair from 1976 to 1979 and is presently the coordinator of graduate studies. He was twice selected as a Fulbright-Hays Professor, first as a visiting research fellow in Taiwan (1981–1982) and then as a professor at the University College in Galway, Ireland (1985–1986). In 1990 Engstrom was senior research fellow at the Institute of Irish Studies at Queen's University of Belfast, and in 1993 he was a David Bruce Fellow at the Bruce Centre for American Studies, Keele University, England. His distinguished career includes successful research efforts in many areas, but Engstrom's primary focus has been on elections.

Engstrom has presented numerous papers at political science meetings, including the American and International Political Science Associations; the Midwest, Southern, and Southwestern Political Science Associations; and the Citadel Symposium on Southern Politics. He has chaired panels at many political science meetings during his career and has presented numerous lectures on such topics as cumulative and limited voting as remedies for minority vote dilution, the role of social scientists in voting rights litigation, vote dilution in judicial elections, reapportionment and black political power, and the evolution of the Voting Rights Act. In 1994 he conducted a lecture tour of African nations under the sponsorship of the U.S. Information Agency. Among other topics he spoke on comparative election systems. Engstrom chairs the

Section on Representation and Electoral Systems of the American Political Science Association. Among his organizational affiliations are associate membership in the Centre for the Study of Irish Elections and the Southern Political Science Association's Committee on the Status of Blacks. He is currently engaged in research dealing with the recent history of redistricting in Louisiana; cumulative voting elections in 15 Texas local government jurisdictions; and proportional representation, electoral manipulation, and reform in Ireland. Engstrom has published articles on several election reform topics, including racial gerrymandering, vote dilution, at-large versus district elections, cumulative voting, proportional representation, alternative judicial election systems, multiseat electoral systems, the single transferable vote, and the Voting Rights Act.

Engstrom's published research has been cited in several rulings of the U.S. Supreme Court, including the landmark voting rights decision *Thornburg v. Gingles* (1986). He has served as an expert witness in numerous court cases involving the voting rights of African Americans, Hispanic Americans, Native Americans, and Native Alaskans. He has established himself as a leading author on the use of modified multiseat electoral systems—such as limited, cumulative, and preference voting—as alternative remedies for dilutive electoral arrangements in the United States. In 1993 Engstrom received the George W. Lucas Community Service Award from the New Orleans National Association for the Advancement of Colored People for his contributions to assuring voting rights for minorities.

Bernard N. Grofman (1944–)

Bernard Grofman, a professor of political science and social psychology in the School of Social Sciences at the University of California, Irvine, has published extensively on such subjects as voting rights, voter turnout, and reapportionment. Born in Houston, Texas, he received a B.S. (1966), M.A. (1968), and Ph.D. (1972) from the University of Chicago. Grofman began his academic career at the State University of New York at Stony Brook, where he joined the Political Science Department in 1970. He remained there until 1976. His research focused on social science methodology, including mathematical model building, legislative processes, and decision-making processes. In the late 1960s and early 1970s he began publishing articles on voting, including "Some

Notes on Voting Schemes and the Will of the Majority" (*Public Choice*, 1969), "Voting Tactics, a Neglected Study" (*Parliamentary Journal*, 1971), and "A Note on Some Generalizations of the Paradox of Cyclical Majorities" (*Public Choice*, 1972).

In 1976 Grofman moved from the State University of New York at Stony Brook, to the University of California at Irvine, assuming an associate professor position in the Political Science Department. In 1980 he was promoted to full professor. In the 1980s his work in electoral systems began to blossom. He edited *Representation and Redistricting* (1982), in which questions of districting and minority representation were investigated; *Choosing an Election System* (1984); and *Electoral Systems and Their Political Consequences* (1986). His scholarly articles continued to demonstrate his interest in minority representation. Examples are "Fair and Equal Representation" (*Ethics*, 1981), "Criteria for Districting: A Social Science Perspective" (*UCLA Law Review*, 1985), and "Multivariate Methods and the Analysis of Racially Polarized Voting: Pitfalls in the Use of Social Science by the Courts" (*Social Science Quarterly*, 1991). In recent years Grofman has served as an expert witness in several cases involving redistricting litigation or as a court-appointed expert on reapportionment.

Grofman, along with Chandler Davidson, initiated a research project to investigate the consequences of the Voting Rights Act. The research was funded by the National Science Foundation and the Rockefeller Foundation. Grofman and Davidson edited *Controversies in Minority Voting: The Voting Rights Act in Perspective* (1992), an examination of the 1965 Voting Rights Act and its amendments, and *Quiet Revolution in the South: The Impact of the Voting Rights Act 1965–1990* (1994), which focuses on the effects of election reform on minority group representation. Grofman has also edited *Legislative Term Limits: Public Choice Perspectives* (1996), a balanced treatment of the probable effects of term limits on rates of legislative turnover and the operation of representation.

Minority Representation and the Quest for Voting Equality (1992), which Grofman coauthored with Lisa Handley and Richard Niemi, provides an excellent overview of minority voting rights and an examination of congressional and court-established standards of vote dilution. The authors conduct a mathematically sophisticated investigation of the totality of circumstances test and offer a way to measure racially polarized voting. Grofman has devoted much of his professional career to assuring that the Voting Rights Act remains an effective tool for minorities in exercising the right to vote and to gain representation on legislative bodies.

Stanley A. Halpin, Jr. (1940–)

Stanley Halpin has had long experience with working for electoral reform. As part of his public interest law practice, he has engaged in numerous legal cases dealing with voting rights. After receiving his B.A. in 1962 from the University of Southwestern Louisiana, Halpin went on to Tulane University Law School, where he earned his J.D. in 1965. From 1969 to 1972 Halpin served as staff counsel and chief counsel for the Lawyers Constitutional Defense Committee of the American Civil Liberties Union of New Orleans. From 1972 to 1980 he concentrated on a public interest law practice in New Orleans. He engaged in some 40 voting rights cases on behalf of African Americans, including *East Carroll Parish School Board v. Marshall,* argued before the U.S. Supreme Court in 1976. The Court decided that single-member districts must be used to elect school board members, barring any unusual circumstances. In the meantime Halpin furthered his education, and in 1978 he received a Ph.D. in political science from George Washington University. His dissertation was titled "The Anti-Gerrymander: The Impact of the Voting Rights Act upon Parish Redistricting in Louisiana." From 1980 to 1983 Halpin served as a litigation training specialist for the New Mexico Legal Services Support Project in Albuquerque. In 1981 he took part in litigation invalidating New Mexico's redistricting efforts, which were determined to constitute racial gerrymandering against Native Americans and Hispanic Americans. The case resulted in a federal-court-drawn plan under which an additional number of Hispanic Americans and Native Americans were elected to the state legislature. The state was required to obtain a federal predetermination that its 1990 redistricting was not racially discriminatory. In 1983, in recognition of his public interest practice, Halpin received the Benjamin Smith Civil Liberties Award of the American Civil Liberties Union. From 1983 to 1988 Halpin directed the Farmworkers Legal Assistance Project of Louisiana, an organization that provided legal services with regard to employment questions for indigent seasonal and migrant farmworkers. As part of his public interest law practice Halpin took part in ensuring fair electoral districting for Native Americans and Hispanic Americans in the 1990 redistricting of the New Mexico legislature. In Louisiana he engaged in a challenge of congressional districts on behalf of African American plaintiffs, which resulted in the election of William Jefferson, Louisiana's first black congressman since Reconstruction.

Halpin was a visiting assistant professor in the Political Science Department at the University of New Orleans, where he taught constitutional law and judicial process, and a lecturer at the Tulane School of Social Work, where he taught a graduate course in law and society. He is presently a professor at the Southern University Law Center in Baton Rouge and the coordinator of the Institute of Human and Civil Rights. He conducts research on voting rights law and has published articles on such topics as minority voting rights in Louisiana and racial gerrymandering. He has made presentations on such subjects as cumulative voting, limited voting and other remedies for minority vote dilution, the Voting Rights Act, and minority representation in Louisiana.

Julia Ward Howe (1819–1910)

Born to a prominent family, Julia Ward Howe added her incisive wit, disarming sense of humor, and superior organizational skills to the fight for woman suffrage. Her family provided her with excellent educational opportunities, which allowed her to develop her innate talents. After her marriage to Samuel Gridley Howe in 1843, she and her husband traveled to Europe, a journey that provided the young woman with a cosmopolitan outlook. When the couple settled in Boston, Howe had the opportunity to converse with some of the leading intellectual and literary personages of the period. In the 1850s and 1860s she directed her talents in a literary direction, publishing a number of volumes, none of which were especially notable. However, she gained wide recognition as the composer of "The Battle Hymn of the Republic."

After her children were grown and her husband had died Howe concentrated her energies on various movements, including woman suffrage. Though she had played a secondary role along with her husband in the abolition movement, she subsequently took a more prominent part in the fight for woman suffrage. She helped to establish the New England Woman's Club in 1868 and served as the organization's president nearly uninterruptedly from 1871 to 1910, the year of her death. She also became the president of the New England Woman Suffrage Association when it was formed in 1868. In 1869 Howe took part in the meeting that established the American Woman Suffrage Association and became an active participant in that organization. She joined with such other women as Lucy Stone to follow a state-by-state strategy in the campaign for woman suffrage, as opposed to the National Woman Suffrage Association's national campaign. In 1870 Howe called for an international meeting of women to promote the peaceful resolution of international conflict. At a meeting in New York City that December Howe addressed a group of women attempting to organize an international women's conference to further world peace. In 1871 she became president of the American chapter of the Woman's International Peace Association. Her efforts in 1872 to bring about a women's peace conference in London, England, proved unsuccessful.

Like many women of the time Howe pursued many social reforms and began her social activism in the abolition movement. In her later years the objective of election reform was a major, but by no means the only, cause that engaged Howe's energies. Her use of the essay and her lectures did much to keep the cause of woman suffrage viable during a time of few victories and many frustrations. Her life of service provided inspiration to others seeking equal social and political rights for women.

Laughlin McDonald (1938–)

Laughlin McDonald has been the director of the Southern Regional Office of the American Civil Liberties Union (ACLU) in Atlanta, Georgia, since 1972. The Southern Regional Office specializes in voting rights litigation and has provided representation to African Americans and Native Americans in many voting rights cases throughout the nation. McDonald has argued cases before the U.S. Supreme Court, one of which significantly expanded and defined the scope of preclearance of state and local alterations in voting rules under Section 5 of the Voting Rights Act.

Born in South Carolina, McDonald graduated from Columbia University in 1960. After completing his J.D. degree at the University of Virginia Law School in 1965, he served as corporate counsel for the Sea Pines Plantation Company in Hilton Head Island, South Carolina. In the late 1960s he worked as a staff attorney for the ACLU Southern Regional Office. In the early 1970s McDonald taught criminal law at the University of North Carolina Law School as a visiting professor and entered private law practice in Columbia, South Carolina, before rejoining the ACLU as director of the Southern Regional Office.

In addition to his participation in litigation related to voting rights, McDonald has testified frequently before Congress on voting rights issues. In 1981 he appeared before the Subcommittee on Civil and Constitutional Rights of the House Judiciary Committee, and the following year he testified before the Senate Judiciary Committee's Subcommittee on the Constitution. On each occasion he presented information regarding the extension and amendment of the Voting Rights Act of 1965. In 1984 and 1985 he testified before the Subcommittee on Civil and Constitutional Rights of the House Judiciary Committee during its hearings on the Voting Rights Act and runoff primaries. In 1988 McDonald appeared before the Senate Committee on Rules and Administration in hearings regarding the proposal for a universal voter registration act.

McDonald has published a number of articles on voting rights, including treatments of the disfranchisement of African Americans in South Carolina, the need for preclearance, universal voter registration as a means of reducing nonparticipation, and vote dilution. He has also authored two books, *Racial Equality* (1977) and *The Rights of Racial Minorities* (second edition, 1993). He coauthored *Litigation under the Voting Rights Act* (1986), a publication of the Center for Constitutional Rights, and wrote *Voting Rights in the South: Ten Years of Litigation Challenging Continuing Discrimination against Minorities* (1982), published by the ACLU.

McDonald has received a number of awards for his work on behalf of voting rights, including honorable mention in 1982 from *The American Lawyer* for Best Performance of the Year in Civil Rights, the John Bolt Culbertson Civil Liberties Award from the South Carolina ACLU in 1988, the Pro Bono and Professional Responsibility Award in 1989 from the American Bar Association's Litigation Section, and the Gate City Bar Association's R. E. Thomas Civil Rights Award in 1990.

Cynthia McKinney (1955–)

In 1992 Cynthia McKinney became Georgia's first African American woman to win a seat in the U.S. House of Representatives. Her victory was attributed to a reapportionment plan in accordance with the Voting Rights Act that created a majority-minority district that McKinney herself had been lobbying to create. When the eleventh district was established, with blacks composing over 60 percent of the population, McKinney moved to De Kalb County and ran for the new open seat. The district extended for 250 miles across the state and included all or part of 22 counties. Her district became one of the foci for a controversy over the legal appropriateness of racial gerrymandering. Whereas to some the creation of majority-minority districts is a vital method for allowing minorities to gain representation, to others such districts amount to the continuation of an unacceptable policy based on racial distinctions.

In 1978 McKinney received a B.A. degree in international relations from the University of Southern California. She was elected to the Georgia House of Representatives for the first time in 1988. While in the Georgia House, McKinney fought vigorously for redistricting plans that would increase black representation in Congress as well as in state and local offices. After garnering the highest percentage of votes in the 1992 primary and winning the runoff for the Democratic nomination in the eleventh district, McKinney overwhelmed her Republican opponent in the general election, receiving 73 percent of the vote. Her district was subsequently challenged in the courts, resulting in a June 1995 decision that led to the redrawing of district lines. Although she was forced to run in a majority white district in the 1996 election, McKinney won reelection. Contrary to the claims of those who have argued that her victory indicates that majority-minority districts are unnecessary to assure fair representation of minorities, the congresswoman has claimed that her success in politics was made possible by the creation of the eleventh district. She has argued that her initial election allowed her to contribute to a depolarization of race relations and to demonstrate to her constituents the ability to represent both black and white voters. The advantage of incumbency, McKinney suggested, permitted her to run for reelection in the newly created fourth district without having to compromise her political views.

The procedure for drawing congressional districts, McKinney has argued, is flawed and needs reform. She has supported alternative voting systems that would obviate the need for racial gerrymandering and avoid further court battles. In 1967 a federal law was enacted that required states to use single-member congressional districts. In October 1995 McKinney introduced legislation that would allow states to employ alternatives to the single-member district system to elect members of the U.S. House of Representatives. Mckinney supports the use of multimember districts along with an alternative voting system, such as cumulative voting, preference voting, or limited voting, noting that the Constitution nowhere requires that representatives be elected according to a single-member district, winner-take-all system. Under these alternatives, voters would have the opportunity to take part in electing more than one person to represent them in Washington. Several cities and counties already employ these alternative voting systems.

Louise Overacker (1891–1982)

Louise Overacker, a noted political scientist, focused much of her research efforts on campaign and electoral reform, making significant contributions to a clearer understanding of the process and potential difficulties of campaign finance. She lent her impressive record as a political scientist to the question of campaign finance reform. In the 1920s Overacker conducted research on the primary election process and in 1932 completed *Money in Elections*, a landmark treatise on campaign financing. She examined efforts to bring about finance regulation, identified the results of such efforts, and suggested potentially more effective controls on campaign funding procedures. In her treatment of the subject, Overacker tapped a variety of sources, including information she derived from her own participation in congressional hearings that were held in 1931 on the regulation of campaigns. She placed the subject of campaign finance within the context of a theory of political parties and the electoral process, noting the ways in which political campaign finance practices threatened existing political institutions and how specific money-raising procedures might weaken the democratic electoral process. She believed that it was of great importance that citizens be aware of the sources of funds and of how campaign money is used. Overacker suggested consideration of such reforms as public funding of political parties and candidates, greater oversight of the handling of donations, and an effective procedure for enforcing new legislation. However, she did not recommend limitations on levels of campaign contributions or spending.

After receiving her Ph.D. from the University of Chicago in 1925, Overacker taught at Wellesley College for 22 years. She served on the executive council of the American Political Science Association in 1926 and 1956 and as that organization's second vice president in 1939. In 1950 Overacker became a member of the association's Committee on Political Parties and assisted in drafting a report that recommended reforms of the American party system. In 1957 she was chosen as a fellow of the American Academy of Arts and Sciences.

In the 1930s Overacker continued her research on campaign funding. For instance, she investigated the effects of the depression on the level and sources of campaign donations. After passage of the Hatch Act in 1939, legislation that among other things prohibited political parties from soliciting political contributions and other assistance from federal employees, Overacker investigated the effects of the new legislation on the 1940 presidential election. During this period she also examined the political activities of labor unions, including the consequences of legislation forbidding unions from making campaign contributions. In 1946 Overacker published *Presidential Campaign Funds.* Although this book focused on presidential politics, she expected her conclusions to be relevant to congressional and state elections as well. Though noting the rising cost of campaigns, she concluded that such costs themselves were not related directly to corruption. Of greater concern was the source of contributions. Without direct regulation of campaign funding, she advocated publicity as a means of controlling donations. Because the decentralized structure of political party organizations in the United States limited the ability to track funding adequately, Overacker recommended more consolidated and responsible party structures.

Mark P. Petracca (1955–)

Since 1991 Mark Petracca has focused much of his scholarly activities on term limits for public officials, becoming a noted advocate of the claimed advantages of such limits. A native of Quincy, Massachusetts, Petracca received his A.B. in government from Cornell University (1977) and A.M. (1979) and Ph.D. (1986) in political science from the University of Chicago. He joined the political science department at the University of California, Irvine, in 1986 and is currently an associate professor there. In 1987 he was a visiting professor in the department of international politics at Beijing University in China.

Petracca has lectured extensively in defense of term limits and has contributed commentary to newspapers around the nation, including the *Christian Science Monitor, Houston Chronicle,*

Los Angeles Times, and *Chicago Tribune.* He has testified before the House Judiciary Committee's Subcommittee on Civil and Constitutional Rights (1993) and the Senate Judiciary Committee's Subcommittee on the Constitution (1995).

Petracca supports term limits as a means of restoring the idea of rotation in office as a fundamental principle of representative government and combatting the professionalization of legislative politics. He supports a constitutional amendment to establish a national term limit standard. The amendment would limit the number of terms served by members of the U.S. House and Senate to an amount of time less than the present average length of service and would specify the amount of time that a former legislator must remain in private life before being eligible to run again for office in the same legislative house.

Petracca prefers a limit of less than twelve years for members of the House because a twelve-year, or six-term, limit would do little to introduce the principle of rotation in office and to eliminate professionalism. He recommends the gradual introduction of limits so that the House will not experience a massive replacement of members in the same year, which would leave the legislative chamber devoid of experienced legislators.

Richard H. Pildes (1957–)

A professor at the University of Michigan Law School, Richard Pildes for many years has advocated election reform. He received his B.A. degree from Princeton University in 1979, majoring in theoretical physical chemistry. He was well regarded as a student of chemistry, receiving a fellowship from the National Science Foundation, the McKay Physical Chemistry Prize, and the Foster Chemistry Prize; he graduated Phi Beta Kappa before entering law school. He served as editor of the *Harvard Law Review* from 1981 to 1983 and received his J.D. from Harvard Law School in 1983. From 1984 to 1985 Pildes served as a judicial clerk to U.S. Supreme Court Justice Thurgood Marshall. After entering private practice in Boston for a brief period, he joined the faculty of the University of Michigan Law School in 1988. For brief periods in 1995 and 1996 Pildes served as a visiting lecturer on comparative constitutional law at the Zussman Institute for Israeli Judges in Jerusalem. He also served as visiting professor of law at the University of Chicago and the University of Texas. He has been counsel to the Council of State Governments, the National Governors Association, the National Conference of State Legislatures, the National Association of Counties, the International City/County Management Associations, the National League of Cities, and the U.S. Conference of Mayors for litigation before the U.S. Supreme Court.

Pildes has published extensively on subjects relevant to electoral reform, including articles dealing with cumulative voting and the Supreme Court decision in *Shaw v. Reno* on racial redistricting. He contributed a chapter on cumulative voting to a volume dealing with representation and reapportionment and has just coauthored with Pamela Karlan a casebook titled *The Law of Democracy.* His writings have also appeared in popular publications, including pieces on political gerrymandering, racial redistricting, and alternative voting systems. In 1993, when Lani Guinier came under strong criticism for her election reform proposals, Pildes came to her defense in an article that appeared in the *Wall Street Journal.* He has also made presentations on various aspects of electoral reform, including cumulative voting, the *Shaw v. Reno* decision, the politics of race, racial aspects of redistricting, and the future of voting rights. In 1996 Pildes presented research results, titled "Voting Rights and Racial Gerrymandering," at a panel of the Law and Political Process Group at the American Political Science Association meeting.

Pildes has taught courses and seminars on voting rights and political participation, conceptions of democracy in American constitutional thought, comparative conceptions of democracy, and the legislative process. He has made numerous national and local radio appearances, including on National Public Radio, to discuss recent Supreme Court decisions. He is the cofounder of the Michigan Legal Theory Workshop. Pildes has served as a legal expert to assist in the court-ordered redistricting of the Ohio legislature and prepared a brief for the U.S. Supreme Court in a case challenging the redistricting of the St. Louis City Council.

Frances Fox Piven (1931–)

In cooperation with Richard Cloward, Frances Fox Piven has worked toward government reform of voter registration laws. Believing that the 1965 Voting Rights Act, which contained provisions restricting possible attempts of state and local governments to deny the right to vote, was insufficient to guarantee suffrage rights, Piven has advocated a more positive role for government in encouraging voter registration. She has focused her attention on enfranchising low-income and minority Americans. As co-founder and board secretary of the Human Service Employees Registration and Voter Education Campaign (Human SERVE), Piven has for over a decade advocated registering people to vote when they apply for welfare, food stamps, Medicaid, unemployment benefits, and driver's licenses. The efforts of Human SERVE came to partial fruition in May 1993 when President Bill Clinton signed into law the National Voter Registration Act (the so-called motor-voter bill).

Piven received her M.A. in city planning in 1956 and a Ph.D. in social science in 1962 from the University of Chicago. After serving as a senior research associate for Mobilization for Youth, the predecessor of the Office of Economic Opportunity Community Action Programs, she joined the faculty of the School of Social Work at Columbia University. In collaboration with Richard Cloward, she has published books on such topics as the functions of public welfare; class, race, and poverty; poor people's movements; and President Ronald Reagan's welfare policies. In 1992 she published *Labor Parties in Postindustrial Societies*. In 1988 Piven published *Why Americans Don't Vote*, coauthored with Richard Cloward. Piven and Cloward argue that commonly accepted explanations for low voter turnout in the United States that focus on the individual characteristics of citizens, such as apathy and alienation, are inadequate. Instead they stress electoral laws that have discouraged people from registering and exercising their right to vote.

Piven's work in social and political science has been well recognized. In 1991 she received the Founders Award from the Society for the Study of Social Problems for her contributions to the study and solution of social problems. In 1995 she received the first Lifetime Achievement Award in Political Sociology from the American Sociological Association. Along with Cloward, Piven has received awards for her work to achieve voter registration reform. In 1986 she received the Bryant Spann Memorial Prize from the Eugene V. Debs Foundation for coauthoring a two-part article on voter registration, "Trying to Break Down the Barriers" and "How to Get Out the Vote in 1988," which appeared in the November 2 and 23, 1985, issues of *The Nation*. In 1994 she received the Jim Waltermire Award from the National Association of Secretaries of State for her work to increase voter participation. In 1996 Piven was given the James Bagley Lehman Award for Excellence in Public Advocacy from the Tides Foundation for her efforts to expand citizen participation.

Robert Richie (1962–)

Robert Richie is executive director of the Center for Voting and Democracy, a nonprofit organization that conducts research and distributes information on electoral reforms that promote voter participation and fair representation. Richie, an expert on both international and domestic electoral systems, has directed the center since its founding in 1992. Born in Washington, D.C., Richie entered Haverford College in 1980 but took three years away to engage in such activities as interning with the Washington, D.C., Public Defenders Service and being a camp counselor for troubled adolescents. He graduated from Haverford with a B.A. in philosophy in 1987.

Richie's great uncle, George Hallett, was the leading proponent of proportional representation (PR) in the United States for many decades and author of *Proportional Representation: The Key to Democracy* (1940). Richie was working for a nonelectoral nonprofit law and policy center in Washington, D.C., when he met his future wife, Cynthia Terrell. Terrell was a political consultant who believed that the most direct route to encouraging better policy was through electing candidates who support those policies. She encouraged Richie to take electoral politics more seriously.

Together they worked for Jolene Unsoeld, congresswoman from Washington, in her 1990 reelection campaign. After winning the closest congressional race in the nation in 1988, Unsoeld was the target of the best-funded challenge to a House incumbent in 1990. Richie prepared and packaged research on her opponent. Although all the research was factual, the process demonstrated the pressures facing candidates in winner-take-all elections to oversimplify issues. Unsoeld ultimately won by a comfortable margin, but in the process she downplayed some of the issues of particular interest to her core supporters in order to appeal to "swing voters." Richie's new belief in the significance of electoral politics was tempered by an increased understanding of serious flaws in the current method of election.

Richie became involved in an effort to reform the charter in the county where he was living. Familiar with Hallett's arguments for PR, he wrote a cover article for a widely distributed monthly publication on why the county should adopt PR. In the course of researching the article he discovered that there was no existing national organization promoting PR. Terrell and Richie received a small grant for a new group called Citizens for Proportional Representation (CPR) to pursue a local initiative campaign on PR. However, they learned that Washington state law prohibited PR for this level of election.

Terrell and Richie volunteered on a campaign for PR in the Cincinnati, Ohio, City Council elections. Although the campaign fell short of victory, an article by Richie in the national publication *In These Times* about the campaign helped identify other national allies. That winter, Richie met Matthew Cossolotto, a former congressional aide who had formed an organization also called Citizens for Proportional Representation. With Cincinnati activist Bill Collins they scheduled a founding meeting for June 1992 to establish a national organization. The meeting was a success, attracting PR supporters from 17 states. Richie moved to Washington to work full-time as the organization's director. In 1993 the name Citizens for Proportional Representation was changed to the Center for Voting and Democracy.

Richie has worked with the staff of Congresswoman Cynthia McKinney in developing the Voters' Choice Act, a bill to allow states to use proportional systems. He has addressed the Voting Section of the U.S. Department of Justice, the Texas Commission on Judicial Efficiency, the annual meetings of the National Association of Counties and the National Conference of State Legislatures, and foreign visitors through the U.S. Information Agency. Richie helped organize three national conferences on PR and worked with activists supporting proportional representation in several states. He worked closely with government officials and community leaders seeking to reform New York's community school board elections, and he toured New Zealand at the invitation of election reformers during a successful referendum campaign in that country to adopt a proportional voting system.

Richie is a frequent source for print, radio, and television journalists, and his commentary appears in such publications as the *New York Times, Washington Post, New Republic, Nation,* and *Christian Science Monitor.* He has been a guest on numerous radio and television programs, including C-SPAN and MSNBC. He edits a regular column for the *National Civic Review* along with the Center for Voting and Democracy's newsletter and other publications, such as its two *Voting and Democracy* reports and

Dubious Democracy, an analysis of congressional elections from 1982 to 1994.

Anna Howard Shaw (1847–1919)

Anna Howard Shaw became one of the most effective advocates of woman suffrage in the late nineteenth and early twentieth centuries. Her leadership and oratorical skills contributed significantly to the cause. Born in England, she came to the United States with her family in 1851. While her family lived in Lawrence, Massachusetts, they participated in the abolition movement, offering their home as a station on the Underground Railroad. In 1859, when her father moved the family to Michigan, Shaw began to take part in the many activities necessary to maintain a farm. She educated herself by reading books her father gave her. After attending a school for two years she became a teacher. After the Civil War religion attracted her interest, and in 1871 she received a license from the Methodist church to preach. In 1873, over the objections of her Unitarian family, Shaw enrolled in a Methodist high school, and in 1876 she graduated from the divinity school at Boston University. After her ordination in 1880 in the Methodist church, Shaw went on to earn a degree in medicine in 1886.

In 1885, forsaking her church position, Shaw helped to establish the Massachusetts Woman Suffrage Association and started speaking on the suffrage issue. Also joining the temperance movement, she became head of the Franchise Department of the Woman's Christian Temperance Union. Having already worked with Lucy Stone in the American Woman Suffrage Association, she joined the rival National Woman Suffrage Association when Susan B. Anthony saw her great leadership potential. When the two organizations merged in 1890 Shaw served as a national lecturer, and in 1892 she became the organization's vice president. Because of her excellent speaking abilities she was elected president of the National American Woman Suffrage Association (NAWSA) in 1904. As president she engaged in lobbying activities in Washington and in states holding referenda on extending the vote to women, and she spoke at numerous conferences.

Although an able representative for the cause of woman suffrage, Shaw tended to create dissension within the movement. In 1915, due in part to threatened factionalism in the NAWSA, she decided not to run for reelection as president but remained a national board member. Shaw became active in public service during World War I as chairman of the Woman's Committee of the U.S. Council of National Defense and after the war spoke in favor of the League of Nations. Shaw lived to see congressional approval of the woman suffrage amendment but died before final state ratification.

Elizabeth Cady Stanton (1815–1902)

Elizabeth Cady Stanton, the daughter of a judge, became one of the foremost advocates of women's rights. In her youth she learned about the second-class status of women, overhearing stories in her father's law office of women forced to endure maltreatment with no relief to be had under existing laws. In 1840 she accompanied her husband, an abolitionist, to the world antislavery convention in London, England. At the convention she met other American women who shared a desire to further their rights as women. They would form the core of a woman suffrage movement in the United States. In July 1848 Stanton succeeded in organizing a women's rights convention in Seneca Falls, New York, where she was then residing with her husband. At the convention Stanton introduced a woman suffrage resolution and succeeded in obtaining its adoption over objections that the women would be ridiculed for it. She met Susan B. Anthony in 1851, and the two women commenced a lifelong collaboration in support of woman suffrage. In 1869 the National Woman Suffrage Association was established and the members chose Stanton as the organization's president, a position she held until the formation of the National American Woman Suffrage Association in 1890. In 1887, while Stanton was in Europe, the U.S. Senate for the first time voted on a constitutional amendment proposing woman suffrage. The amendment was defeated, with only 16 senators supporting the measure. While the National American Woman Suffrage Association met in Washington in February 1890, Stanton testified before a Senate committee that once again was exploring the possibility of woman suffrage. In the 1880s Stanton collaborated with Susan B. Anthony and Matilda Joslyn Gage in preparing a history of the woman suffrage movement. From 1881 to 1886 the women published three volumes of *History of Woman Suffrage.*

Unlike most in the early suffrage movement, Stanton's concerns went far beyond gaining the right to vote. She insisted on the right of women to act for themselves, not only in the voting booth but in all aspects of life, insisting on physical, intellectual, financial, and legal autonomy. In 1902, shortly before her death, Stanton wrote her last letters to President and Mrs. Theodore Roosevelt, appealing for their support for woman suffrage at the national level. When Stanton died, newspapers across the nation took notice. She had challenged the common understandings of the place of women in her society. Although final victory for woman suffrage was not achieved until 18 years after her death, with the ratification of the Nineteenth Amendment, Stanton was able to live her life, especially in her later years, much as she chose. Her life stood as a model for those women seeking greater recognition for women's rights after the victory of suffrage had been achieved.

Edward Still (1946–)

A lawyer in Birmingham, Alabama, Edward Still has played a prominent role in many reapportionment and voting rights cases. Born in Augusta, Georgia, Still received his B.A. degree from the University of Alabama in 1968 and a J.D. degree from the university's law school in 1971. After practicing in a partnership for four years, he set up his own law office in Birmingham in 1975. While still in law school, he joined the board of directors of the Legal Aid Program at Tuscaloosa. In the late 1970s Still contracted with the Birmingham Area Legal Services Corporation to provide legal services to the poor. In 1996 and 1997 he taught American legal history and election law at the University of Alabama School of Law. He has been a guest lecturer on the history of voting rights litigation and on election methods at Cumberland Law School; Birmingham-Southern College; the University of Alabama, Birmingham; Pomona College; and the University of Massachusetts, Boston. Still served as general counsel for the Alabama State Democratic Executive Committee from 1980 to 1986 and organized a statewide network of lawyers for election-day ballot security and polling place problems during the 1984, 1988, and 1992 presidential elections.

Still has contributed to an understanding of alternative electoral systems through his extensive publication on electoral reform. Among the subjects of his articles are the impact of the Voting Rights Act of 1965 on Alabama, alternatives to the single-member district system, cumulative and limited voting in Alabama, the gerrymander, and minority vote dilution. He is a member of the Section on Representation and Electoral Systems of the American Political Science Association (APSA) and has participated in discussions at APSA meetings on such topics as proportional representation, the problems of gerrymandering, and the Voting Rights Act of 1965. Still has played an active role in the Center for Voting and Democracy, an organization that provides information about alternative electoral systems. A charter member of the organization, he joined the board of directors in 1993 and began serving as chair in 1996.

Among the many reapportionment cases in which Still has been involved are *Bolden v. City of Mobile*, which led to a decision in 1982 to reapportion the Mobile City Commission. *Adams v. City of Gadsden*, settled in 1985, resulted in the abandonment of the commission form of government and the establishment of a mayor and seven-member council, elected from single-member districts. *Dillard v. Moore* ultimately led to reapportionment of nearly 200 county commissions, county school boards, and city and town councils. The many voting rights cases in which Still has been engaged involve such subjects as a local law restricting campaigning on election day, an Alabama constitutional provision barring certain misdemeanants from voting, an Alabama constitutional provision disfranchising "wife beaters," and limitations placed on the availability of absentee ballots. Still has also taken part in a number of cases dealing with freedom of speech and freedom of religion.

Still's tenaciousness as a lawyer has been honored by author Isaac Asimov, who wrote a limerick that begins:

> Don't mess round with Lawyer Ed Still,
> For he puts those opposed through the mill.

Lucy Stone (1818–1893)

Lucy Stone worked throughout her life to achieve equal rights for women, including the right to vote. Although her father firmly believed in the subordinate status of women, Stone developed a desire to excel. Initially without her father's assistance, she entered Oberlin College, working as a teacher to pay tuition. She graduated in 1847. Stone became involved in the abolitionist movement and possessed a talent for presenting effective talks on the subject. She also focused on the lowly status of women in society and in 1850 helped to initiate a women's rights convention. Her marriage to Henry Brown Blackwell revolved around the women's rights cause, for he agreed to assist her in her life's work. Stone decided not to take her husband's name.

Following the Civil War Stone joined in the unsuccessful attempt to have the Fourteenth Amendment include rights for women as well as for former slaves. Stone became involved in establishing organizations to further the suffrage rights of women. In 1866 she joined the executive committee of the newly established American Equal Rights Association and in 1867 she helped to establish the New Jersey Woman Suffrage Association, serving as the organization's president. In 1868 she participated in the formation of the New England Woman Suffrage Association and provided leadership for the Massachusetts Woman Suffrage Association. When disagreements developed in the American Equal Rights Association Stone became one of the founders of the American Woman Suffrage Association. Years later her daughter, Alice Stone Blackwell, played a major role in bringing about the merger of the American Woman Suffrage Association and the National Woman Suffrage Association. Stone's group focused on a state-by-state strategy for achieving woman suffrage. In 1867, for instance, she had taken part in the efforts in Kansas to amend the state constitution to assure voting rights to women as well as to African Americans. In all of these activities, Stone's husband remained a valuable supporter. In 1872 Stone and her husband became editors of the *Woman's Journal,* a publication she had helped to establish in 1870. This periodical served as a major voice for women's rights in the late nineteenth century.

Stone stands with that group of prominent women who worked valiantly for woman suffrage prior to the ratification of the Nineteenth Amendment in 1920 that finally granted voting rights to women. Although she did not live to see the final achievement of her goal, Stone's active life of lecturing, appearances before legislative hearings, participation in legislative work, and magazine editing presented the nation with one of the stronger arguments for election reform that would enfranchise half the American population.

William Simon U'Ren (1859–1949)

William U'Ren, a major leader in the Progressive movement, contributed to electoral reform through his advocacy of such innovations as the Australian ballot and the initiative and referendum. Born in Lancaster, Wisconsin, he moved frequently with his family. At the age of 17 U'Ren began to work in Colorado mines and gained employment as a blacksmith in Denver. In 1880, while reading law, he campaigned for Republican candidates and gained first-hand knowledge of corrupt campaign and electoral practices. After being admitted to the bar in 1881 U'Ren practiced law in Colorado communities and for a short time edited a small-town newspaper. In 1888, trying to find relief from a respiratory illness, he journeyed to Honolulu and worked as a foreman on a sugar plantation. On his return to the mainland in 1889 U'Ren went to Oregon and quickly became involved in a movement to introduce the Australian ballot to the state. Through the efforts of the Oregon Australian Ballot League, a secret-ballot measure became law in 1891.

In 1892 U'Ren read J. W. Sullivan's *Direct Legislation by the Citizenship through the Initiative and Referendum* and decided that this electoral reform would open the way to significant improvement in the political process. In 1893 he worked with the Milwaukie, Oregon, Farmers' Alliance to establish a committee that would campaign for adoption of the initiative and referendum. In 1896 U'Ren gained election to the state legislature, where he persuaded fellow legislators to support direct legislation measures. Although U'Ren was not reelected, he continued to work for election reform by engaging in the formation of the Non-Partisan Direct Legislation League of Oregon in 1898. His efforts came to fruition in 1902 when legislation was approved that established the initiative and referendum in Oregon. Continuing his reform efforts, U'Ren established the Direct Primary Nomination League in 1903. As a result of his efforts, Oregon approved a direct primary provision in 1904. Part of U'Ren's drive for a direct primary was "Statement No. 1," a provision to have the selection of U.S. Senators by state legislators reflect the choice of the citizens of the state. In 1905 U'Ren founded and subsequently served as secretary of the People's Power League, an organization that successfully lobbied the state legislature to approve a measure to enforce "Statement No. 1." The league also employed the recently adopted initiative and referendum measure to propose laws, especially a recall provision and a corrupt practices act.

U'Ren remained active in political reform movements for the remainder of his life, participating in such organizations as the National Municipal League and the National Short Ballot Organization. He was also active in the American Political Science Association. His influence in political reform extended beyond his home state. For instance, he helped to gain Woodrow Wilson's support for the initiative and referendum. After serving a single term in the state legislature, U'Ren never again won election to public office, running unsuccessfully for governor of Oregon in 1914, finishing third, and for the Oregon state legislature in 1932, 1934, and 1935. In recognition of his reform efforts the University of Oregon conferred upon him an honorary M.A. in public service.

Victoria Woodhull (1838–1927)

Although Victoria Woodhull did not play a central role in the woman suffrage movement, her ability to gain publicity for the cause qualifies her as an important figure in the fight for women's rights. In her early years she participated with other family members in a traveling show throughout the state of Ohio. The family offered a mixture of spiritualism and patent medicine, the "Elixir of Life." Victoria married Canning Woodhull when she was only 16 years old. After the couple divorced in 1864, Woodhull continued her travels with another man, James H. Blood. In 1868 she moved to New York City with her sister, Tennessee Claflin, where they made the acquaintance of Cornelius Vanderbilt. He and the two women had a mutual interest in spiritualism. With Vanderbilt's assistance, the two sisters began a stockbrokerage business and did well in the market. Woodhull was attracted to the "Pantarchy" movement, headed by Stephen Pearl Andrews. This socialist group contributed to Woodhull's less-than-orthodox approach to women's rights. She supported the various principles of the movement, including the rejection of conventional marriage and advocacy of free love, the collective care of children, and common ownership of property.

In 1870 Woodhull and her sister began *Woodhull and Claflin's Weekly*, a publication that among its causes supported women's rights. Woodhull remained at the fringes of the woman suffrage movement until she gained wide publicity in January 1871 by testifying in favor of women's right to vote before the Judiciary Committee of the U.S. House of Representatives. She was a highly successful spokesperson on this as well as other topics. That same year, Woodhull published her social and political views in a volume of collected essays, *Origin, Tendencies, and Principles of Government.* The height of her fame as an advocate of woman suffrage came in 1872, when she became the first woman to offer herself as a candidate for the presidency of the United States. With the backing of the National Radical Reformers, a women's rights splinter group, and her own publication, Woodhull became the nominee of the Equal Rights party. Although her attempt to vote in the general election proved unsuccessful, the event added to her reputation as a daring woman.

Woodhull's efforts on behalf of woman suffrage were subsequently overshadowed by her involvement in the Henry Ward Beecher affair. In 1872 Woodhull claimed in her publication that Beecher, a popular New York City minister, had had an affair with a married woman. Woodhull and her sister, Tennessee, were arrested on obscenity charges but were ultimately acquitted. In 1877 Woodhull and her sister sailed for England, where each married. Except for occasional visits to the United States, they spent the remainder of their lives in England. Like other notable women of the nineteenth century, Woodhull led the way to the enfranchisement of women not only by her direct efforts to achieve the suffrage goal but by demonstrating that women could live active lives in the public realm.

Survey Data and Quotations  4

Survey and Other Data

This chapter provides public opinion survey data, up-to-date information on campaign finance and election reform, and a summary of campaign finance regulations at the state level. Also included are survey data of attitudes toward public financing of congressional campaigns, term limits, and the influence of money in elections. Major U.S. Supreme Court cases—on campaign finance, political participation, term limits, and redistricting—are identified and summarized. In addition, the influence of money on American politics is linked to political action committee (PAC) expenditures in federal elections. Many reformers have expressed deep concern about the increased influence of PACs on candidate success and election outcomes. The most expensive races in the U.S. House of Representatives and the U.S. Senate are identified. The data point out the concrete linkage between money and success in politics, which to many indicates the need for finance reforms.

National voter turnout from 1960 through 1996 is provided as one indicator of political participation. Although voting is one of several ways to participate in politics,

101

scholars often look at voter turnout as a sign either of system legitimacy or of the level of citizen apathy. Those who supported the motor-voter bill contended that if voter registration was easier and less time consuming, more Americans would vote. This proposition may be tested by examining whether the voter turnout rate rose in 1996.

Campaign Finance Law

The Federal Election Campaign Act of 1974 placed limits on contributions by individuals and groups to candidates, party committees, and PACs. At the state and federal levels, campaign financing is once again hotly debated partly due to citizen movements across the country protesting the influence of special interests. In the 1996 elections, voters in Arkansas, California, Colorado, Maine, and Montana gave overwhelming approval to campaign finance reform initiatives. Trying to reduce the role of money in politics, these initiatives sharply limit the amount of campaign contributions.[1] Interest groups, such as Common Cause and the Center for a New Democracy, are leading advocates of campaign finance reform at the federal and state levels.

Table 4.1 outlines campaign finance regulations at the state level. All states have some report filing requirements, while 36 of them place some limits on contributions from one or more type of donor: individual, candidate, PAC, corporate, labor union, and state-regulated industry contributions to political campaigns. However, half the states do not restrict the giving or solicitation of contributions during a state legislative session. Twenty-five states completely prohibit anonymous contributions, and 25 place no limits on political party contributions to state campaigns. Cash expenditures in campaigns are unlimited in 22 states while the other states allow varying amounts of cash donations.

Since 1972, 42 referenda or initiatives dealing with campaign reform have been placed on state ballots, with 75 percent of these efforts occurring since 1985. In 33 of the 42 cases, voters approved the measures. Of these 42 proposals, 16 addressed the issue of public financing. Twelve of these ballot issues succeeded. In the 1990s various states have had initiatives calling for $100 political contribution limits for state legislative office. In November 1994 three states enacted these limits.[2]

TABLE 4.1
Campaign Finance Regulations at the State Level

Report Filing Requirements	States
Required for political committees only	AL, IL
Required for political committees and candidates	48 remaining states
Contents filed include information on all contributors/expenditures	50 states
Individual Contributions	
Unlimited	AL, CO, ID, IN, IA, MS, NE, NM, ND, OH (except judicial elections), PA, TX, UT, VA
Limited	Remaining 36 states
Candidate contributions	
Limited	DE, HI, NV, NJ, TN, WA, WV, WI
Unlimited	Remaining 42 states
Candidate's Family — Contributions	
Unlimited	AL, CO, ID, IL, IN, IA, MI (except governor's race), MS, NE, NC, ND, OH, PA, SD, TX, UT, VT, VA, WY
Unlimited for spouse only	AZ, ME, MD, NM, NY
General restrictions	26 remaining states
Corporate Contributions	
Unlimited	CO, ID, IL, MO, NM, TX (except 60 days before election), UT, VA
Limited	AL, AK, AR, CA, DE, FL, GA, HI, IN, KS, LA, ME, MD, MS, NE, NV, NJ, NY, SC, VT, WA
Prohibited completely	AZ, CT, IA, KY, MA, MI (for candidates), MN, MT, NH, NC, ND, OH, OK, OR, PA, RI, SD, TN, WV, WI, WY
Labor Union Contributions	
Unlimited	AL, CO, ID, IL, MS, MO, NM, TX (except 60 days before election), UT, VA
Limited	AK, AR, CA, DE, FL, GA, HI, IN, IA, KS, KY, LA, ME, MD, MA, MI, MN, MT, NE, NV, NJ, NY, OK, SC, SD, TN, VT, WA, WV
Prohibited completely	AZ, CT, NH, NC, ND, OH, OR, PA, RI, WI, WV
PAC Contributions	
Unlimited	AL, CO, ID, IL, IN, IA, MS, MO, NM, ND, OH (except judicial elections), PA, SD, TX, UT, VA, WY
Prohibited completely	CT
Limited	32 remaining states
State-Regulated Industries	
Unlimited	CO, ID, IL, ME, MO, NM, SD, TX (to political parties except 60 days before election)

(continues)

TABLE 4.1 (continued)

Report Filing Requirements	States
State-Regulated Industries (continued)	
Limited	AL, AK, AR, CA, DE, FL, HI, IN, KS, LA, MD, NE, NV, NJ, NY, SC, UT (to insurers only), VT, VA (pari-mutuel betting only), WA
Prohibited completely	AZ, CT, GA, IA, KY, MA, MI (except through PACs), MN, MS, MT, NH, NC, ND, OH, OK, OR, PA, RI, TN, WV, WI, WY
Contributions/Solicitations during Legislative Session	
Unlimited	CA, DE, FL, HI, ID, IL, ME, MI, MS, MT, NE, NH, NJ, NY, ND, OH, OK, PA, RI, SC, SD, VA, WV, WI, WY
Limited	AZ, CO, CT, IN, IA, KS, KY, LA, MD, NV, NM, TN, TX, UT, VT, WA
Prohibited completely	AL, AK, AR, CO, GA (for statewide candidates and General Assembly), MN (statewide candidates and General Assembly), MO, NC, OR
Solicitation of Government Employees	
Unlimited	AZ, DE, MD, NE, TX, VA, WY
Prohibited completely	HI, KY, LA, MA, NV, NM, OH, PA, RI, VT
Limited	33 remaining states
Government Employee Contributions	
No restrictions	AL, AZ, CA, DE, GA, ID, KS, ME, MT, NE, NV, NH, NJ, NC, OH, TX, VT, WY
Prohibited completely	HI
Restrictions for certain employees	31 remaining states
Cash Contributions	
Unlimited	AL, GA, ID, IL, IN, IA, ME, MN, MS, NV, NH, ND, OR, SD, TN, UT, VA, WY
Prohibited completely	AZ
Limited	31 remaining states
Anonymous Contributions	
Unlimited	AL, FL, IN, ME, MS, SD, TN, UT, VT, VA, WY
Limited	AR, CA, CO, CT, ID, KS, KY, MN, MO, NV, NM, OK, WA, WI
Prohibited completely	AK, AZ, DE, GA, HI, IL, IA, LA, MD, MA, MI, MT, NE, NH, NJ, NY, NC, ND, OH, OK, PA, RI, SC, TX, WV
Political Party Contributions	
Unlimited	AL, AK, AZ, CO, CT, ID, IL, IN, IA, KS, LA, MD, MS, NV, NM, NC, ND, OH (except judicial elections), PA, SD, TX, UT, VT, VA, WI
Limited to $25,000 or less	AR, CA, DE, GA, KY, ME, MA, MN, MO, MT, NH, NJ, OK, OR, WV
Limited to $25,000 or more	FL, HI, MI, NE, RI, SC, TN, WA

(continues)

TABLE 4.1 (continued)

Report Filing Requirements	States
Political Party Contributions (continued)	
Prohibited in primaries, otherwise unlimited	NY, WY
Expenditure Limits (Personal Use of Contributors' Money)	
Unlimited	AL, AK, AZ, AR, CO, DE, ID, KS, ME, MD, MI, MN, MT, NE, NH, NY, NC, OR, PA, SD, TN, TX, UT, VT, VA, WI
Allowed under certain conditions	CT, IL, IA, LA, ND, WA, WV, WY
Prohibited completely	CA, FL, GA, HI, IN, MA, KY, MO, NJ, NM, OH, OK, RI, SC, VA
Walking Around Money	
Limited	CT, LA, NJ, WV
Prohibited completely	MD
Unlimited	45 remaining states
Cash Expenditures	
Unlimited	AK, AZ, DE, GA, HI, ID, IL, IN, KS, ME, MD, MS, NV, NH, ND, RI, SD, TN, TX, UT, WI, WY
$50 or less	AR, FL, KY, MA, MI, MO, MT, NE, OK, OR, PA, VA, WA
$50 to $100	AL, CA, CO, CT, LA, NM, NY, SC
Prohibited — by check only	IA, NJ, OH, VT, WV
Other	NC, MN

Source: Edward D. Fiegenbaum and James A. Palmer, *Campaign Finance Reform* (Washington, DC: Federal Election Commission, 1996).

In the wake of the Supreme Court's rejection in *Buckley v. Valeo* of expenditure limits as a means of reducing the influence of money and monied interests in campaigns, many states have enacted public financing mechanisms for state elections. Table 4.2 specifies states with special tax or public financing provisions, including the source of funding and the distribution method. Thirteen states have voluntary checkoff systems similar to the federal government's $3 checkoff. Another six states have surcharge provisions that allow taxpayers to contribute money to election campaigns over and above their tax liability. Minnesota provides a tax refund to taxpayers who make political contributions. Six states allow tax deductions for political contributions, and several states use some combination of direct appropriations, checkoff, or surcharge. Nine of the states allocate their monies to the taxpayer's designated political party while two states—North Carolina and Ohio—simply divide the money equitably between the major political parties. The remaining states either allocate

TABLE 4.2

States with Special Tax or Public Financing Provisions

States	Source of Fund	Distribution Method
AL	Surcharge	Taxpayer's designated party
AZ	Surcharge, donations	Taxpayer's designated party
CA	Surcharge, state matching funds	To political parties and statewide general election candidates
FL	Taxes, donations, assessments on political committees	Gubernatorial, lt. governor and cabinet members
HI	Checkoff, appropriations	To all nonfederal candidates
ID	Checkoff	Taxpayer's designated party
IN	Revenues from personalized motor vehicle license plates	State and county parties
IA	Checkoff	Taxpayer's designated party
KY	Checkoff	Taxpayer's designated party
ME	Surcharge	Taxpayer's designated party
MD	Appropriations, fines, tax	Gubernatorial and lt. governor candidates
MA	Checkoff	To candidates who abide by expenditure limits and who raise qualifying contributions in statewide primaries and general elections
MI	Checkoff	Gubernatorial and lt. governor candidates
MN	Checkoff, appropriations	Statewide and legislative candidates
NE	Appropriations, tax refund, amount paid to campaign finance limit fund	Statewide candidates and legislative candidates
NJ	Appropriations, checkoff	Gubernatorial candidates
NM	Checkoff	Taxpayer's designated party
NC	Checkoff, surcharge	Divided among parties
OH	Checkoff	Divided among parties
RI	Checkoff	Divided among parties and statewide candidates
UT	Checkoff	Taxpayer's designated party
VA	Surcharge	Taxpayer's designated party
WI	Checkoff	Gubernatorial, legislative, and state supreme court candidates

Source: Edward D. Fiegenbaum and James A. Palmer, *Campaign Finance Reform* (Washington, DC: Federal Election Commission, 1996).

the money directly to statewide candidates or specify particular types of offices that qualify for public financing.

Public Opinion on Campaign Finance Laws

Survey data taken in April 1996 indicate that campaign finance laws are not a high priority item (see Table 4.3). Survey respondents agreed that a fixed amount of money for congressional

TABLE 4.3
Public Opinion on Priority Issues for Congress
and the President, Including Campaign Finance Laws
(percentage)

Issues	Top Priority	High Priority	Very Important	Somewhat Important	Not Important	No Opinion
Welfare	22	27	28	17	5	1
Immigration	17	16	29	26	10	2
Health care coverage for workers who change or lose their jobs	27	27	30	12	3	1
A higher minimum wage	18	19	27	22	13	1
A balanced budget amendment	31	26	28	11	2	2
Campaign finance laws	8	16	20	32	19	5

Source: *The Gallup Poll Monthly* (April 1996), 29.

campaigns was a good idea (see Table 4.4). However, other polls indicate that public opinion may be somewhat sensitive to the wording of the question and that Americans are not necessarily in favor of public financing of congressional campaigns. The public, although ambivalent about public financing of congressional campaigns, favors limiting the expenditures of congressional candidates.[3]

Those who contribute cash to political campaigns are themselves very concerned about the influence of money in politics. Nine out of ten contributors to the 1996 presidential or congressional races who were interviewed in January 1997 said they favor overhauling the campaign finance system. In the same poll, the general public also favored reforming the system, but both the general public and the contributors were skeptical about public financing of campaigns through tax dollars. Even in this most recent poll, after the campaign finance scandals associated with the Clinton administration were aired, neither the public nor campaign contributors ranked campaign finance reform as a high-priority issue.

More than seven in ten of the 807 randomly selected Americans polled were troubled by candidates who accept contributions from companies that receive government contracts or otherwise do business with the government. A majority of contributors and the general public agreed that special interests who con-

TABLE 4.4
Public Opinion on Public Financing of Congressional Campaigns

Question 1: Fund congressional campaigns and prohibit all private contributions — good or poor idea? (percentage)

Responses	1973	1977	1979	1982	1984	1987	1990
Good idea	56	57	57	55	52	50	58
Poor idea	28	32	30	31	36	42	33
No opinion	16	11	13	14	12	8	10

Sources: Gallup polls for 1973–1987; Greenberg-Lake for 1990 poll.

Question 2: Make funds available to finance campaigns for Congress, with limits on campaign contributions from individuals and political action committees? (percentage)

Responses	1990	1993
Favor	38	38
Oppose	55	53
Not sure	7	9

Source: NBC/Wall Street Journal polls.

Question 3: Approve or disapprove of the proposal to use public funds to pay the costs of congressional campaigns? (percentage)

Responses	1978	1980	1982	1984	1986
Approve	22	23	25	24	21
Disapprove	67	68	65	65	71
Not sure	11	9	9	12	8

Source: Civil Service Incorporated.
General Source: David B. Magleby and Kelly D. Patterson, "Congressional Reform," Public Opinion Quarterly 58 (1994), 423–427.

tribute to political campaigns end up having too much influence.[4] (See Table 4.5.)

Public Attitudes toward Term Limits

Public opinion rankings of 20 key issues reveal that, unlike campaign finance reform, congressional term limits is a highly ranked item that almost 75 percent of Americans support. (See Table 4.6.) Since 1977, a majority of Americans favor limiting a U.S. senator to two terms of office. Opinion on term limits since 1990 has generally been in favor of term limits by a 2 to 1 margin,

TABLE 4.5
Political Campaign Contributors: Can Money Buy Influence?

Question 1: Bothered by political contributions from companies that do business with the government or are regulated by Congress or a government agency? (percentage)

A lot	59
Some	20
Just a little	11
Not at all	10

Question 2: Members of Congress decide what to do based on what their contributors want, rather than what they really believe? (percentage)

All the time	5
More than half the time	26
About half the time	38
Less than half the time	18
Not very often	11

Question 3: Ever contributed to a candidate specifically because you hoped to influence their position on an issue or wanted them to do something specific for you? (percentage)

No	90
Yes	9
No opinion	1

Source: *Washington Post* survey based on telephone interviews with 414 randomly selected political campaign contributors derived from lists from the FEC, conducted on January 9–23, 1997. In *Gallup Poll Monthly* (February 1997).

and large proportions of Republicans and Democrats as well as Independents support congressional term limits.[5] (See Table 4.7.)

Public support of term limits is also reflected in the enactment of term limits by states for state legislators. Table 4.8 identifies states that have placed term limitations on state legislators from 1990 through 1995. Twenty-one states have enacted term limits. Voters in Mississippi rejected term limits for state legislators in November 1996. Alaska and North Dakota are the only other initiative states that have not passed term limits for state legislators.[6]

Public Attitudes toward Political Action Committees

The presence of PACs in funding congressional campaigns has increased dramatically since the late 1970s. One reason why the

TABLE 4.6
1996 Public Opinion Rankings of 20 Key Issues
Respondents Would Support on Election Day
(percentage)

Rank Order	For	Against	No Opinion
1. Balanced budget amendment	83	14	3
2. Raising the minimum wage	83	15	2
3. English as official language	82	16	2
4. Life sentences for drug dealers	80	17	3
5. Death penalty for murder	79	18	3
6. Congressional term limits amendment	**74**	**23**	**3**
7. Prayer in public schools amendment	73	25	2
8. Reducing government agencies	71	23	6
9. Two-year cutoff for welfare without work	71	24	5
10. Mandatory job retraining	69	25	6
11. Doctor-assisted suicide	68	29	3
12. School choice	59	37	4
13. Teaching creationism in public schools	58	36	6
14. Ban on partial birth abortions	57	39	4
15. Ban on assault rifles	57	42	1
16. Five-year freeze on legal immigration	50	46	4
17. Federal flat tax system	49	39	12
18. Reducing social spending	44	53	3
19. Reducing defense spending	42	54	4
20. Abortion ban except to save mother's life	42	56	2

Source: *Gallup Poll Monthly* (May 1996), 3.

public wishes to limit PAC contributions to political campaigns is the fear that PACs may exert a disproportionate amount of influence in congressional decisions on important public policy matters. Many may be concerned that raising money has become more important than appealing for votes and that special interest control over the public agenda is getting out of hand. Table 4.9 indicates that in 1980 and 1993 survey respondents expressed a desire to place limits on the amount of money that a candidate can receive from PACs. It is unclear, however, whether the public would like greater limits than those already enacted in the Federal Election Campaign Acts.

Public attitudes toward PACs vary depending on the type of PAC. Business PACs are viewed more negatively than are PACs representing environmental or women's groups. Corporate and labor PACs also fall into great disfavor. The latter are also

TABLE 4.7
Public Opinion on Congressional Term Limits

Question 1: Favor or oppose a new constitutional amendment that limits congressional terms? (percentage)

Date of Poll	For	Against	No Opinion
April 1996	74	23	3
June 1995	67	29	4
November 1994	73	24	3

Question 2: Favor or oppose limiting senators to two terms? (percentage)

Date of Poll	For	Against	No Opinion
November 1990	67	30	3
April 1981	61	32	7
November 1977	60	30	10
May 1971	49	39	12
January 1969	45	45	10
December 1965	50	38	12
Jan./Feb. 1964	49	38	13
February 1955	43	43	14

Question 3: Limit the number of years members of Congress should serve? (percentage)

1995 Response	Democratic	Republican
Yes, term limits	61	62
No, voter's choice	38	37
No opinion	1	1

Question 4: How important is it that Republicans keep their promises on specific measures? (Dec. 1994) (percentage)

Issue	Major	Minor	None	No Opinion
Reduce deficit	82	14	3	1
Pass budget amendment	71	21	7	1
Pass tax cuts	69	23	7	1
Pass term limits	**39**	**41**	**16**	**4**

Question 5: Members of U.S. House of Representatives limited to 6 or 12 years? (March 1995) (percentage)

Response	Democratic	Republican
6	58	50
12	39	47
Less than 6	—	1
Between 6 and 12	1	1
More than 12	—	0
No opinion	2	1

(continues)

TABLE 4.7 (continued)

Question 6: Limit the number of terms a senator or member of Congress can be elected? (asked of registered voters only) (percentage)

Response	Jan. 1990	Nov. 1990	Dec. 1990	Nov. 1991	Apr. 1992	Oct. 1992
Should limit	67	72	74	75	80	79
Shouldn't limit	28	24	22	21	18	17
Not sure	5	4	4	4	2	4

Sources: Questions 1–5 were drawn from Gallup polls; question 6 was taken from an NBC/*Wall Street Journal* poll. Patricia Southwell and David Waguespuck, "Support for Term Limits and Voting Behavior in Congressional Elections," *Social Science Journal* 34 (1997), 81–89; *Gallup Poll Monthly* (April 1995), 15–16; Jeffrey A. Karp, "Explaining Public Opinion Support for Legislative Term Limits," *Public Opinion Quarterly* 59 (Fall 1995), 373–391.

TABLE 4.8
Enactment of Term Limits by States for State Legislatures, 1990–1995

State	House		Senate		
	Year Effected	Year Limits	Year Effected	Year Limits	Year Enacted
ME	1996	8	1996	8	1993
CA	1996	6	1998	8	1990
CO	1998	8	2000	8	1990
AR	1998	6	2002	8	1992
MI	1998	6	2002	8	1992
MT	1998	6	2002	8	1992
OR	1998	6	2002	8	1992
WA	1998	6	2002	8	1992
WY	1998	6	2002	12	1992
FL	2000	8	2002	8	1992
MO	2000	8	2002	8	1992
OH	2000	8	2002	8	1992
SD	2000	8	2000	8	1992
AZ	2000	8	2000	8	1992
ID	2002	8	2002	8	1994
MA	2002	8	2002	8	1994
NE	—	—	2004	8	1994
OK	2002	12	2004	12	1990
NV	2006	12	2008	12	1994
UT	2006	12	2008	12	1994
LA	2007	12	2007	12	1995

Source: National Conference of State Legislatures Web site at http://www.ncsl.org/.

TABLE 4.9
Public Opinion on Limiting PAC Contributions

Question: Do you think there should be a limit on the total amount that a candidate can receive from all PACs? (percentage)

Response	1980	1993
Think so	68	73
Don't think so	29	12
It depends/not sure	3	15

Sources: 1980 Harris poll and 1993 Greenberg-Lake poll, in David B. Magleby and Kelly D. Patterson, "Congressional Reform," *Public Opinion Quarterly* 58 (1994), 423–427.

more likely to receive criticism from reformers, which is to be expected since these PACs represented 60 percent of all PAC spending in the 1992 congressional elections.[7]

Major U.S. Supreme Court Decisions on Campaign Finance

Table 4.10 provides the evolution of case law on campaign finance, summarizing decisions since the U.S. Supreme Court ruling in *Buckley v. Valeo* in 1976. Although various politicians and reformers disagree with the *Buckley* ruling, which struck down expenditure limits as a violation of the First Amendment, the Supreme Court has continued to uphold *Buckley* and to further expand on its reasoning. While upholding contribution limits the Court has rejected attempts to limit independent expenditures, as noted in the 1995 case *Colorado Republican Federal Campaign Committee v. FEC*. In this case, the Federal Election Commission (FEC) sought to limit the amount of money political parties could spend independently of a candidate's campaign. The Supreme Court declared that federal campaign finance limits of this sort are unconstitutional.

Major U.S. Supreme Court Decisions on Political Participation

Since 1944 the Supreme Court has expanded political participation for minorities and the poor by striking down mechanisms designed to limit their opportunity to vote. Table 4.11 describes several major

TABLE 4.10
Major U.S. Supreme Court Decisions on Campaign Finance

Date	Case	Holding
1976	*Buckley v. Valeo* 424 U.S. 1	Upheld the constitutionality of the Federal Election Campaign Act except for provisions limiting campaign spending and what an individual could spend on his or her own campaign
1981	*California Medical Association v. FEC* 453 U.S. 182	Upheld the constitutionality of limits on contributions to a PAC to $5,000 per year per contributor
1986	*FEC v. Massachusetts Citizens for Life* 479 U.S. 238	Held that a Massachusetts law's banning of corporate expenditures was unconstitutional as applied to independent expenditures made by narrowly defined types of nonprofit corporations that take positions on abortion, busing, gun control, and other issues
1990	*Austin v. Michigan State Chamber of Commerce* 494 U.S. 652	Ruled that Michigan state law prohibiting independent expenditures by corporations was constitutional
1991	*U.S. v. McCormick* 500 U.S. 257	Overturned the Hobbs Act conviction of a West Virginia state legislator who introduced legislation after accepting $2,900 from a lobbyist, claiming that such conduct is unavoidable in privately financed election campaigns
1995	*Colorado Republican Federal Campaign Committee v. FEC* 64 U.S.L.W. 4663	Held that federal campaign finance limits on the amount of money political parties spend independently of a candidate's campaign are unconstitutional

cases that have opened the voting booth to millions of Americans. By 1966 white primaries, poll taxes, and literacy tests, used primarily in the South to deny the vote to blacks and the poor, had been declared unconstitutional. Lengthy, excessive residency requirements, which disproportionately disadvantaged students and other mobile individuals, were struck down in 1972. These cases and others have contributed to enfranchising greater numbers of people.

Major U.S. Supreme Court Decisions on Term Limits

U.S. Term Limits (USTL), founded in 1992, has assisted activists at the state and local levels as they try to limit terms of office for congressional, state, and local political candidates. A test case came to the Supreme Court in 1995 when Arkansas limited the terms of office served by its members of Congress by prohibiting

TABLE 4.11
Major U.S. Supreme Court Cases on Political Participation

Date	Case	Holding
1944	*Smith v. Allwright* 213 U.S. 649	Held that white primaries violated the Fifteenth Amendment and Texas could not prevent blacks from participating by holding white only state conventions
1966	*Harper v. Virginia State Board of Education* 383 U.S. 663	Held poll taxes unconstitutional under the equal protection clause of the Fourteenth Amendment
1966	*South Carolina v. Katzenbach* 383 U.S. 301	Upheld suspension of literacy tests under the Voting Rights Act of 1965
1970	*Oregon v. Mitchell* 400 U.S. 112	Upheld the Voting Rights Act extension that lowered the voting age to 18 for national elections but declared that state and local elections were not governed by this provision
1972	*Dunn v. Blumstein* 405 U.S. 330	Struck down residency requirements in excess of 30 days as a prerequisite to register to vote
1983	*United States v. Grace* 461 U.S. 171	Upheld distribution of leaflets and picketing on public sidewalks as constitutional under the First Amendment
1996	*Morse v. Republican Party of Virginia* 64 U.S.L.W. 4207	Held that political parties in states covered by the federal Voting Rights Act must get federal preclearance to charge fees to delegates attending nomination conventions

the name of an otherwise eligible candidate for Congress from appearing on the general election ballot if that candidate had already served three terms in the U.S. House of Representatives or two terms in the U.S. Senate. The U.S. Term Limits movement sponsored the case when implementation of Arkansas's term limit provision was challenged.

U.S. Term Limits v. Thornton, arising out of the dispute over Arkansas's amendment to its state constitution, which limits access to the general election ballot and in effect limits congressional terms of office, was decided in a 7 to 2 vote. Justice John Paul Stevens, writing for the majority, struck down this imposition of congressional term limits, stating that state-imposed qualifications would undermine the right of the people to vote for whomever they wish and that "the right to choose representatives belongs not to the States but to the people."

As a result of this path-breaking decision advocates of term limits have turned their attention to Congress and have lobbied to get members of Congress to propose a constitutional amendment that would limit congressional terms. The term limits movement has sponsored enactment of "informed voter laws." Voters in nine states—Alaska, Arkansas, Colorado, Idaho, Maine, Missouri, Nebraska, Nevada, and South Dakota—adopted referenda that instruct members of Congress to support a constitutional amendment instituting term limits or face voter retaliation if they refuse to follow the instructions. Arkansas's informed voter law was challenged in the Arkansas Supreme Court, which declared it unconstitutional. The U.S. Supreme Court's refusal to hear an appeal means that the Arkansas provision is now dead.

Major U.S. Supreme Court Decisions on Redistricting

Although the Supreme Court originally declared that redistricting and apportionment issues were political questions best resolved by state legislatures, not the courts, the process of redrawing state legislative and congressional district lines has come under court scrutiny. The Supreme Court and lower federal courts are often the final arbiters of redistricting plans proposed by state legislatures. Various forms of gerrymandering—for partisan purposes, for protecting incumbents, and for racial equality—have been upheld. Table 4.12 describes the evolution of case law in this very complex area.

In *Baker v. Carr* (1962), the Supreme Court held that reapportionment disputes are justifiable on the grounds that voters in more populous districts were denied equal protection under the law when their votes sometimes counted less than those voters in less populated, usually rural districts. *Reynolds v. Sims* and *Wesberry v. Sanders* held that the principle of one person, one vote applied to state legislative and congressional districts.[8] Since 1964 the Supreme Court has dealt primarily with the technical matters associated with implementing the one person, one vote principle.

Other issues, such as minority vote dilution, arose. In the 1986 case *Thornburg v. Gingles,* the Supreme Court issued a three-pronged test for deciding whether the Voting Rights Act requires states to create majority-minority districts when they reapportion. The 1990 census required redrawing of electoral districts as shown in Table 4.13. Majority black districts were drawn in Alabama, Florida, North Carolina, South Carolina, Louisiana, Texas, and Virginia, some of which have been challenged as unconstitutional

TABLE 4.12

**Major U.S. Supreme Court Cases on
Reapportionment, Gerrymandering, and Vote Dilution**

Date	Case	Holding
1962	*Baker v. Carr* 369 U.S. 186	Malapportioned state legislative districts may violate the equal protection clause of the Fourteenth Amendment
1964	*Reynolds v. Sims* 377 U.S. 533	Both houses of a bicameral state legislature must be apportioned according to population, thus establishing the criterion of one person, one vote for legislative apportionment
1964	*Wesberry v. Sanders* 376 U.S. 1	Congressional districts must be roughly equal in population
1970	*Hadley v. Junior College District of Kansas City* 397 U.S. 50	Upheld one person, one vote principle and applied it to all elections including national, state, and local elections
1973	*White v. Weiser* 412 U.S. 783	Electoral districts must be as equal in size as mathematically possible
1980	*Mobile v. Bolden* 446 U.S. 55	Plaintiffs must prove that at-large voting systems not only have a discriminatory effect but were designed with the intent to further racial discrimination
1986	*Thornburg v. Gingles* 478 U.S. 30	Established a three-prong test for deciding whether the Voting Rights Act required the creation of majority-minority districts; plaintiffs could seek relief if the minority was geographically compact, politically cohesive, and racial bloc voting by whites effectively deprived blacks and other minorities of an equal chance to elect candidates of their choice
1986	*Davis v. Bandemer* 478 U.S. 109	Ruled that although political party gerrymandering could be challenged such challenges must (1) show that a redistricting plan makes winning elections more difficult and (2) provide evidence that the majority of voters' will is continually thwarted or minority voters are denied a fair chance to influence the political process
1993	*Shaw v. Reno* 509 U.S. 630	Upheld limits on the way states comply with the Voting Rights Act, stating that white residents could challenge North Carolina's congressional redistricting plan using the equal protection clause of the Fourteenth Amendment when a district's shape was so strange that it could only be interpreted as an attempt to segregate voters on the basis of race
1995	*Miller v. Johnson* 115 S.Ct. 2475	Struck down Georgia's racially gerrymandered congressional redistricting plan, stating that a district could be challenged, regardless of its shape, if race was the sole factor in the redistricting process
1996	*Shaw v. Hunt* 64 U.S.L.W. 4437	Struck down North Carolina's congressional district 12, holding that the creation of this majority black district was not based on a compelling state interest
1996	*Bush v. Vera* 64 U.S.L.W. 4452	Struck down three majority-minority districts in Texas, asserting that race was the predominant factor in drawing the district boundaries and did not serve a compelling state interest

TABLE 4.13

House Reapportionment

(1990 census population counts)

State	Percent Population Difference from 1980 to 1990	Seats (and Change from 1980)	State	Percent Population Difference from 1980 to 1990	Seats (and Change from 1980)
AL	3.8	7	MT	1.6	1 (−1)
AK	36.9	1	NE	0.5	3
AZ	34.8	6 (+1)	NV	50.1	2
AR	2.8	4	NH	20.5	2
CA	25.7	52 (+7)	NJ	5.0	13 (−1)
CO	14.0	6	NM	16.3	3
CT	5.8	6	NY	2.5	31 (−3)
DE	12.1	1	NC	12.7	12 (+1)
FL	32.7	23 (+4)	ND	−2.1	1
GA	18.6	11 (+1)	OH	0.5	19 (−2)
HI	14.9	2	OK	4.0	6
ID	6.7	2	OR	7.9	5
IL	0.0	20 (−2)	PA	0.1	21 (−2)
IN	1.0	10	RI	5.9	2
IA	−4.7	5 (−1)	SC	11.7	6
KS	4.8	4 (−1)	SD	0.8	1
KY	0.7	6 (−1)	TN	6.2	9
LA	0.3	7 (−1)	TX	19.4	30 (+3)
ME	9.2	2	UT	17.9	3
MD	13.4	8	VT	10.0	1
MA	4.9	10 (−1)	VA	15.7	11 (+1)
MI	0.4	16 (−2)	WA	17.8	9 (+1)
MN	7.3	8	WV	−8.0	3 (−1)
MS	2.1	5	WI	4.0	9
MO	4.1	9	WY	−3.4	1

Source: U.S. Department of Commerce, Bureau of the Census.

racial gerrymandering. Since 1993 the Supreme Court has demonstrated a willingness to impose limits on how states comply with the Voting Rights Act of 1982, stating that if race is the sole factor in the redistricting process the state districting plan could be challenged and struck down as unconstitutional.

PAC Expenditures and the Costs of Elections

As indicated in Table 4.14, PAC expenditures in federal elections have risen dramatically from $60 million in 1979–1980 to

TABLE 4.14
Total PAC Expenditures in Federal Elections, 1979–1996

Year	Total PAC Expenditures (in millions of dollars)
1979–1980	$60
1981–1982	$88
1983–1984	$113
1985–1986	$140
1987–1988	$159
1989–1990	$159
1991–1992	$189
1993–1994	$189
1995–1996	$265[a]

Source: Larry Makinson, *The Price of Admission: Campaign Spending in the 1994 Elections* (Washington, DC: Center for Responsive Politics, 1995).
[a]PAC expenditures for 1995–1996 were estimated based on FEC analyses from January 1, 1995, through June 30, 1996.

an estimated $265 million in 1995–1996. Between 1974 and 1992 the number of PACs grew from 600 to 4,729, with most of the growth occurring among business and corporate PACs—the ones toward which the public has the most negative attitudes. PAC contributions to congressional candidates has risen from $12.5 million in 1974 to $178.3 million in 1992.[9] In general PAC activity and visibility has increased, and this in turn has created concern among the public about special interests and their influence on American politics.

Table 4.15 lists the top 20 PAC contributors for 1993–1994 and 1995–1996. Many organizations have remained consistent contributors. As PAC contributions and expenditures rise, there has also been an increase in the overall costs of elections. Spending on election campaigns rose from less than $150 million in 1952 to more than $3 billion in 1992 ($2.2 billion was spent on national elections, and the remainder went to state and local candidates and ballot issues). Inflation, the rise of media campaigns, and increased competition explain a large portion of the increased costs of campaigns, but the rise in the number of PACs and special interests also explain this trend.[10]

Table 4.16 lists the ten most expensive races for the House of Representatives and Table 4.17 lists the ten most expensive races for the Senate. In nine of the ten most expensive House races, the candidates who spent the most money won (six of the ten were

**TABLE 4.15
Top 20 PAC Contributors, 1993–1996**

1993–1994 (rank ordered)

United Parcel Service
Teamster's Union
American Medical Association
American Federation of State, County, Municipal Employees
National Education Association
Association of Trial Lawyers of America
United Auto Workers
National Rifle Association
National Association of Realtors
National Auto Dealers Association
American Institute of Certified Public Accountants
Machinists/Aerospace Workers Union
International Brotherhood of Electrical Workers
American Bankers Association
Marine Engineers Union
Laborers Union
Carpenters Union
Food and Commercial Workers Union
Letter Carriers Union
National Association of Life Underwriters

1995–1996 (rank ordered)

Democratic Republican Independent Voter Education Committee
Association of Trial Lawyers of America
International Brotherhood of Electrical Workers
American Federation of State, County, Municipal Employees
United Auto Workers
National Education Association
National Automobile Dealers Association
Laborers' Political League
National Association of Home Builders
United Parcel Service
AT&T
American Medical Association
United Food and Commercial Workers International Union
National Rifle Association
American Institute of Certified Public Accountants
Realtors PAC
Machinists Non-Partisan Political League
Carpenters Union
Transportation Political Education Committee
American Federation of Teachers

Source: Larry Makinson, *The Price of Admission: Campaign Spending in the 1994 Elections* (Washington, DC: The Center for Reponsive Politics, 1995).

TABLE 4.16
Ten Most Expensive Races for the U.S. House of Representatives
(total spent, January 1, 1995–October 16, 1996)

1. Georgia = $6,852,466
   *Representative Newt Gingrich (R) $4,512,307
   Michael Coles (D) $2,340,159
2. Missouri = $2,658,373
   *Representative Richard Gephardt (D) $2,609,500
   Deborah Wheelehan (R) $48,873
3. Texas = $2,424,206
   *Ronald Paul (R) $1,621,342
   Charles Morris (D) $802,864
4. California = $2,413,353
   *Ellen Tauscher (D) $1,541,370
   Representative William Baker (R) $871,983
5. Iowa = $2,392,028
   *Representative Greg Ganske (R) $1,818,715
   Connie McBurney (D) $573,313
6. Tennessee = $2,292,817
   *Representative Bart Gordon (D) $1,299,399
   Steven Gill (R) $993,418
7. Michigan = $2,148,538
   *Debbie Stabenow (D) $1,168,679
   Representative Richard Chrysler (R) $979,859
8. California = $2,019,050
   *Representative Vic Fazio (D) $1,620,871
   Timothy LeFever (R) $398,179
9. Nevada = $2,005,580
   *Representative John Ensign (R) $1,562,501
   James Coffin (D) $443,079
10. Ohio = $1,860,649
    Representative Frank Crameans (R) $1,409,609
    *Ted Strickland (D) $451,040

*denotes winning candidates
Source: Common Cause Web site at http://www.commoncause.org/.

incumbents as well). In the Senate top-ten most-expensive races, the candidates who spent the most money won in seven out of the ten races (five of the ten were incumbents).

According to an analysis of candidate financial activity through October 16, 1996, House incumbents in the 1996 elections possessed a 4 to 1 financial advantage over challengers, with $282 million in campaign funding compared to $75 million for challengers. PACs contributed more funds to incumbents than to challengers, thus fueling the incumbency advantage. In the Sen-

TABLE 4.17
Ten Most Expensive Races for the U.S. Senate
(total spent, January 1, 1995–October 16, 1996)

1. North Carolina = $19,677,060
   *Senator Jesse Helms (R) $13,321,423
   Harvey Gantt (D) $6,355,637
2. Massachusetts = $16,387,109
   *Senator John Kerry (D) $10,423,966
   Governor William Weld (R) $5,973,143
3. Virginia = $13,137,804
   Mark Warner (D) $8,022,301
   *Senator John Warner (R) $5,115,503
4. New Jersey = $11,370,133
   *Representative Robert Torricelli (D) $6,484,585
   Representative Dick Zimmer (R) $4,885,548
5. Minnesota = $9,845,815
   *Senator Paul Wellstone (D) $6,382,050
   Rudy Boschwitz (R) $3,463,765
6. Georgia = $9,252,978
   *Guy Millner (R) $7,524,350
   Max Cleland (D) $1,728,628
7. Texas = $8,710,282
   *Senator Phil Gramm (R) $8,293,101
   Victor Morales (D) $417,181
8. Michigan = $8,240,760
   *Senator Carl Levin (D) $5,766,795
   Ronna Romney (R) $2,473,965
9. Illinois = $7,186,688
   *Representative Richard Durbin (D) $4,003,384
   Al Salvi (R) $3,183,304
10. South Dakota = $6,569,729
    Senator Larry Pressler (R) $4,046,973
    *Representative Tim Johnson (D) $2,522,756

*denotes winning candidates
Source: Common Cause Web site at http://www.commoncause.org/.

ate a similar trend occurred, with only 1 of the 20 incumbents seeking reelection going down to defeat.[11]

Voter Turnout and Voter Registration

As Table 4.18 indicates, between 1960 and 1996 the national percent turnout of the voting-age population has slowly declined in federal elections. This trend applies not only to midterm elections, in which turnout has been traditionally lower, but also to

TABLE 4.18
National Voter Turnout in Federal Elections, 1960–1996

Year	Voting Age Population	Registration	Turnout	Percent Turnout of Voting Age Population
1996	196,509,000	148,697,265	96,397,564	49.06
1994	193,650,000	130,246,259	75,105,860	38.78
1992	189,529,000	133,821,178	104,405,155	55.09
1990	185,812,000	121,105,630	67,859,189	36.52
1988	182,778,000	126,381,202	91,594,693	50.12
1986	178,566,000	118,399,984	64,991,128	36.40
1984	174,468,000	124,150,614	92,652,680	53.11
1982	169,938,000	110,671,225	67,615,576	39.79
1980	164,597,000	113,043,734	86,515,221	52.56
1978	158,373,000	103,291,265	58,917,938	37.21
1976	152,309,190	105,037,986	81,555,789	53.55
1974	146,336,000	96,199,020[a]	55,943,834	38.23
1972	140,776,000	97,328,541	77,718,554	55.21
1970	124,498,000	82,496,747[b]	58,014,338	46.60
1968	120,328,186	81,658,180	73,211,875	60.84
1966	116,132,000	76,288,283[c]	56,188,046	48.39
1964	114,090,000	73,715,818	70,644,592	61.92
1962	112,423,000	65,393,751[d]	53,141,227	47.27
1960	109,159,000	64,833,096[e]	68,838,204	63.06

[a]Registrations from Iowa are not included.
[b]Registrations from Iowa and Missouri are not included.
[c]Registrations from IA, KS, MS, MO, NE, and WY are not included. DC is not an independent state.
[d]Registrations from AL, AK, DC, IA, KS, KY, MS, MO, NE, NC, ND, SD, TN, WI, and WY are not included.
[e]Registrations from AL, AK, DC, IA, KS, KY, MS, MO, NE, NM, NC, ND, OK, SD, WI, and WY are not included.
Source: Federal Election Commission Web sites at http://www.fec.gov/pages/htmlto5.htm and http://www.fec.gov/pages/96to.htm.

presidential elections. Reformers have tended to blame low voter turnout on structural barriers such as difficult voter registration procedures. With the passage of the motor-voter bill registration has been made easier. Even though more citizens than ever were registered to vote in 1995 and 1996, the voter turnout was still lower than it had ever been for a presidential election year—49 percent. This figure may lead reformers to examine other causes of and possible solutions to low voter turnout.

Voter satisfaction with the status quo, the failures of the political parties to mobilize voters, and voter disillusionment with negative campaigning are other possible explanations for declining voter turnout. Some states, such as Oregon, responding to perceived structural barriers to voting, have used all-mail ballots, allowing voters to mail in their ballots at their convenience as long as they arrive by the deadline. In such instances, voter turnout has been substantially higher. Other states have made it more convenient to register by establishing registration periods that last until election day. However, most states require registration at least 25 days before the election. Still other reformers call for election day registration to reduce the time spent by voters in the registration process.

Quotations

These quotations present the attitudes of a wide range of individuals—including elected and appointed public officials, interest group representatives, and students of political reform—toward campaign finance reform, electoral reform, redistricting, term limits, and gerrymandering.

Buckley v. Valeo

I think *Buckley v. Valeo* was wrongly decided. And we should reconsider it. . . . I'd want to put some restrictions on individuals loaning themselves money; the [Representative Michael] Huffington example [the California Republican who set a record in 1994 by spending more than $28 million of his own money on his unsuccessful Senate campaign] presents a really serious problem, because it more and more allows people of great wealth to move away from any restrictions. And the public *likes* that. All the arguments that it will produce a gilded Congress of rich people doesn't affect people very much. They sort of like it when [Ross] Perot says, "I'm buying the election for you."
former House Speaker Tom Foley, quoted in
Martin Schram, *Speaking Freely: Former
Members of Congress Talk about Money in
Politics* (1995)

Even under *Buckley,* limits on contributions are permitted. But such limits only apply to cash contributions. Thus, the owner of a newspaper could openly campaign for one candidate in the pages of his publication, but a wealthy citizen could not provide equivalent support to the other candidate to allow him to respond.

Ira Glasser, executive director of the
American Civil Liberties Union, House of
Representatives Subcommittee on the
Constitution (February 27, 1997)

[The Supreme Court's ruling in *Buckley v. Valeo* represents] the stupidity of how we define freedom of expression. Go back to the flag burning amendment. We define flag burning as freedom of expression. . . . It just turns the English language constructs on its head. Flag burning is not speech, it is conduct. We're all seduced by the television age. We allow our image, demonstrations that are covered by the press, to be called speech. Now extend it to the campaign financing thing—they say money is speech. It's not. We've made this incredible leap across the linguistic barriers.

Representative Wyche Fowler, quoted in
Martin Schram, *Speaking Freely: Former
Members of Congress Talk about Money in
Politics* (1995)

Under a system of private financing of elections, a candidate lacking immense personal or family wealth must depend on financial contributions from others to provide the resources necessary to conduct a successful campaign. . . . To the extent that large contributions are given to secure a political quid pro quo from current and potential office holders, the integrity of our system of representative democracy is undermined. . . . We find that . . . the weighty interests served by restricting the size of financial contributions to political candidates are sufficient to justify the limited effect upon First Amendment freedoms caused by the $1,000 contribution ceiling [imposed on individuals]. . . . The Act's [FECA of 1974] expenditure ceilings [however] impose direct and substantial restraints on the quantity of political speech. . . . We conclude that the independent expenditure limitation is unconstitutional under the First Amendment.

Per curiam opinion of the U.S. Supreme
Court in *Buckley v. Valeo* 424 U.S. 1 (1976)

Campaign Finance and Ethics

I would argue that the way big money has come to dominate politics has become the ethical issue of our time. I say to all of my colleagues . . . that all of us in office should hate this system. On the one hand, it is a bit like the play *Fiddler on the Roof*—you can argue that, well, no, people should not hate the system because in a way the current system is wired for incumbents. . . . But I really think all of us should hate this system, because even if you believe in your heart of hearts, even if you are absolutely convinced that the compelling need to raise money never has affected any position you have taken on any issue, even if you believe that . . . it sure does not look that way to the people. If we want people to believe in this political process . . . then we better get this big money out of politics and we better turn this system upside down—it is upside down right now—we better turn this system right side up.

> Senator Paul Wellstone, *Congressional Record* (January 23, 1997)

I never thought I would live to see a major drug dealer give 20,000 bucks in Florida and then be invited to a big Democratic reception by the vice president of the United States, Al Gore, and then be invited to the White House for a reception. Now keep in mind you can't get into the White House unless the Secret Service clears you. This guy had been convicted, arrested twice in the '80s. It's in the computer.

> Ross Perot, PBS, *The NewsHour with Jim Lehrer* (November 28, 1996)

It's not hypocritical to say that we have to change the campaign finance system we have and [at the same time] continue to raise money under the system that exists . . . unless you all think that we ought to just kind of throw up our hands and say, well, we're going to discontinue waging a campaign on behalf of the President's ideas and candidates that the President supports.

> Mike McCurry press briefing (March 11, 1997)

What we have here is a pattern and practice. . . . You have the Werthen Bank, which was owned at one point by this family in Indonesia. They give $3.5 million in loans to Clinton in 1992, when his campaign is in the very lowest days of Genifer Flowers, draft-dodging charges, [at this] lowest point, this group comes through with $3.5 million. . . . That's the quid. What's bad is the quo. The quo is billions, F-16 fighters for Indonesia; the quo is billions of business contracts for the cronies of all these people; the quo is the United States turns its back on awful human rights abuses, genocide in East Timor. . . . When Bill Clinton was running for president . . . he said, George Bush is terrible for not having done something about what the Indonesians were doing in East Timor. Now that all these millions have gone through [his campaign], Mickey Kantor stops the investigations of human rights abuses in East Timor.

> Haley Barbour, chair, 1996 Republican
> National Committee, PBS, *The NewsHour*
> *with Jim Lehrer* (October 21, 1996)

Campaign Finance Reform

We must make our democracy stronger by enacting real, bipartisan campaign finance reform. [*Applause*] Talk is no longer enough; we must act and act now. And the American people will be watching the leaders of both parties to see who is willing not just to talk, but to act. I am willing to act. And I ask others to join me. [*Applause*]

> Remarks by President Bill Clinton, Old State
> House in Little Rock, Arkansas (November
> 5, 1996)

I would have to raise $100,000 a week, starting today, for the next year. And Mrs. Ford won't let me bring anyone to sleep in our spare bedroom.

> Retiring Senator Wendell Ford (1997)

We see people in a situation where you've given your $1,000 maximum. They want to give more money, so they give a gift to their teenage son, who gives a gift to the candidate. . . . What we really need to do is dump some of these [campaign finance] laws, deregulate the system, require full disclosure. Now people are trying to hide their contributions. If we open up, let people contribute, those contributions come into the open, and then if the voters think it's important, the voters can decide. Do the voters care where Bill Clinton's getting his money, do they care where Bob Dole's getting his money? They can decide that.

> Bradley Smith, Cato Institute scholar and
> law professor, Capital University,
> Columbus, Ohio, PBS, *The NewsHour with*
> *Jim Lehrer* (October 18, 1996)

These people who have given huge contributions are not giving money to get good government. They are giving money because they want access to influence in the political process. It's corrupting, the American people understand it, and it has really got to be changed.

> Ann McBride, president of Common Cause,
> PBS, *The NewsHour with Jim Lehrer* (October
> 18, 1996)

A poll conducted by . . . Public Opinion Strategies . . . asks three questions: "Which of the following do you really think controls the Federal Government in Washington?" Registered voters responded: the lobbyists and special interests, 49 percent; Republicans in Congress, 25 percent; have not thought much about it, 14 percent; the President, 6 percent; the Democrats in Congress, 6 percent. When asked [whether] "those who make large campaign contributions get special favors from politicians," respondents said: this is one of the things that worries you most, 34 percent; worries you some, 20 percent; worries you not too much, 5 percent; and worries you not at all, 3 percent. Finally, when asked [whether] "we need campaign finance reform to make politicians accountable to average voters rather than special interests," the [registered] voters stated: this was very convincing, 59 percent; somewhat convincing, 31 percent; not very convincing, 5 percent; not at all convincing, 4 percent; and don't know, 2 percent.

> Senator John McCain, *Congressional Record*
> (June 24, 1996)

Public financing is just about the only answer to it. And it would be a very good thing for the country. It wouldn't be too good for the incumbents. They wouldn't like it, because there's nothing more than being an incumbent and . . . [reading] that your Republican opponent doesn't have a dime and hasn't even had a fund raiser. . . . A non-incumbent has a helluva time. I'd put in public financing . . . 100 percent. I think it's good for democracy. I'd like to see school teachers [be able to afford to run for Congress]. I'd like to see more laboring men and women. I'd like to see more housewives, . . . people who don't have the expertise, don't know how to run for public office, . . . people who don't have access to money.

> Representative Don Edwards, quoted in
> Martin Schram, *Speaking Freely: Former*

Members of Congress Talk about Money
in Politics (1995)

Public financing [of congressional races] would be a catastrophe.
They hate us now, and they'd hate us even worse if we had it. . . .
I don't think there is *an* answer. But I think disclosure is essential.
My people are entitled to know who gives me money and they're
entitled to ask about it. And if I can't answer, they're entitled to
run me out.
> Senator Malcolm Wallop, quoted in Martin
> Schram, *Speaking Freely: Former Members of*
> *Congress Talk about Money in Politics* (1995)

Electoral College Reform

The American electoral college is a deplorable political institution. . . . If the electoral college were only a neutral and sure
means for counting and aggregating votes, it would be the subject of little controversy. The electoral college, however, is neither
certain in its operations nor neutral in its effects. . . . In short, the
electoral college is a flawed means of determining the president.
Its workings at best are neither smooth nor fair, and at worst contain the potential for constitutional crisis.
> Lawrence D. Longley, quoted in Judith A.
> Best, *The Choice of the People? Debating the*
> *Electoral College* (1996)

It is not possible here to discuss all the dangers that alarm critics
of the Electoral College. . . . But the present remarks are limited to
the main danger that the reformers fear; namely, the popular-
vote-electoral-vote discrepancy. This is the loaded pistol pointed
to our heads, the threat that necessitates radical constitutional revision. Now the funny thing about this loaded pistol is that the
last time it went off, in 1888, no one got hurt. . . . As far as I can
tell, there was hardly a ripple of constitutional discontent . . . and
nothing remotely resembling the crisis predicted by present-day
critics of the Electoral College.
> Martin Diamond, "The Electoral College
> and the American Idea of Democracy," in
> Walter Berns, ed., *After the People Vote: A*
> *Guide to the Electoral College* (1992)

A constitution is not simply the highest and most solemn law a people can make, it is an organic arrangement of interdependent balanced parts. It is like a solar system where the entire system is dependent upon each planet being in its place, each moving in its own orbit around the sun, and if you change a part, you change the whole. The fundamental principles of the American Constitution [such as the electoral college] are like the sun in the solar system. Why does the Electoral College keep on winning? Because the electoral vote system is a model of our federal Constitution— a novel system, "a great discovery," that creates one society out of many societies. The reason is there for us to see on every nickel we spend. It is our national motto: *E Pluribus Unum*.
　　Judith A. Best in *The Choice of the People?*
　　Debating the Electoral College (1996)

Money and Elections

A poor man's soapbox does not equal a rich man's wallet.
　　Senator Bill Bradley, quoted by Ellen Miller,
　　PBS, *The NewsHour with Jim Lehrer* (October
　　18, 1996)

I have a great concern over what campaigns are costing these days. You know, I ran my first campaign [in 1956] for $15,000. And then by the time I got to my toughest campaign in '82, it was $600,000. . . . When I look around the country and see some of these multimillion-dollar races, I just have to be concerned about that. The time that you spend raising money, and the number of fund raising events that I was obliged to attend or at least stop by—gosh, you'd have five or six a night. It just wears you out doing that. Now they've started the breakfast routine. You can make more at a breakfast because you don't have to pay as much for the stuff you serve them.
　　House Minority Leader Robert Michel,
　　quoted in Martin Schram, *Speaking Freely:*
　　Former Members of Congress Talk about Money
　　in Politics (1995)

He once turned to me and said, "I can't think, I can't act, I can't govern; all I do is raise money." We called it trial by handshake because . . . it was physically exhausting for him to do that. Donors basically give money because they want to be the presi-

dent; they want a photo; they want a handshake; they want a pen; they want a momento.
> Dick Morris, former adviser to President Clinton and political strategist, PBS, *The NewsHour with Jim Lehrer* (March 24, 1997)

According to data provided by the Congressional Research Service, the combined cost of all House and Senate races in the 1994 election cycle was $724 million, a sixfold increase from 1976. Even more troubling, though, at least from the perspective of our colleagues, is that the average cost of winning a senatorial campaign rose from barely $600,000 in 1976 to more than $4 million in 1994. . . . And that, of course, is just the average. In 1994 nearly $35 million was spent by two general election candidates in California, while the candidates in the Virginia race spent $27 million.
> Senator Robert Byrd, *Congressional Record* (June 25, 1996)

When I was running for president a few months ago, in New Hampshire I was on a talk show, an interview show, it was interrupted for a commercial. And there, right in the middle of my important public discourse, appeared Steve Forbes's commercial. I had just been talking about the flat tax, which I had done a ton of work on, and have produced legislation on it, and there Steve Forbes came on with his flat tax. And he came on with so many 30-second sound bite commercials that the people of New Hampshire knew about Forbes's flat tax, didn't know a thing about Arlen Specter's flat tax. And it didn't come from the cerebrum, it came from the pocketbook.
> Senator Arlen Specter, PBS interview, "So You Want to Buy a President?" (January 30, 1996)

The Ernie is something that I established for the award for the worst fund-raiser. I once did a fund-raiser where we did not raise enough money to pay for the luncheon, and therefore we had negative cash flow. So any time I went on a fund-raising trip, we always gave the Ernie within the staff and the group to the fund-raiser who was the most disappointing.
> Senator Bill Bradley, PBS interview, "So You Want to Buy a President?" (January 30, 1996)

Consider that in his run for the Republican presidential nomination, [Steve] Forbes spent $400,000 per delegate that he won in the Republican primaries. Our colleague, Phil Gramm, spent $20 million to win ten delegates. For Bob Dole, his victory in Iowa caucuses cost him about $35 a vote.

> Senator Christopher Dodd, *Congressional Record* (June 25, 1996)

Money and Political Participation

We keep spending more and more money every election cycle, and participation goes down, down, down. . . . If we want people to at least have more confidence in the political process than they do now, if we want people to believe in us, if we want people to believe in the legislation that we pass, which is a product of this process, then people have to believe that politics in Washington, D.C., is not dominated by big money. People have to believe the Congress belongs to them, that the Capitol belongs to them, that all of us, Democrats and Republican, belong to them.

> Senator Paul Wellstone, *Congressional Record* (March 6, 1997)

Motor-Voter Registration

Supporters of motor voter have argued that easing voter registration procedures would invigorate voter turnouts. However, as last year's elections clearly displayed, the law did not meet its goal. Although massive numbers of new voters were placed on the rolls under motor voter, they did not take the initiative to cast their ballots. In fact, a mere 49 percent of eligible Americans voted, the lowest voter turnout since 1924. More than 90 million registered voters failed to vote. While voter apathy under motor voter is unsettling, there is another more compelling reason to rethink the soundness of the law. It has allowed voter fraud on a national scale. The law does not contain a provision to preclude illegal registration and voting. . . . It requires States to keep registrants who fail to vote or who are unresponsive to voter registration correspondence to be maintained on voter registration rolls for years. As a result, children, cats, dogs, a pig, deceased people, and non-citizens registered to vote.

> Representative Bob Stump, *Congressional Record* (January 7, 1997)

Political Action Committees (PACs)

In the U.S., some view a PAC ban as a cure-all to campaign finance problems. However, according to figures released by the Federal Election Commission, PAC contributions have remained at fairly equal levels over the past few election cycles. Aggregate PAC contributions totaled $149 million in 1990, rose to $178 million in 1992 and remained at $178 million in 1994. During the same period, overall campaign spending has risen from $446 million in 1990 to $724 million in 1994—a 62 percent increase. So even though campaign costs have skyrocketed in recent years, the level of PAC contributions has remained relatively constant.

> Senator Russell Feingold, *Congressional Record* (September 7, 1995)

When you raise money from PACs, members have almost a mental checklist of the things they need to do to make sure their PAC contributors continue to support them. Maybe in committees, maybe submitting floor statements—usually not spoken, maybe just submitted into the record. All sorts of mechanical things. Not aggressive, substantive buying of the legislative process. But there's no question that money has a certain impact on the process.

> Representative Vin Weber, quoted in Martin Schram, *Speaking Freely: Former Members of Congress Talk about Money in Politics* (1995)

Foreign citizens are already prohibited from contributing to U.S. political campaigns. Yet, every year foreign interests spend millions of dollars to influence the American political process. This money often comes in the form of political action committee contributions from foreign-controlled corporations or their trade associations. Just as foreign individuals are prohibited from contributing to U.S. campaigns, so should be PACs that are controlled by foreign corporations and trade associations, for, in fact, under U.S. law, corporations are considered persons. Due to a loophole in the FECA, American subsidiaries of foreign-owned companies may operate PACs—the only restriction being that the PAC cannot solicit funds from foreign nationals or permit them to be involved in the policymaking decisions of the PAC. Consequently, many of the world's largest multinational corporations and financial institutions contribute to U.S. campaigns through their U.S.-based subsidiaries.

Representative Marcy Kaptur, *Congressional Record* (February 5, 1997)

Poll Tax

Voter qualifications have no relation to wealth nor to paying or not paying this or any other tax. . . . We say the same whether the citizen, otherwise qualified to vote, has $1.50 in his pocket or nothing at all, pays the fee or fails to pay it. The principle that denies the State the right to dilute a citizen's vote on account of his economic status or other such factors by analogy bars a system which excludes those unable to pay a fee to vote or who fail to pay.

Justice William O. Douglas, majority opinion, *Harper v. Virginia State Board of Elections* 383 U.S. 663 (1966)

Proportional Representation and Cumulative Voting

The evidence is compelling that single seat legislative districts— the voting system used in most U.S. elections—discriminate against women. . . . Under the present system, a small number of discriminatory or fearful voters can deny a female candidate a seat. Under PR, the parties would be sponsoring several candidates, and throwing a woman or two into the mix would not be the huge gamble it apparently is in a winner-take-all race. Voters would be much more likely to spend their votes on women if they felt those candidates actually stood a chance of winning. And, having a better chance of winning, women would be more encouraged to run for office.

Wilma Rule, Steven Hill, and Sandy Fernandez, "Voting for a Change," *Ms.* (September/October, 1996)

Cumulative voting offers striking advantages. Most obviously, it avoids the drawing of radically defined political districts that so trouble the [Voting Rights] Act's critics. It might also diminish conflicts between minority groups struggling over district boundary lines, such as between blacks and Hispanics in many places. In fact, cumulative voting reduces gerrymandering opportunities in general. Because it relies on several candidates competing in at-large elections, it requires geographically broad electoral units. The fewer the district lines to be drawn, the fewer the invitations to gerrymander.

Richard H. Pildes, "Gimme Five," *The New Republic* (March 1, 1993)

To listen to organizers of Citizens for Proportional Representation (CPR) tell it, there's almost nothing PR can't cure. Low voter turnout? PR will energize everyone. Gerrymandering? Impossible. Not enough blacks and women in Congress? PR fixes that. Racial and political polarization? One organizer told me proportional representation would have prevented the Los Angeles riots. At lunch with several of the attendees, I brought up the problems that have been perceived with PR. I had thrown a lighted match into a powder keg. "That's all part of the myth!" one of them nearly shouted. Elements of The Myth include that PR is overly complex; that it helped bring Hitler and Mussolini to power, and that it leads to unstable coalition governments.

John A. Barnes, "Proportional Deception," *National Review* (July 20, 1992)

Interest representation . . . fulfills the dual vision of the Voting Rights Act that minority groups should enjoy equal voting weight and equal voting power. Instead of emphasizing arbitrary territorial boundaries, which waste the votes of both minority and majority groups, interest representation favors allowing voters of the same interests to join in voting for candidates of choice, regardless of where the voters live in the jurisdiction. This at-large system, however, would be modified in one critical respect. The winner-take-all feature of majority rule would be discarded in favor of cumulative voting, which allows voters to cumulate their votes in order to express the intensity of their preferences. In this fashion, interest representation strives to ensure that groups that are politically cohesive, sufficiently numerous, and strategically mobilized will be able to elect a representative to the legislative body.

Lani Guinier, *The Tyranny of the Majority: Fundamental Fairness in Representative Democracy* (1994)

Americans have suffered under our two-party system for so long that we tend to view its problems and limitations as unfortunate but inevitable. In reality, of course, many of these problems are inevitable only under single-member plurality voting rules. The adoption of proportional representation in the United States would go a long way toward addressing these shortcomings. PR would allow the development of a multiparty system with a variety of genuine political alternatives. Minor parties would no longer be unfairly penalized, and they would be able to elect representatives in numbers that reflect their political strength in the electorate. In short, PR would be an antitrust law for the party system. It would discourage party monopolies and oligopolies and allow for free competition among parties. It would create a level playing field on which all parties could vie fairly for public support.

> Douglas J. Amy, *Real Choices/New Voices: The Case for Proportional Representation Elections in the United States* (1993)

With cumulative voting, candidates have every incentive to get all people's votes for themselves. This easily could lead to negative campaigning—particularly among candidates similar in philosophy. . . . Japan provides a lesson in such campaigning, as its limited voting system—in which voters have one vote in districts of three-to-five members—has led to both bitter intra-party competition and to smaller parties avoiding such competition by nominating only one candidate. . . . Cumulative voting has another serious problem: because of the danger of vote-splitting, it might not represent the population accurately, undercutting both majority rule and representation of minorities.

> Rob Richie, "Does Cumulative Voting Pass Guinier's Fairness Test?" (Center for Voting and Democracy Web site at http://www.igc.apc.org/cvd/)

Racial Gerrymandering

A reapportionment plan that includes in one district individuals who belong to the same race, but who are otherwise widely separated by geographical and political boundaries, and who may have little in common with one another but the color of their skin bears an uncomfortable resemblance to political apartheid. For these reasons we conclude that a plaintiff challenging a reapportionment statute under the Equal Protection Clause may state a claim by alleging that the legislation, though race-neutral on its face, rationally cannot be understood as anything other than an effort to separate voters into different districts on the basis of race, and that the separation lacks sufficient justification. . . . Racial gerrymandering, even for remedial purposes, may balkanize us into competing racial factions; it threatens to carry us further from the goal of a political system in which race no longer matters.

> Justice Sandra Day O'Connor, majority
> opinion, *Shaw v. Reno* (1993)

Until today the court has analyzed equal protection claims involving race in electoral districting differently from equal protection claims involving other forms of governmental conduct. . . . As long as members of racial groups have the commonality of interest implicit in our ability to talk about concepts like "minority voting strength" and "dilution of minority votes," and as long as racial bloc voting takes place, legislators will have to take race into account in order to avoid dilution of minority voting strength in districting plans they adopt. A second distinction between districting and most other governmental decisions in which race has figured is that those other decisions using racial criteria characteristically occur in circumstances in which the use of race to the advantage of one person is necessarily at the obvious expense of a member of a different race. . . . In districting, by contrast, the mere placement of an individual in one district instead of another denies no one a right or benefit provided to others.

> Justice David H. Souter, dissenting opinion,
> *Shaw v. Reno* (1993)

As everyone knows, for most of this century and some of the past century blacks were effectively disenfranchised across most of the South. They couldn't vote. That was largely fixed by the Voting Rights Act of 1965, which did away with literacy tests and other gimmicks to prevent blacks from voting. But another problem came into focus, which is racially polarized voting. Blacks tend to be isolated if districts are drawn in the usual, traditional way, in majority white districts in which blacks can't get elected and the candidates they prefer can't get elected because of block voting by whites and blacks. In order to address that problem in the 1982 Amendments to the Voting Rights Act, Congress clearly indicated that at least sometimes you can take race into account to draw majority black or majority Hispanic districts for purposes of ensuring, in the words of the Act, . . . that blacks and Hispanics will have as good an opportunity as white people to elect representatives of their choice.

Stuart Taylor, PBS, *The NewsHour with Jim Lehrer* (December 5, 1995)

Even today, with the new districts hanging on by a thread, minorities remain under-represented in Congress and every state legislature. African-Americans are 12 percent of the population but have only 7 percent of the seats in Congress, while Latinos make up 10 percent of the population but have only 3 percent of congressional seats.

Jamin B. Raskin, "Gerrymander Hypocrisy: Supreme Court's Double Standard," *Nation* (February 6, 1995)

Redistricting and Reapportionment

Redistricting since the 1990 census has marked tremendous gains for women and minorities. 1992 . . . was very historic for Florida. For the first time in over 120 years, an African-American [Representative Corrine Brown] was elected to Congress from Florida. At the same time . . . Representative Carrie Meek and Representative Alcee Hastings were also elected to represent Florida in Congress. Sixteen new African-American members, most from the South, were seated in the House of Representatives and one African-American Senator, Carol Moseley-Braun, was seated, expanding the number of congressional Black Caucus members to 40, the largest ever. There are now 57 women, 19 Hispanics, 8 Asians and 1 American Indian. This is the highest number of minorities to ever serve in the history of the U.S. Congress.

Representative Corrine Brown, *Congressional Record* (November 29, 1995)

While it may not be possible to draw congressional districts with mathematical precision, that is no excuse for ignoring our Constitution's plain objective of making equal representation for equal numbers of people the fundamental goal for the House of Repre-

sentatives. That is the high standard of justice which the Founders set for us.
Justice Hugo Black, majority opinion,
Wesberry v. Sanders 376 U.S. 1 (1964)

Legislators represent people, not trees or acres. Legislators are elected by voters, not farms or cities or economic interests. As long as ours is a representative form of government, and our legislatures are those instruments of government elected directly by and directly representative of the people, the right to elect legislators in a free and unimpaired fashion is a bedrock of our political system. . . . And, if a State should provide that the votes of citizens in one part of the State should be given two times, or five times, or 10 times the weight of votes of citizens in another part of the State, it could hardly be contended that the right to vote of those residing in the disfavored areas had not been effectively diluted.
Chief Justice Earl Warren, majority opinion,
Reynolds v. Sims 377 U.S. 533 (1964)

Term Limits

Asking an incumbent member of Congress to vote on term limits is a bit like asking a chicken to vote for Colonel Sanders.
Representative Bob Inglis, *Reader's Digest*
(October 1995)

Politicians are ambitious. There's no way we're ever going to change that. But the genius of our political system is that it ties political ambition to public approval. . . . That will change under term limits. Knowing they won't have to keep going back and asking the voters to reelect them, members of Congress will be less responsive to their constituencies. And with fewer opportunities for advancement within Congress itself, they will look outside the institution to fulfill their goals. Sitting members busy plotting their next political campaign or jockeying for executive appointment won't be very committed to their legislative duties. Their responsibilities will be neglected, their constituents ignored, and their congressional office seen as simply a step on the ladder, rather than a significant and meaningful career in itself.
Victor Kamber, *Giving Up on Democracy: Why Term Limits Are Bad for America* (1995)

Several times in debating the issue of term limits I've had an opponent suggest that limits will cost America its most experienced legislators. Invariably, such a comment draws loud applause from the audience. Which should not necessarily be interpreted as disrespect for those in Congress who have been in office a long time, as much as a uniquely American response to the idea of a ruling elite. Besides, many people reason, it was the experienced legislators who have brought us the huge deficit and such undesirable episodes as the $300 billion S&L bailout. . . . I could imagine a Congress picked by lottery that would have refused to pass federal deposit insurance as part of the necessary move to deregulate the thrift industry.

> Edward H. Crane, president of the Cato
> Institute, testimony to the Subcommittee on
> the Constitution, U.S. Senate (January 25,
> 1995)

The term limit movement amounts to a radical distrust of democracy. It is cynical and pessimistic, devoid of optimism and hope that built this country. It's also a rejection of professionalism in politics. Have you ever been in a storm at sea? I was—and I was terrified until I looked up at the bridge and the skipper was there sucking on his pipe—an old Norwegian 45 years at sea and that was reassuring. When the neurosurgeon has shaved your head, and made the pencil line across your skull and he approaches with the electric saw—ask him, won't you, one question: Are you a careerist?

> Representative Henry Hyde, speech before
> Congress (March 29, 1995)

USTL [U.S. Term Limits] spokesperson Jeff Langan calls term limits the "biggest grassroots movement ever in the United States." But if proponents describe support for term limits as a spontaneous, populist prairie fire driven by local outrage over entrenched congressional incumbents, a *Common Cause Magazine* analysis of campaign finance reports filed in the 14 states suggests that something else is fueling the fire: More than three-fourths of the movement's financing in 1992 came from four national groups and a relatively small number of wealthy individual donors.

> Amy E. Young, "The Money behind the
> Movement," *Common Cause* (Summer 1993)

The average length of terms for Members of the 104th Congress is 7.5 years. However . . . high turnover rates are largely confined to junior Members. As an example, during the 103rd Congress average length of service for senior Members—those serving more than 6 terms—was 21 years. . . . During the 19th century, less than 3 percent of the Members elected to serve in the House served over 12 years. In the Senate, only 11 percent served more than 12 years. In contrast, during the 20th century the percentage of Members serving for more than 12 years has skyrocketed to 27 percent in the House and 32 percent in the Senate. Studying the data since the post World War II era is even more alarming. From 1947 to present, 37 percent of House Members and 42 percent of Senate Members have served longer than 12 years.

> Representative Douglas Peters, *Congressional Record* (March 29, 1995)

Make no mistake about it, term limits are not the "end" but they are the "means" to an "end" of a smaller, less intrusive, and less expensive federal government. Congress will never, not in a million years, limit itself, unless it has to.

> Milton Friedman, Web page of Citizens for Federal Term Limits, Idaho campaign

The Founders [of the U.S.] debated the issue of term limits at the constitutional convention and ultimately decided that the sole responsibility for choosing the people who would represent them should be left to the people, and not be controlled or limited by the Government. Thomas Jefferson said it best in a letter to William Charles Jarvis on September 28, 1820: "I know no safe depository of the ultimate power of society but the people themselves; and if we think them not enlightened enough to exercise their control with a wholesome discretion, the remedy is not to take it from them, but to inform their discretion."

> Representative John Porter, *Congressional Record* (March 29, 1995)

Term limits . . . deprive Congress of members with experience and judgment and institutional memory. All things considered, I believe term limits would cause Congress to get worse, not better.

> Representative John Spratt, letter to constituents (Americans for Limited Terms

Web site at http://www.termlimits.org:80/
quotebank.shtml)

Last week, we heard about the cycle of dependency and people living off the taxpayer's money. And who was saying it?
The same Republicans who have been getting a government
salary for 20 to 25 years, and today are going to talk and fake
about phony 12-year term limits. Last week, Republicans said
"you get 2 years to learn job skills on your own, no job training." But the gentleman from Florida (Bill McCollum), sponsor
of a 12-year limit, says he needs a longer learning curve to
master the job.
Representative Luis Gutierrez, *Congressional
Record* (March 31, 1995)

I've never been for term limits. If people want to throw us out,
they know how to do it.
Senator Robert Dole, *Associated Press* (March
3, 1992)

Our founding fathers' vision of a "citizen legislature" where
members would be able to serve in Congress, and then return to
their communities to live under the laws they have written has
given way to year-round meetings and hurried weekend plane
trips to and from our districts and states.
Senator Robert Dole, *Los Angeles Times* (June
27, 1993)

Every one of the Founding Fathers was a professional. None of
them were amateurs who showed up on Tuesday and said, "I
have this inspiration, let me just do it, because my creative juices
are flowing." All of the Founding Fathers would have repudiated
that model and said, "that's exactly what you meant by 'moboc-
racy.' That's the mob."
Speaker of the House Newt Gingrich, *The
Weekly Standard* (September 18, 1995)

Term limits are fundamentally undemocratic. . . . They would do
nothing to deliver services better, or cut government waste, or
solve any of the social problems that desperately need solving.
Representative Lee Hamilton, *Washington
Report* (May 5, 1995)

Voting Rights

It was we, the people; not we, the white male citizens; nor yet we, the male citizens; but we, the whole people, who formed the Union. And we formed it, not to give the blessings of liberty, but to secure them; not to the half of ourselves and the half of our posterity, but to the whole people—women as well as men. And it is downright mockery to talk to women of their enjoyment of the blessings of liberty while they are denied the use of the only means of securing them provided by this democratic-republican government—the ballot. . . . Are women persons? And I hardly believe any of our opponents will have the hardihood to say they are not. Being persons, then, women are citizens; and no State has a right to make any law, or to enforce any old law, that shall abridge their privileges and immunities. Hence, every discrimination against women in the constitutions and laws of the several States is today null and void, precisely as in every one against negroes.

Susan B. Anthony, speech in New York
(1873)

Notes

1. Center for a New Democracy news release, "Voters in Five States Use Ballot Initiatives to Enact Tough Campaign Finance Reforms," November 6, 1996.

2. Citizen's Research Foundation, *Political Moneyline* 3 (August 1996) (newsletter).

3. David B. Magleby and Kelly D. Patterson, "Congressional Reform," *Public Opinion Quarterly* 58 (1994), 419–427.

4. Richard Morin and Mario A. Brossard, "Poll: Everyone Wants a New Direction," *Washington Post* (February 9, 1997), A1.

5. Magleby and Patterson, "Congressional Reform," 422.

6. Nancy Rhyme, "Term Limits Update," *National Conference of State Legislatures LegisBrief* 4 (February 1996), 1–2.

7. Magleby and Patterson, "Congressional Reform," 421.

8. Mark E. Rush, *Does Redistricting Make a Difference? Partisan and Electoral Behavior* (Baltimore, MD: Johns Hopkins University Press, 1993), p. 13.

9. Paul S. Herrnson, *Congressional Elections: Campaigning at Home and in Washington* (Washington, DC: CQ Press, 1993), p. 107.

10. Congressional Quarterly, "Campaign Finance Reform: Are Tighter Laws Needed to Police the System?" *CQ Researcher* 6 (February 9, 1996), 124.

11. Common Cause news release, "95 Percent of Incumbents Win Re-election in 1996, Aided by Dramatic Fundraising Advantage over Challengers, According to Common Cause," November 7, 1996.

Directory of Organizations and Agencies

5

The organizations listed here vary widely in political ideology and intent. Included are both profit-making and nonprofit organizations, government agencies, and intergovernmental associations. The common denominator is that all are working for an improved campaign and election process. Among the concerns of these organizations are increased political participation, term limits, campaign finance, voter education, alternative election systems, more efficient election administration, vote fraud and election crime, voter registration, and voting rights. A few historical associations, especially those involved in the campaign for woman suffrage and those that lobbied for progressive reforms, and some contemporary organizations no longer active have also been included.

American Association of Political Consultants (AAPC)
900 2nd Street NE, No. 204
Washington, DC 20002
(202) 371-9585
President: Ralph D. Murphine

Established in 1969, this organization includes individual and corporate members

145

that engage full-time in political counseling and other activities related to electoral politics. Persons who are active part-time in consulting, who are political science teachers or students, or who have aspirations to political activity may become associate members. AAPC conducts meetings every two years to provide information on innovative campaign tactics and other political developments.

Publications: The AAPC distributes *Politea* four times a year, a yearly *Membership Roster,* and a political resource directory.

American Association of Women (AAW)
2118 Wilshire Boulevard, Suite 174
Santa Monica, CA 90403
(310) 395-0244
President and Editor: Leslie C. Dutton

This organization strives to engage women in public policy debate and holds workshops and conferences for career women, working mothers, and former public officials. The AAW has demonstrated concern for election procedures that fail to hold poll officials accountable for voting irregularities.

Publications: American Association of Women Newsletter, published two to four times each year, and *AAW Issue Papers,* an occasional publication.

American Voter Coalition (AVC)
11901 Santa Monica Boulevard, Suite 531
Los Angeles, CA 90025
(310) 281-8683
Director: Julia A. E. Wright

The AVC is a national nonpartisan organization dedicated to increasing participation in the political process through voter education and registration. This group is active in a number of programs that include a national voter registration day; eliciting commitments from U.S. House, Senate, presidential, and gubernatorial candidates to refrain from using negative campaign advertisements; and the establishment of a national voter database as a research tool for academia, civic groups, and the media.

Publications: None.

American Woman Suffrage Association (AWSA)

This early organization committed to voting rights for women was established in 1869. For a time, the AWSA competed with a rival organization, the National Woman Suffrage Association, for the loyalty of those seeking suffrage expansion. The leadership of the AWSA concentrated primarily on lobbying states to grant woman suffrage rather than appealing to the national government to initiate a constitutional amendment. Although a man, Henry Ward Beecher was chosen as the first president; Lucy Stone became a major figure in the organization. In 1870 Mrs. Stone established the *Woman's Journal*, which eventually became the official publication of the National American Woman Suffrage Association.

Americans for Limited Terms (ALT)
2135 Sherman Avenue
Evanston, IL 60201
(847) 475-8186
President: Bob Costello

ALT works to end the present system of representation, in which incumbents in state and federal offices make an extended career of their public service. The organization wishes to replace this system with a political structure that allows for the election of citizen legislators who serve limited terms in office. ALT investigates candidate positions on state and local term limit proposals and makes those positions available to the public through the media so that citizens may better evaluate their vote choices. The organization believes that more frequent rotation in office will end the seniority system, the careerism of elected officials, and the constant electioneering of incumbents.

Americans for the National Voter Initiative Amendment (ANVIA)
3115 N Street NW
Washington, DC 20007
(202) 333-4846
Director: Edward A. Dent

With a membership of 35,000, ANVIA supports the adoption of an amendment to the U.S. Constitution that would permit direct voter action to initiate legislation at both the federal and state levels. Founded in 1979, the organization sponsors informational seminars at colleges and universities, issues press releases, and conducts direct mail campaigns. Members lobby government officials and testify before state legislatures and the U.S. Congress on behalf of the voter initiative amendment.

Publications: None.

Americans for the Voter Initiative
See Americans for the National Voter Initiative Amendment.

Black Women's Roundtable on Voter Participation (BWRVP)
410 7th Street SE
Washington, DC 20006
(202) 659-4929
Executive Director: Sonia R. Jarvis

Established in 1983, this program of the National Coalition on Black Voter Participation conducts a series of forums. The roundtable seeks to develop women's leadership skills in the black community through nonpartisan political participation and encourages black women's involvement in discussions concerning the influence of the women's vote in elections, stressing volunteer coalitions that seek to increase voter registration, voter education, and voter turnout.

Publications: None.

Center for a New Democracy (CND)
410 7th Street SE
Washington, DC 20003
(202) 543-0773
Executive Director: Donna F. Edwards

The center works with citizens groups to reform campaign finance laws and increase citizen participation in the electoral process. Founded in 1991, the CND conducts research on such topics as barriers to citizen participation and government responsiveness to public opinion.

Publications: CND Update is a monthly newsletter that covers campaign finance reform efforts around the country.

Center for Living Democracy (CLD)
RR 1, Black Fox Road
Brattleboro, VT 05301
(802) 254-1234
(802) 254-4331
Codirector: Frances Moore Lappe

This organization, founded in 1990 as the Institute for the Arts of Democracy, is concerned with the broader aspects of democratic politics. The CLD advocates more active participation in democratic politics and distributes information detailing the potential for successful democratic participation.

Publications: Newsletter.

Center for Responsive Politics (CRP)
1320 19th Street NW, 7th Floor
Washington, DC 20036
(202) 857-0044
Executive Director: Ellen S. Miller

The CRP was founded in 1983 to work for a more efficient and productive Congress and political process. The center compiles data, conducts surveys, and holds educational seminars for the purpose of disseminating information on congressional operations and American politics. Among the center's objectives are campaign finance reform, improved ethics in government, more effective public policy, congressional and media reform, and the establishment of a national library on money and politics. The center also provides computer services with databases on campaign finance, financial disclosure, lobbyists, and soft money.

Publications: Beyond the 30-Second Spot: Enhancing the Media's Role in Congressional Campaigns; The Fat Cat's Laundromat: Soft Money and the National Parties; New Directions in Voter Participation; Open Secrets: The Dollar Power of PACs in Congress; The Price of Admission: An Illustrated Atlas of Campaign Spending in the 1988 Convention Elections; Soft Money: A Loophole for the '80s; and The View from Capitol Hill: Lawmakers on Congressional Reform.

Center for Voting and Democracy (CVD)
6905 5th Street NW, Suite 200
Washington, DC 20012

(202) 882-7378
President: Matthew Cossolotto

The center focuses on a proportional representation electoral system that ensures political parties and candidates legislative seats in proportion to the percentage of the popular vote they receive as an alternative to the single member district "winner-take-all" voting system. Founded in 1992 as Citizens for Proportional Representation, the center believes that proportional representation will produce fairer levels of representation for women and for ethnic, racial, and ideological minorities. To promote its objective the center advocates the formation of national and state-level commissions on voting system reform, conducts educational and research programs, and pursues litigation in Voting Rights Act cases.

Publications: Voting and Democracy Report is an annual survey of voting systems and representation. *Voting and Democracy Review* is a bimonthly newsletter on voting systems and developments in electoral reform. The Center for Voting and Democracy also distributes various brochures and pamphlets on voting systems.

Cincinnatus Political Action Committee
See Citizens for a Fair Vote Count.

Citizen Action
See Citizen Action Fund.

Citizen Action Fund (CAF)
1730 Rhode Island Avenue NW, Suite 403
Washington, DC 20036
(202) 775-1580
Executive Director: Ira Hook

Founded in 1979 as Citizen Action, the organization strives to have the concerns of the majority of Americans heard in economic, environmental, and political decision making. With 32 state groups and a membership of three million, the CAF works for economic democracy and social justice. The organization calls for job creation, safe and affordable energy, fair taxes, equal voting rights, and communities and workplaces free of toxic hazards. Toward these ends, the CAF conducts research, training, and educational conferences.

Publications: News, a quarterly newsletter, provides updates on public policy issues and political campaigns.

Citizens for a Fair Vote Count
P.O. Box 11339
Cincinnati, OH 45211
(513) 984-4284
Director: James J. Condit, Jr.

Originally established as Cincinnatus Political Action Committee in 1972, this organization campaigns for the reinstatement of the printed ballot in every American election. Computer and machine voting are considered to be a major source of fraud in contemporary elections. The organization claims that Voter News Service, the polling company for the major news networks, and computer programming companies are responsible for vote fraud in key elections. The present system of presidential debates and other methods of maintaining two-party dominance also come under criticism.

Publications: Cincinnatus News Service is the organization's monthly newsletter, which contains reports of vote fraud and accounts of the organization's efforts to uncover fraud and to lobby for the printed ballot.

Citizens for Proportional Representation
See Center for Voting and Democracy.

Citizens' Research Foundation (CRF)
University of Southern California
Research Annex
3716 South Hope Street
Los Angeles, CA 90007
(213) 743-5211
Director: Herbert E. Alexander

The CRF strives to increase political participation through providing citizens a better understanding of political finance. Established in 1958 as the Political Research Foundation, the organization conducts studies on a variety of campaign finance–related topics, including public funding of political campaigns, federal and state election reform, and the conditions of successful fund-raising.

Publications: The CRF publishes its studies on the role of money in politics and the financing of presidential elections. The organization also publishes a quarterly newsletter, *Political Moneyline,* which includes reports on campaign spending and legislative efforts to institute political reform.

Coalition for Free and Open Elections (COFOE)
P.O. Box 20263
London Terrace Station
New York, NY 10011
(212) 691-0776

The COFOE, founded in 1985, opposes restrictive state regulations that govern the establishment of minor political parties. The organization argues that these regulations protect the two dominant parties from competition and therefore act as limitations on electoral democracy. The COFOE advocates more liberal voter registration laws and systems of proportional representation that would give third parties a greater chance to gain public office. The coalition distributes information about state electoral policies to interested citizens.

Publications: Ballot Access News, published monthly, contains information about legislative action and judicial decisions concerning the conduct of elections.

Commission on Presidential Debates (CPD)
601 13th Street NW, Suite 310 S
Washington, DC 20005
(202) 872-1020
Committee Chairman: Frank Fahrenkopf

In addition to sponsoring presidential debates, this nonpartisan commission, founded in 1987, conducts voter education programs.

Publications: The CPD makes news packets available to interested citizens.

Committee for the Study of the American Electorate (CSAE)
421 New Jersey Avenue SE
Washington, DC 20003
(202) 546-3221
Director: Curtis B. Gans

Founded in 1976, the committee conducts studies that chronicle and seek to explain the decline in political participation in the United States. The group also organizes conferences with recognized authorities in the field of American political participation.

Publications: None.

Common Cause (CC)
2030 M Street NW
Washington, DC 20036
(202) 833-1200
President: Ann McBride

With a membership of 250,000, a staff of 120, a budget of $11 million, and 48 state-level groups, Common Cause organizes lobbying efforts designed to promote campaign reform that the group considers necessary to reduce the influence of political action committees in the U.S. Congress. Founded in 1970 as the Urban Coalition Action Council, Common Cause supports issues such as partial public financing of congressional elections, improved ethics in government, nuclear arms control, oversight of defense spending, and tax reform. The organization has sponsored the People against PACs and Clean Up Congress projects.

Publications: Common Cause Magazine covers topics concerning ethics in government.

Congressional Quarterly, Inc. (CQ)
1414 22nd Street NW
Washington, DC 20037
(202) 887-6353

For over 50 years CQ has provided information about the American political process, including analyses of campaigns and elections. CQ provides valuable sources for investigating all aspects of campaigns and elections.

Publications: CQ publishes timely volumes on the three branches of government and the various issues currently facing the nation. Among these publications is *Guide to U.S. Elections*, a historical summary of elections for president, Congress, and state governorships. Among CQ's periodical publications are *Campaign Practices Reports*, a detailed look at campaign issues and finance regulations, *Congressional Insight,* an examination of the day-to-day workings of the U.S. Congress, and *CQ Weekly Report,* which covers the personalities and events in current American politics.

Council of State Governments (CSG)
Iron Works Pike
P.O. Box 11910
Lexington, KY 40578-9989
(606) 231-1939

The CSG, an organization representing all three branches of state government, provides research and other services to member governments and represents state government in Washington. Its various activities include an annual national meeting and four regional meetings, committee investigations on issues of concern to members, and management seminars. Because state governments are still a major source of policy making regarding election administration, communication and cooperation among the states facilitated by the CSG can be an important factor in the coordination of election procedures.

Publications: The Book of the States, issued yearly, contains valuable information on state election results and many other subjects. *Innovations* provides information about new state programs. *Journal of State Government,* issued bimonthly, contains articles detailing research.

Election Center (EC)
444 North Capitol Street NW, Suite 349
Washington, DC 20001
(202) 638-1445

The EC offers services for registration and election officials at the state, county, and municipal levels. The EC promotes national election conferences each year and acts as a communication channel for the exchange of information about election administration practices among officials. The organization has sponsored groups to investigate computer security and voting equipment certification. It also keeps election officials informed about legislative and regulatory changes that may affect their policies.

Publications: Election Center Reports, issued monthly, contains information regarding policy developments related to voter registration and elections and report on pending federal legislation.

Election Crimes Branch (ECB)
Public Integrity Section
U.S. Department of Justice
1400 New York Avenue NW
Washington, DC 27518
(202) 514-2601
Director: Craig Donsanto

Created in 1980 to supervise the enforcement of federal laws against criminal misconduct in the electoral process, the ECB is part of the Public Integrity Section of the Criminal Division at the U.S. Department of Justice. The agency conducts investigations of such election law violations as election fraud, intimidation and coercion of voters, violation of campaign financing and reporting provisions in federal law, solicitation of illegal contributions or activities from public employees, and violations of restrictions on the use of public funds for lobbying. The branch prosecutes some 150 criminal cases each year. Its personnel conduct training sessions for federal law enforcement officials who will investigate possible election crimes and recommend antifraud techniques to state and local election officials. The branch has cooperated with the Federal Election Commission in efforts to maintain ballot security.

Publications: Federal Prosecution of Election Offenses, a critical source for federal investigators and prosecutors, is published every two years.

Election Data Services, Inc. (EDS)
1522 K Street NW, Suite 320
Washington, DC 20005
(202) 789-2004
Director: Kimball W. Brace

EDS is an independent consulting firm that provides information to public officials about voting equipment and the electoral process. Among its services, EDS helps local officials to select voting equipment; offers customized computer software to count ballots and present election results; holds workshops for election officials on such topics as new voting equipment, the evaluation of future technological advances, and redistricting methodology; assists state governments with redistricting plans; and maintains county-level data regarding voter registration and turnout, election results, and election equipment.

Publications: None.

Election Research Center (ERC)
1321 Connecticut Avenue NW, 2nd Floor
Washington, DC 20036
(202) 659-9590
Director: Richard M. Scammon

The ERC is a nonprofit organization that provides verified results of federal and gubernatorial elections. The organization can also provide election results from other democratic nations.

Publications: Since 1956, the ERC has published the *America Votes* series, a summary of election results, in cooperation with Congressional Quarterly, Inc.

Fair Campaign Practices Committee (FCPC)

The FCPC is a group representing major political parties and major religious faiths. Its goal is to work with the press, political parties, candidates for public office, schools, churches, and civic groups in order to increase public awareness of "smear and similar tactics" in political campaigns. Though presently inactive, since its establishment in 1954 the committee worked on a variety of projects including problems in political campaigns, election laws, and candidate and voter education efforts.

Federal Election Commission (FEC)
999 E Street NW
Washington, DC 20463
(202) 376-3120

The FEC is an independent regulatory agency within the federal government that Congress established in 1974 through amendments to the Federal Election Campaign Act. The commission administers federal campaign finance laws, including public funding of presidential elections, contributions and spending in federal elections, and disclosure of campaign finance information submitted by political action committees. The commission, which meets approximately twice a week, is composed of six voting commissioners appointed by the president and confirmed by the Senate for six-year, overlapping terms. The clerk of the House of Representatives and the secretary of the Senate serve as ex officio nonvoting members of the commission. The FEC has a staff of approximately 250 people.

Publications: A monthly newsletter, campaign manuals, a series of publications on various aspects of election law, and the *Journal of Election Administration,* now a once-yearly publication.

Federal Voting Assistance Program (FVAP)
Office of the Secretary of Defense
1B457, Pentagon
Washington, DC 20301
(703) 697-5737
Director: Phyllis Taylor

Established in 1955 under the Federal Voting Assistance Act and expanded in 1968 and 1975 under the Overseas Citizens Voting Rights Act and in 1986 under the Uniformed and Overseas Voting Rights Act, the FVAP helps members of the armed forces, their spouses and dependents, members of the merchant marine and their spouses and dependents, and any qualified U.S. citizen residing overseas to register and vote. The program recommends an official postcard form to states for use in absentee registration and voting. It acts as an ombudsman for local election officials and for those wishing to vote absentee under provisions of federal law, and it works with states to improve absentee registration and voting programs.

Publications: The FVAP publishes the *Voting Assistance Guide,* which describes each state's absentee voting regulations, lists mailing addresses of local election officials and includes the Uniformed and Overseas Citizens Absentee Voting Rights Act. The program also publishes a brochure titled *How to Vote Absentee.*

Frontlash
815 16th Street NW
Washington, DC 20006

(202) 783-3993
Executive Director: Cheryl Graeve

Founded in 1968, Frontlash claims 38 affiliated state groups. Its purpose is to increase the political participation of young people, minorities, senior citizens, and workers through voter registration and "get out the vote" drives. Frontlash conducts conferences, seminars, and workshops and organizes campus leaflet drops and phone banks in order to foster among young citizens and others an understanding of what the group believes is the importance of a strong, growing, and democratically governed labor movement in the United States. The group takes stands on many public policy issues, including health care, education, housing, job training, and veterans' benefits. In order to further its goals Frontlash advocates increasing citizen electoral participation by reforming what it considers restrictive voter registration and election laws.

Publications: Frontlash Update is a quarterly newsletter that keeps members informed about the group's activities.

Funders Committee for Citizen Participation (FCCP)
437 Madison Avenue, 27th Floor
New York, NY 10022
(212) 371-3200
Contact: Jerry Mannion

Formerly the Funders Committee for Voter Registration and Education, the FCCP is a group representing 25 community, corporate, and private foundations. Established in 1983 and affiliated with the Council on Foundations, the committee's purpose is to broaden the base of support for nonpartisan voter education and voter registration, particularly among underrepresented groups such as blacks, Hispanics, women, and young people. In order to encourage greater political participation among these groups, the FCCP collects and disseminates information through its sponsorship of briefings on issues relating to citizen participation in the United States.

Publications: Funding Citizen Participation is a semiannual newsletter on the group's activities.

Funders Committee for Voter Registration and Education
See Funders Committee for Citizen Participation.

Honest Ballot Association (HBA)
North Shore Towers, Building 3 Arcade
272-30 Grand Central Parkway
Floral Park, NY 11005
(516) 466-4100

HBA, founded in 1909, focuses on ensuring that elections are free from dishonest practices. Its goals include prevention of fraudulent voter registration, repetitive voting, and voter coercion. The organization trains individuals to be pollwatchers, who assume responsibility for monitoring election procedures to determine their honesty and efficiency. In addition to public elections, the organization monitors elections for such organizations as labor unions and corporations.

Publications: HBA distributes pamphlets that provide basic facts about election laws.

Initiative America (IA)
3115 N Street NW
Washington, DC 20007
(202) 333-4846
Director: Edward A. Dent

This election reform organization, founded in 1977, lobbies for the passage of legislation that will allow for greater citizen participation in the initiation and passage of legislation at the state and federal levels. IA attempts to educate the public regarding the need for such reform.

Publications: None.

Institute for the Arts of Democracy
See Center for Living Democracy.

International Association of Clerks, Recorders, Election Officials, and Treasurers (IACREOT)
P.O. Box 1012
Camden, NJ 08101-9998
(609) 963-0109

This organization, founded in 1971, provides the opportunity for county, municipal, and state government officials, including those concerned with the conduct of elections, to share information and ideas regarding their respective operations. It provides representation for the membership in Washington and the state capitals. IACREOT conducts annual meetings at which new administrative procedures are demonstrated and organizes workshops in various areas of administration, including elections.

Publications: The News, a quarterly newspaper for exchanging information among members.

International Foundation for Electoral Systems (IFES)
1101 15th Street, 3rd Floor
Washington, DC 20005
(202) 828-8507
Chairman: Charles T. Manatt

Established in 1987, the IFES observes elections in countries that request its help and strives to improve electoral procedures to help guarantee free and fair elections. The organization offers advice to election officers about establishing regularized electoral procedures, which include appropriate statutes, training for poll workers, efficient and honest vote-counting methods, security procedures, and voter education programs.

Publications: Elections Today, a quarterly; a newsletter; and reports on specific activities.

League of Women Voters Education Fund (LWVEF)
1730 M Street NW, Suite 1000
Washington, DC 20036
(202) 429-1965
Executive Director: Judith A. Conover

The LWVEF serves as an educational unit of the League of Women Voters of the United States. The organization conducts studies on citizen participation and voter services as well as on a variety of substantive issues such as health care and social welfare.

Publications: Along with the *LWVEF Annual Report* and a publications catalogue, the organization distributes reports on substantive issues as well as on election reform, such as the *Motor Voter Status Report.*

League of Women Voters of the United States (LWVUS)
1730 M Street NW, Suite 1000
Washington, DC 20036
(202) 429-1965
Executive Director: Gracia Hillman

Founded in 1920 as an outgrowth of the National American Woman Suffrage Association following ratification of the Nineteenth Amendment granting voting rights to women, the League of Women Voters promotes responsible citizen participation in government. Formerly the National League of Women Voters, the organization's regional, state, and local groups distribute voter guides that offer information about political candidates and their issue positions. Although the LWVUS does not offer support for candidates or political parties, members involve themselves in various political and social issues.

Publications: The league distributes two bimonthly publications, *National Voter* and *Report from the Hill,* an annual report, handbooks, and voter guides at election time.

Lobbyists and Lawyers for Campaign Finance Reform (LLCFR)
Arnold and Porter
1200 New Hampshire Avenue NW
Washington, DC 20036
(202) 872-6805
Executive Officer: William J. Baer

This organization of lawyers and lobbyists founded in 1987 seeks the passage of legislation to limit campaign expenditures for congressional elections.

Publications: None.

National American Woman Suffrage Association

Formed in 1890 from the union of the National and American Woman Suffrage Associations, this organization played a major role in the final achievement of woman suffrage. Its early leaders, Elizabeth Cady Stanton and Susan B. Anthony, fought initial battles at the national level, petitioning Congress to propose a constitutional amendment granting voting rights to women. After ratification of the Nineteenth Amendment in 1920, the organization's leadership established the National League of Women Voters.

National Association of Counties (NACo)
440 First Street NW
Washington, DC 20001
(202) 393-6226
Executive Director: John P. Thomas

Representing more than two-thirds of the nation's counties, NACo is a major agent of county government on the national level. The organization assists member counties, which are the primary level of election administration, to improve their operations. NACo investigates innovative ways to provide services. An annual meeting is held each summer, and a legislative conference meets each winter.

Publications: County News, a biweekly newspaper, keeps members informed about national policy changes and trends in county administration.

National Association of County Recorders, Election Officials, and Clerks (NACRC)
c/o Ardis Schmitt, CPO
200 South Cascade Avenue
Colorado Springs, CO 80903
(719) 520-6216
President: Mary Harkrader

This organization, representing elected and appointed county officials, advocates the more effective operation of county government offices, including voter registration and election administration. NACRC, an affiliate of the National Association of Counties, conducts workshops on a number of subjects, including elections, and provides information on new computer and voting technologies. Members are kept informed about forthcoming legislation and rules changes. The organization maintains an election committee.

Publications: Bulletin, a quarterly available to members only, reports on legislative actions and the activities of the organization.

National Association of Secretaries of State (NASS)
Iron Works Pike
P.O. Box 11910

Lexington, KY 40578-9989
(606) 231-1913

The NASS, an affiliate of the Council of State Governments, was formed in 1904 as a means of communication among the secretaries of state of the several states. Because secretaries of state are often the chief election officer of a state, the organization has been involved in such election reform efforts as "get out the vote" programs, the investigation of campaign finance regulation, cooperative reporting of election results, and observation of election procedures in other countries. The NASS holds two conferences each year, at which meetings are held to discuss state problems.

Publications: NASS News, the organization's quarterly newsletter; *The Office and Duties of the Secretary of State;* and *NASS: A Heritage,* a historical series.

National Coalition on Black Voter Participation (NCBVP)
1629 K Street NW, Suite 801
Washington, DC 20006
(202) 659-4929
FAX: (202) 659-5025
Executive Director: Sonia R. Jarvis

This coalition of labor and religious organizations, black caucuses, fraternities and sororities, and political groups was founded in 1976. The NCBVP acts to increase African American voter registration and to encourage voter education. The organization conducts studies of African American voting patterns.

Publications: Operation Big Vote Newsletter is published bimonthly. The organization also distributes a manual titled *How to Organize and Implement a Successful Nonpartisan Voter Participation Campaign.*

National Conference of State Legislatures (NCSL)
1050 17th Street, Suite 2100
Denver, CO 80265
(303) 623-7800

An organization that represents all 50 states, the NCSL was established to provide services, such as research and technical assistance, to state legislators. The organization also represents state interests before the federal government. The NCSL works with legislators on legislative questions, including election policy, providing professional staff and research resources, conducting workshops, and offering training sessions.

Publications: State Legislatures, a magazine issued ten times per year, reports on state policy developments. *Conference Reports,* issued quarterly, contains information about the organization's activities. *Legislative Reports,* published approximately 15 times per year, covers a variety of issues of current interest.

National League of Women Voters

See League of Women Voters of the United States.

National Municipal League

Committed to ending corruption in city government, this historic reform organization was established in 1894. By 1896 there were 180 League-affiliated chapters, and by 1900 a chapter existed in almost every large city. The league's first president, James C. Carter, was founder and five-time president of the New York Bar Association. In order to accomplish its goal the league advocated that city government reform its election systems in a number of ways. These reforms included replacing ward with at-large elections, replacing partisan with nonpartisan elections, holding local elections at times different from state and federal elections, reducing the size of city councils, instituting election methods that provided for proportional representation, and introducing the initiative, referendum, and recall.

National Publicity Law Association (NPLA)

This early organization included such prominent figures as William Jennings Bryan, Samuel Gompers, and Charles Evans Hughes. Formed in 1905, the association's goal was the enactment of a federal law to require that candidates disclose campaign funding sources and spending.

National Short Ballot Organization

Formed in 1909 by Richard Chiles and Woodrow Wilson, this early reform group advocated reducing the number of county and municipal elective offices. By limiting the number of elected municipal positions to the mayor and city council, for example, the organization believed that elected officeholders would take greater care in the selection of other public officials and thus increase the level of professionalism in government. In 1920 it was decided to consolidate the National Short Ballot Organization with the National Municipal League.

National Student Campaign for Voter Registration (NSCVR)
218 D Street SE
Washington, DC 20003
(202) 546-9707
Contact: Gene Karpinski

This organization, founded in 1975 and promoted by public interest groups, works with student governments and other organizations in the effort to increase student participation in elections. The NSCVR claims that its voter registration drives on college campuses have resulted in over one million new registrants. The organization collects data on voting behavior and conducts a speakers' bureau.

Publications: NSCVR distributes *The Student Advocate,* a monthly publication; *Voter Registration Manual,* a biennial; and a periodic newsletter.

National Woman Suffrage Association (NWSA)

This rival organization to the American Woman Suffrage Association began in 1869 and continued until the merger with its competitor in 1890. The NWSA, under the leadership of Elizabeth Cady Stanton and Susan B. Anthony, took stands on social issues that went beyond attaining the vote. The major focus of this organization was the achievement of suffrage at the national level.

100% Vote/Human SERVE
622 113th Street, Room 410
New York, NY 10025
(212) 854-4053
Executive Director: Richard Cloward

This organization, formerly called Human SERVE Fund and Human SERVE Campaign, is a coalition of state and national organizations concerned with voter registration reform. "SERVE" stands for Service Employees Registration and Voter Education. The organization focuses its efforts on altering voter registration systems by making voter registration more convenient for the average citizen. It has advocated automatic registration by various governmental and social service agencies. SERVE gathers data regarding levels of voter registration and voter turnout. The organization was a major supporter of the National Voter Registration Act.

Publications: SERVE distributes a newsletter several times a year, as well as the publication *Why Americans Don't Vote.*

Operation Big Vote (OBV)
c/o National Coalition on Black Voter Participation
1629 K Street NW, Suite 801
Washington, DC 20006
(202) 659-4929
Executive Director: James J. Ferguson

This organization, founded in 1976, encourages increased African American voter participation. It is associated with the National Coalition on Black Voter Participation. Focusing its efforts on communities with large African American populations, OBV encourages voter participation and cultivates greater concern for politics among voters. The organization provides various services, including training, grants for nonpartisan local projects, and fund-raising advice.

Publications: OBV publishes handbooks and manuals on voter registration and participation.

People's Lobby (PL)
c/o Floyd Morrow
653 Nathan Lane
Santa Rosa, CA 95407-5110
(707) 539-5667
President: Floyd Morrow

This organization, founded in 1968, encourages the more extensive use of referendum, initiative, and recall elections. The PL advocates a constitutional amendment that would establish a national initiative. The organization provides a consulting service for elections campaigns.

Publications: Direct Democracy.

Political Campaign Institute (PCI)
c/o Aristotle Industries
205 Pennsylvania Avenue SE
Washington, DC 20003
(202) 543-6408
President: John Phillips

Composed of a group of both Democratic and Republican campaign advisers, this profit-making organization offers materials, including video tapes, to candidates for public office who wish to receive instruction on winning election campaigns. The group also provides information on the political system to the general public.

Publications: The PCI publishes a monthly magazine, *Campaign Industry News.*

Political Research Foundation
See Citizen's Research Foundation.

Project Vote! (PV)
1511 K Street NW, Suite 326
Washington, DC 20005
(202) 638-9016
Executive Director: Sanford A. Newman

This nonpartisan organization manages voter registration and education programs, especially among minority and low-income Americans. PV organizes voter registration drives among the poor and supports education programs for voters.

Publications: How to Develop a Voter Registration Plan; How to Register Voters at a Central Site.

Southwest Voter Registration Education Project (SVREP)
403 East Commerce Street, Suite 220
San Antonio, TX 78205

(210) 222-0224
President: Andrew Hernandez

This organization, formed in 1975, represents labor, civic, and church groups that cooperate in registering voters among minority group members in southwestern and western states. The SVREP gathers information about Hispanic American and Native American political participation in the Southwest. The organization works for reapportionment in cities and counties suspected of racial gerrymandering and also trains individuals to conduct voter registration drives.

Publications: The organization publishes a bimonthly newsletter and report as well as *National Hispanic Voter Registration Campaign.*

Urban Coalition Action Council
See Common Cause.

The Voluntaryist (TV)
P.O. Box 1275
Gramling, SC 29348
(803) 472-2730
Co-Organizer: Carl Watner

This libertarian organization, founded in 1982, provides a unique perception of campaigns and elections. TV denies the legitimacy of political power and therefore rejects political activity, even in the libertarian cause. Rather than electoral politics and other traditionally accepted means of change, TV advocates nonpolitical means for achieving the libertarian goal of a free society.

Publications: In addition to *The Voluntaryist,* a monthly newsletter, the organization offers such books as *A Voluntary Political Government; Neither Bullets nor Ballots;* and *Bearing Witness for Silence.*

Vote America Foundation (VAF)
1850 M Street NW, Suite 900
Washington, DC 20036
(202) 833-8550
Chairman: Joe M. Rodgers

This organization, established in 1983 and presently inactive, has attempted to increase voter turnout, especially among younger

Americans. The VAF has employed the mass media to make public service announcements regarding voter turnout.

Publications: The organization has distributed manuals intended to educate and motivate prospective voters.

Voting Section, Civil Rights Division
Department of Justice
P.O. Box 66128
Washington, DC 20530-6128
(202) 724-5767

The Voting Section of the U.S. Justice Department's Civil Rights Division is responsible for enforcing federal civil rights voting laws. The section brings litigation in federal district courts, employs federal observers to monitor elections, and reviews changes in voting regulations and standards made by state and local governments. Each year some 3,000 to 4,000 requests for approval are made, representing as many as 23,000 individual changes. The section is composed of a chief, 4 deputy chiefs, approximately 20 lawyers and 20 equal opportunity specialists, and 20 clerical personnel. Lawsuits filed by the section involve any denial or abridgment of minority voting rights (such as vote dilution through the use of at-large and multimember district election systems) under the Voting Rights Act.

Publications: None.

Selected Print Resources

Books

The works listed in this section are divided into six subgroups. The first includes sources that examine the role of money and political action committees in campaigns, fund-raising strategies, and attempts to introduce finance reform. The second presents sources on campaign strategy, corrupt practices, and suggestions for campaign reform, and the third includes more general works that deal with the relationship between the electoral system and the operation of democracy and representation. The fourth contains sources on election administration and the electoral procedures used to select public officials. The fifth section, on the mass media and politics, presents works that probe the influence of the media on the electoral process. The final section includes sources that investigate various attempts to expand the right to vote, particularly the struggle for woman suffrage and voting rights for minorities.

Campaign Finance

Alexander, Herbert E. *Financing Politics: Money, Elections, and Political Reform.* Fourth ed. Washington, DC: Congressional Quarterly, 1992.

171

Alexander examines a number of topics related to campaign finance, including the history of campaign finance law, the development and operation of political action committees, donations from wealthy contributors, and independent campaign expenditures by organizations not directly associated with a candidate.

Alexander, Herbert E., and Anthony Corrado. *Financing the 1992 Election.* Armonk, NY: M. E. Sharpe, 1995.

This ninth volume in a series provides a wealth of information about the financing of presidential and congressional elections. Employing data from the Federal Election Commission and other sources, the authors derive reliable estimates of total spending in all national, state, and local elections. The analysis of the 1992 presidential campaign presents a detailed description of the race, including accounts of the candidates' fund-raising and spending strategies and the role of the media. The authors conclude that candidate spending limits instituted in 1974 have not been effective and relate recent legislative attempts to bring about reform.

Baker, Ross K. *The New Fat Cats: Members of Congress as Political Benefactors.* New York: Priority Press, 1989.

Baker focuses on so-called leadership political action committees (PACs), organizations established by individual members of Congress who employ resources donated to them by PACs to support colleagues and other candidates for Congress. Leadership PACs add to the already existing threat that PACs pose to political parties and contribute to the growing cynicism of citizens. Baker discusses reform proposals that attempt to get congressional candidates to accept expenditure limits for voluntary participation in publicly financed campaigns. Other possible reforms include better oversight of campaign fund expenditures and an increase in the amount that the parties' congressional campaign committees are allowed to contribute to candidates.

Bennett, James T., and Thomas J. DiLorenzo. *Destroying Democracy: How Government Funds Partisan Politics.* Washington, DC: Cato Institute, 1985.

Examining interest group activity from a conservative perspective, the authors focus on organizations such as the League of Women Voters, the National Association for the Advancement of

Colored People, and the Campaign for Economic Democracy that receive government funding. They believe that such groups pose a threat to democratic politics. While pointing to the special treatment received by unions in the political process, the authors neglect to document the advantages enjoyed by business groups.

Biersack, Robert, Paul S. Herrnson, and Clyde Wilcox, eds. *Risky Business? PAC Decisionmaking in Congressional Elections.* Armonk, NY: M. E. Sharpe, 1994.

The contributors to this volume describe the activities of 19 political action committees, presenting information on their founding and history.

Brown, Clifford W., Jr., Lynda W. Powell, and Clyde Wilcox. *Serious Money: Fundraising and Contributing in Presidential Campaigns.* Cambridge: Cambridge University Press, 1995.

"Serious money" refers to political contributions from individuals that range from $201 to $1,000, the federal legal limit. Brown, Powell, and Wilcox discuss various aspects of fund-raising within the context of existing reform legislation. The authors note that as primaries and caucuses become more "front loaded," occurring earlier in the primary season, timely fund-raising becomes increasingly important. As inflation erodes the value of the $1,000 maximum contribution, candidates are forced to seek contributions from a larger number of people.

Clawson, Dan, Alan Neustadt, and Denise Scott. *Money Talks: Corporate PACs and Political Influence.* New York: Basic Books, 1992.

The authors, all sociologists, investigate business PAC money raising and campaign donation policies. They discuss the pressure placed on corporate employees to make contributions to PACs and the access to public officials gained by campaign donations. Claiming that corporations have come to dominate the political process, the authors recommend limits on campaign fund-raising and expenditures.

Congressional Quarterly. *Congressional Campaign Finances: History, Facts, and Controversy.* Washington, DC: Congressional Quarterly, 1992.

This brief overview of campaign finance provides an investigation of contributions and expenditures in congressional campaigns and summarizes the relevant federal regulations. The historical development of campaign finance is discussed, along with the reforms of the 1970s. The final chapter describes more recent reform efforts, and an appendix presents the Federal Election Campaign Act of 1971, with its 1974, 1976, and 1979 amendments, and the Revenue Act of 1971, which established a system of public funding for presidential elections.

Corrado, Anthony. *Creative Campaigning: PACs and the Presidential Selection Process.* Boulder, CO: Westview, 1992.

Corrado's treatment of the development of precandidacy political action committees by presidential hopefuls provides an instance of the difficulties involved in instituting campaign reform. A loophole in the law permits presidential candidates to avoid campaign contribution limits and disclosure requirements by collecting large amounts of money through personal political action committees. Corrado concludes that this practice can create difficulties for campaign finance regulation and suggests easing regulations on campaign contributions and state primary spending limits.

Cutler, Lloyd N., Louis R. Cohen, and Roger M. Witten, eds. *Regulating Campaign Finance.* Beverly Hills, CA: Sage, 1986.

This collection of essays covers a wide range of views on campaign finance regulation. Authors opposing regulation point to its lack of constitutional justification, the burdensome nature of regulation, and the advantages of market self-monitoring. Other contributors recommend varying regulatory measures, including a constitutional amendment granting Congress increased authority to control campaign finance. The contributors, including academics, politicians, and journalists, provide a good overview of the state of campaign finance in the late 1980s that is largely relevant today.

Drew, Elizabeth. *Politics and Money: The New Road to Corruption.* New York: Macmillan, 1983.

Drew is concerned with the initiation of policies to reform the campaign finance system that ironically was itself established by reform legislation in the 1970s. Political activists have found ways to bypass the new regulations. Despite public financing of presidential campaigns, Drew notes that private money still influences the election process indirectly. Politicians' commitment to raising funds has increased, and political action committees have become a troublesome component in the campaign process.

Eismeier, Theodore J., and Philip H. Pollock III. *Business, Money, and the Rise of Corporate PACs in American Elections.* New York: Quorum Books, 1988.

This analysis of corporate political action committees reveals that about half of these organizations are small, contributing less than $5,000 to ten or fewer candidates. While generally charitable toward PACs, the authors admit that PAC money may make members of Congress less responsive to their districts and express concern that congressional candidates often actively seek out PAC funding. The authors recognize the need for minimal reforms, such as establishing a limit on the total amount of funding from PACs to individual congressional candidates.

Gais, Thomas L. *Improper Influence: Campaign Finance Law, Political Interest Groups, and the Problem of Equality.* Ann Arbor: University of Michigan Press, 1996.

Gais notes that the proliferation of political action committees has altered the system for representing interests at the national level and argues that although interest group activities in American politics are well regulated, Americans still remain displeased with the role special interests play in election campaigns. In partial explanation, the author claims that campaign finance laws discourage less-advantaged groups from organizing while giving preference to business groups.

Gierzynski, Anthony. *Legislative Party Campaign Committees in the American States.* Lexington: University Press of Kentucky, 1992.

Gierzynski examines the development of legislative campaign committees in several states and identifies the strategies commonly used to distribute campaign funds. Interestingly, these legislative party committees concentrate funding on close races, whether the recipient is an incumbent or challenger. Although such committees have helped to fashion a stronger and more competitive party system, the author notes that they have come under severe criticism in some states.

Jackson, Brooks. *Honest Graft: Big Money and the American Political Process.* New York: Knopf, 1988.

Believing that the system of campaign finance needs reform, journalist Jackson provides an interesting account of fund-raising techniques in the 1986 congressional elections. The author presents case studies based on inside information, much of which was provided by Anthony Coelho, chair of the Democratic Congressional Campaign Committee.

————. *Broken Promise: Why the Federal Election Commission Failed.* New York: Priority Press, 1990.

According to Jackson, the Federal Election Commission (FEC), both unwilling and unable to deter violators of federal election law, has failed in its duty to control political contributions. The author claims that the agency is captive to Congress and the two dominant political parties and recommends a major overhaul of the agency, including the establishment of a new five-member panel to avoid tie votes. Terms should be five years, with one commissioner elected each year. Among other changes, the FEC should be protected from political retaliation and should have a staff capable of financial investigations. Realizing that a major restructuring would be unpopular in Congress, Jackson suggests additional, more limited reforms.

Jacobson, Gary C. *Money in Congressional Elections.* New Haven, CT: Yale University Press, 1980.

Basing his study on data from the 1972, 1974, 1976, and 1978 general elections, Jacobson assesses the effects of money in congressional elections. He notes the expansion of political action committees during the late 1970s and the advantages of increased spending for nonincumbent challengers. The author describes the reform effort in the 1960s and 1970s and the resulting campaign finance regulations and discusses the difficult choice for a member of Congress between relying on special interests for campaign funds and supporting a system of public finance.

Kubiak, Greg D. *The Gilded Dome: The U.S. Senate and Campaign Finance Reform*. Norman: University of Oklahoma Press, 1994.

Based on his experience as chief legislative assistant to U.S. Senator David L. Boren, Kubiak recounts the struggle for campaign finance reform over a seven-year period. Employing various documents, interviews, and his own observations, the author describes the relationship between campaign finance and the outcomes of the legislative process.

Magleby, David B., and Candice J. Nelson. *The Money Chase: Congressional Campaign Finance Reform*. Washington, DC: Brookings Institution, 1990.

The authors examine the underlying problems with the present system of campaign finance and determine the possible consequences of reform. Among the reforms they suggest for increasing competition in congressional elections are reducing the influence of special interests, decreasing the need to raise funds, strengthening political parties, instituting full disclosure of campaign contributions and spending, and administering campaign finance laws more effectively.

Makinson, Larry, and Joshua F. Goldstein. *Open Secrets: The Encyclopedia of Congressional Money and Politics*. Third ed. Washington, DC: Congressional Quarterly, 1994.

This large reference work records the sources of congressional campaign contributions, both from individuals and political action committees. Makinson and Goldstein present a thorough and highly informative examination of the connection between political action committee campaign donations and political influence in Congress. Contributions are identified for each member of the House of Representatives and the Senate. The authors include sketches of the House and Senate standing committees as well as major interest group donors and the recipients of their contributions.

———. *The Cash Constituents of Congress: 1992 Elections*. Washington, DC: Congressional Quarterly, 1994.

This book provides summary information from the authors' more extensive work, *Open Secrets*. Makinson and Goldstein present shorter profiles of Senate and House members and identify campaign contributions from individuals and political action committees. Patterns of larger campaign contributions are identified.

Morris, Dwight, and Murielle E. Gamache. *Gold-Plated Politics: The 1992 Congressional Races.* Washington, DC: Congressional Quarterly, 1994.

The authors of the extensive *Handbook of Campaign Spending* present a briefer examination of campaign spending practices. Employing the same research used to produce the larger volume, they analyze the effects of the present system on candidate strategies and activities.

———. *Handbook of Campaign Spending: Money in the 1992 Congressional Races.* Washington, DC: Congressional Quarterly, 1994.

The authors examine campaign spending for all 1992 House and Senate races. They provide data indicating how each campaign used its resources for various categories of spending, including advertising and fund-raising. Sources of information for the book include Federal Election Commission reports and interviews with campaign workers, political consultants, and candidates.

Mutch, Robert E. *Campaigns, Congress, and Courts: The Making of Federal Campaign Finance Law.* New York: Praeger, 1988.

Mutch presents a detailed history of campaign finance legislation, beginning with the 1907 Tillman Act, which prohibited corporate campaign contributions. Early legislation proved ineffective due to lack of enforcement provisions. The author discusses the Federal Election Campaign Act of 1972, revisions enacted in 1974, and the *Buckley v. Valeo* decision of 1976, in which the Supreme Court invalidated provisions of the act limiting the amount of money candidates could spend, except in campaigns where public funds are provided.

Nugent, Margaret Latus, and John R. Johannes, eds. *Money, Elections, and Democracy: Reforming Congressional Campaign Finance.* Boulder, CO: Westview, 1990.

This volume of articles provides analyses of the perceived weaknesses of campaign finance legislation and offers recommendations for reforming finance practices. A difficulty for achieving reform legislation is that Congress has not felt compelled to act because the general public finds it difficult to understand the complex questions involved in campaign finance. Articles deal with such topics as loopholes in the Federal Election Campaign Act, the effect of incumbency on campaign finance, and the development of personal political action committees in Congress.

Overacker, Louise. *Money in Elections.* New York: Macmillan, 1932.

In this early volume, Overacker, an eminent political scientist, offers a detailed analysis of campaign finance. Recognizing the inadequacy of legislation at the time, the author recommends more effective control. She discusses the possibility of restraint through publicizing the names of campaign contributors.

Palda, Filip. *How Much Is Your Vote Worth?* San Francisco: Institute for Contemporary Studies, 1994.

Dismissing the widely expressed concern over large amounts of money in elections, Filip argues that campaign finance reform legislation itself needs reforming. The author observes that contribution limits are just one of many advantages enjoyed by incumbents and that these limitations force candidates to devote an inordinate amount of time raising money. Contrary to existing federal law, Filip claims that contributions are a measure of intensity of support for candidates and that limits actually raise the cost of elections.

Redfield, Kent D. *Cash Clout: Political Money in Illinois Legislative Elections.* Springfield: University of Illinois Press, 1995.

Redfield investigates the role of money in state elections, providing an in-depth case study of the financing of legislative elections in Illinois in 1990 and 1992. The author identifies the major contributors to legislative campaigns in the state. Illinois has no established limits on campaign contributions or expenditures.

Sabato, Larry J. *PAC Power: Inside the World of Political Action Committees.* New York: Norton, 1984.

Though admitting that political action committees have become an important, and in ways worrisome, part of electoral politics, Sabato recommends limiting reform to the undesirable aspects of PACs and encouraging their positive contributions to the political process. For instance, he argues that PACs have helped to strengthen and renew political parties. Sabato's commentary is based on a thorough study of the literature on PACs, a random survey mailed to nearly 400 PACs, and personal interviews with those associated with PACs.

Sorauf, Frank J. *Money in American Elections.* New York: Harper-Collins, 1988.

Sorauf presents a summary investigation of money in congressional and presidential campaigns and also examines campaign finance at the state level. Employing data from the Federal Election Commission, the author focuses on political action committees, political parties, and public funding of campaigns. The problems of campaign finance that have led to intense debates are identified and reforms are suggested, including bringing states into current federal regulations, despite the *Buckley v. Valeo* decision.

———. *Inside Campaign Finance: Myths and Realities.* New Haven, CT: Yale University Press, 1992.

Sorauf provides an excellent brief history and contemporary overview of campaign finance. He argues that politicians often seek campaign resources as actively as contributors attempt to find recipients. While Sorauf suggests moderate, realistic reforms, he rejects common beliefs, originating in the Populist and Progressive movements, that campaign donations can purchase either elections or undue influence.

Whiting, Meredith, E. Patrick McGuire, Catherine Morrison, and Jessica Shelly. *Campaign Finance Reform.* New York: Conference Board, 1990.

This monograph offers a brief description of the Federal Election Campaign Act and the Federal Election Commission (FEC). The authors summarize campaign donation regulations and the duties and authority of the FEC and make several recommendations for reforming the FEC in such areas as the regulation of soft money and public disclosure of contributions and spending.

Campaigns, Corruption, and Reform

Archibald, Samuel J., ed. *The Pollution of Politics: A Research/Reporting Team Investigates Campaign Ethics.* Washington, DC: Public Affairs Press, 1971.

This brief monograph on unethical and illegal campaign tactics is especially interesting because it appeared the year before the Watergate scandal began. Case studies and specific examples are presented. The perhaps surprising theme of the volume is that "dirty politics" does not pay. A final chapter compares the American experience with that of Great Britain and France.

Benson, George C. S. *Political Corruption in America.* Lexington, MA: Lexington Books, 1978.

Benson provides a solid historical treatment of corruption in American politics, depicting corrupt practices in local, state, and national government. The author discusses types of vote fraud, unethical campaign conduct, and the misuse of money in campaigns. To lessen political corruption, Benson recommends better ethical education and more judicious enforcement of existing laws.

Boller, Paul F., Jr. *Presidential Campaigns.* New York: Oxford University Press, 1985.

Boller offers entertaining accounts of presidential campaigns from 1789 to 1984, demonstrating how the presidential selection process has evolved. Boller's commentary indicates that negative campaigning is certainly not a new phenomenon in American politics.

Burrell, Barbara C. *A Woman's Place Is in the House: Campaigning for Congress in the Feminist Era.* Ann Arbor: University of Michigan Press, 1994.

This book focuses on the underrepresentation of women in the U.S. Congress by examining the attempts of women to win congressional seats during the period 1968 to 1992. The author investigates possible ways in which the electoral process might affect the ability of female candidates to run successfully for legislative office. While rejecting various hypotheses that the electoral process discriminates against women, Burrell suggests that the high success of incumbents, usually male, in gaining reelection and the smaller number of women running for office help to explain why disproportionately fewer women gain election to the U.S. Congress.

Callow, Alexander R., Jr. *The Tweed Ring.* New York: Oxford University Press, 1966.

Callow relates the fascinating history of the famous New York City political machine. Organized by William March Tweed and his cronies, the Tweed Ring ruled city and state politics from 1866 to 1871. After a strong reform movement developed, the Tweed Ring finally faced defeat at the hands of reformers in the November 1871 elections. Many of the organization's top people fled, and others, including Tweed, were tried on corruption charges and imprisoned. Callow's work offers a good example of the possibilities and frustrations of reform efforts.

Collier, James M., and Kenneth F. Collier. *Votescam: The Stealing of America.* New York: Victoria House, 1996.

James and Kenneth Collier provide a personal account of their attempts to track down vote fraud in American elections. They attribute much of the fraud, as well as declining voter turnout, to the increased use of computerized voting. They strongly suggest that George Bush won the 1988 New Hampshire primary as the result of vote manipulation and charge Janet Reno with complicity in Florida vote fraud prior to her appointment as U.S. attorney general. The authors urge the reintroduction of the paper ballot.

Cook, Fred J. *American Political Bosses and Machines.* New York: Franklin Watts, 1973.

Cook recounts the development of the political boss and party machine in American cities, describing Tammany Hall and the Tweed Ring in New York; Marcus Alonzo Hanna, the crafty Republican politician; Abraham Ruef, the labor boss; and the political corruption in New Jersey. The author describes examples of election fraud and the attempt of reformers to establish more efficient and honest government.

Dinkin, Robert J. *Campaigning in America: A History of Election Practices.* Westport, CT: Greenwood, 1989.

Dinkin, a historian, describes every presidential election campaign from 1789 to 1988. He focuses on the candidates, parties, and issues in each campaign. Also included are accounts of specific state and local campaigns. Although not a systematic work, the volume offers a great deal of information about the history of election campaigns.

Felknor, Bruce L. *Political Mischief: Smear, Sabotage, and Reform in U.S. Elections.* New York: Praeger, 1992.

Felknor, former executive director of the Fair Campaign Practices Committee, presents a broad historical treatment of unsavory campaign practices. The author exposes the various techniques candidates and their advisers have used to influence voters. Although not a systematic treatment of the subject, the book offers interesting and entertaining anecdotes from the campaign trail.

Finegold, Kenneth. *Experts and Politicians: Reform Challenges to Machine Politics in New York, Cleveland, and Chicago.* Princeton, NJ: Princeton University Press, 1995.

Finegold's historical study of political reform movements in three cities can provide insights into current reform efforts. Contrary to common understanding, the author concludes that reform attempts sometimes involved coalitions across ethnic and class lines. Political experts, independent of business interests, who allied themselves with politicians were important ingredients in the ultimate success of reform efforts.

Fishkin, James S. *Democracy and Deliberation: New Directions for Democratic Reform.* New Haven, CT: Yale University Press, 1991.

Despite reforms instituted over the last two decades to facilitate voting, increasing numbers of Americans have failed to exercise this fundamental right. Fishkin attributes this phenomenon to "disconnection": Citizens simply do not concern themselves with political questions. The author suggests the introduction of deliberative opinion polling as a modified form of the Greek system of lots: Citizens would be chosen randomly to participate in the discussion of issues and the expression of political views. A second possible reform would involve granting to each citizen a voucher (for instance, for $100) to be used to support a candidate or political position.

———. *The Voice of the People.* New Haven, CT: Yale University Press, 1995.

Fishkin elaborates on his criticisms of American democracy, noting that the present system fails to reflect clearly the views of citizens. The author relates his plan for a National Issues Convention that became a reality in 1996. The project was covered in a Public Broadcasting System presentation.

Gross, Martin L. *The Political Racket: Deceit, Self-Interest, and Corruption in American Politics.* New York: Ballantine, 1996.

Gross details the various areas that have contributed to the failure of American politics, including vote fraud, the electoral college, and the use of paid political consultants. The author recommends two constitutional amendments to bring about reform. The first would institute such remedies as popular election of the president; a national presidential primary; congressional term limits; and the establishment of initiative, referendum, and recall elections in all states. A second amendment would create extensive limitations on campaign contributions and spending. Gross has two basic goals for initiating reform: Eliminate all political parties and banish all money from politics.

Guber, Susan. *How to Win Your First Election.* Delray Beach, FL: St. Lucie Press, 1997.

Guber, who served three terms in the Florida House of Representatives and has held numerous other government and public service positions, offers practical campaign advice. This guide to campaigning provides insights into the contemporary campaign and election process. Topics covered include advice to women who are attempting to enter what has been predominantly a male profession, campaign techniques in a multicultural society, and the importance of candidate involvement at the grassroots level.

Holbrook, Thomas M. *Do Campaigns Matter?* Thousand Oaks, CA: Sage, 1996.

The importance of campaigns to electoral outcomes determines in part the need for alterations in financing and other kinds of campaign reform. Recent studies have suggested that certain basic variables, independent of candidates' efforts, can predict election results. Employing public opinion data from several presidential campaigns, Holbrook concludes that campaign events, such as conventions and debates, do play a role in changing public opinion. Therefore, the author concludes that election results can be explained by a combination of longer-term variables in addition to the campaign efforts of candidates and their organizations.

Jamieson, Kathleen Hall. *Dirty Politics: Deception, Distraction, and Democracy.* New York: Oxford University Press, 1992.

In this well-researched study, Jamieson provides an account of negative campaigning from the Eisenhower administration to the 1990s. The author presents in-depth examples from recent campaigns and concludes from her analysis that the strategy of marketing politics tends to personalize politics and avoids coherent argument, all to the detriment of the American political process. She suggests moderate reforms to encourage fairer campaign practices based on the debate of substantive issues and better communication standards in the mass media.

Johansen, Elaine. *Political Corruption, Scope, and Resources: An Annotated Bibliography.* New York: Garland, 1990.

Johansen has collected more than 800 citations from the literature on political corruption, including books, articles, dissertations, government publications, and legal cases. The citations are divided into subject chapters, including election corruption, public opinion, state and local government corruption, and business-government graft. A separate chapter includes publications dealing with the detection of dishonesty, its control, and possible reform. A topic notably lacking from the book is campaign finance.

Luntz, Frank I. *Candidates, Consultants, and Campaigns: The Style and Substance of American Electioneering.* New York: Blackwell, 1988.

Largely a noncritical treatment, this book focuses on the people involved in campaigns, including pollsters, fund-raisers, and consultants, and the various campaign activities, such as direct mailing, polling, the use of focus groups, and advertising. Luntz interviewed many of those engaged in campaigns to gather a detailed catalogue of potentially useful facts about election campaigns.

Mayer, William G., ed. *In Pursuit of the White House: How We Choose Our Presidential Nominees.* Chatham, NJ: Chatham House, 1996.

This book provides a detailed examination of the presidential nomination process. Individual authors deal with such topics as campaign finance, the operation of caucuses and primaries, the preprimary campaign, political party reform, and the role of interest groups in the nomination process.

Miller, Nathan. *Stealing from America: A History of Corruption from Jamestown to Reagan.* New York: Paragon, 1992.

Miller's extensive treatment of corruption in America includes descriptions of election irregularities. As early as 1634, a Massachusetts election was "stolen" when election results that failed to return the leadership to power were set aside, with the avid support of Reverend John Cotton. Miller presents examples of vote buying by both political parties and describes Tammany Hall's offering of naturalization papers to noncitizens for the promise of a favorable vote.

Newman, Bruce I. *The Marketing of the President: Political Marketing as Campaign Strategy.* Thousand Oaks, CA: Sage, 1994.

Newman examines developments in the techniques and technology of political marketing, employing information from the 1992 presidential campaign. The author's approach to the subject takes into account such recent phenomena as the decline of party identification, negative advertising, campaign reporting, and the increased costs of campaigning. Newman discusses the prospects for reform, including the fairness of present campaign and election rules, campaign finance, and the need for a code of ethics to establish the responsibilities of the media, candidates, consultants, and others involved in campaigns. Nonetheless, he concludes that marketing techniques, if used honestly, can strengthen the political process.

O'Shaughnessy, Nicholas J. *The Phenomenon of Political Marketing.* New York: St. Martin's, 1990.

This book provides an examination of U.S. campaigns and elections from the perspective of a British citizen with expertise in management and marketing. Although O'Shaughnessy does not provide any novel findings, he does present a thorough overview of many of the subjects, including political action committees and direct mail campaigns, that have drawn the attention of those concerned with contemporary American elections.

Pfau, Michael, and Henry C. Kenski. *Attack Politics: Strategy and Defense.* New York: Praeger, 1990.

The authors confront one of the more troubling trends in contemporary political campaigns: negative, or attack, messages. Because of the potentially adverse consequences of such tactics, Pfau and Kenski investigate possible ways to counter such attack communications. Their research has led them to recommend a preemption strategy that involves "inoculation" messages that encourage resistance to attitude change resulting from negative messages.

Reinsch, J. Leonard. *Getting Elected: From Radio and Roosevelt to Television and Reagan.* New York: Hippocrene, 1988.

Reinsch traces the changes in presidential nomination and election procedures from 1944 to 1984. In a final chapter he suggests reforms that might reverse the trend of decreasing voter turnout. Recommendations include shifting election day to the weekend (possibly the second Sunday in November), instituting regional primaries, tightening national party convention rules, improving the format for presidential debates, and reforming campaign finance.

Reiter, Howard L. *Parties and Elections in Corporate America.* Second ed. White Plains, NY: Longman, 1993.

Starting with the assumption that the American political process is in need of fundamental reform, Reiter focuses on the political party system as a major component of a flawed system. The author deals with such topics as the limits of voting, nonvoting, campaign finance, presidential and congressional elections, and the possible future development of party politics.

Sabato, Larry J. *The Rise of Political Consultants: New Ways of Winning Elections.* New York: Basic Books, 1981.

Sabato makes his position clear from the start: "Political consultants . . . have inflicted severe damage upon the party system and masterminded the modern triumph of personality cults over party politics in the United States." The author details consultants' activities, including polling, media advertising, and direct mail solicitations. Sabato suggests such reforms as altering media coverage of candidates and strengthening political parties.

Sabato, Larry J., and Glenn R. Simpson. *Dirty Little Secrets: The Persistence of Corruption in American Politics.* New York: Random House, 1996.

Largely through the use of case studies, Sabato and Simpson argue that corrupt practices remain a reality in the American political process despite the reforms instituted by Congress. They offer examples of continuing vote fraud in Alabama, California, Texas, and Philadelphia, Pennsylvania, and suggest that recent reforms such as the National Voter Registration Act have increased the potential for fraud. However, rather than suggesting further restrictions on fund-raising, spending, and campaign practices, the authors recommend "deregulation plus," a reform strategy that would rely primarily on disclosure to improve the campaign and election process.

Simpson, Dick. *Winning Elections: A Handbook in Modern Participatory Politics.* New York: HarperCollins, 1996.

This how-to book on campaign strategy proposes a formula for reform. Simpson argues that a campaign that offers opportunities to average citizens to participate in the political process can provide better results than campaigns that depend on large amounts of money, public relations, and mass media advertising. The author gives advice to candidates on such topics as dealing with the media, communicating with voters, organizing campaign operations, and scheduling events.

Thurber, James A., and Candice J. Nelson, eds. *Campaigns and Elections American Style.* Boulder, CO: Westview, 1995.

This book of essays by political scientists and campaign professionals combines two distinct approaches to election campaigns. While those active in campaigning not surprisingly consider their activities important to election outcomes, political scientists tend to deemphasize the significance of campaigns relative to other factors. The book is an attempt to bridge the gap between students of the political process and practitioners of the art of campaigning.

Troy, Gil. *See How They Ran: The Changing Role of the Presidential Candidate.* Revised ed. Cambridge, MA: Harvard University Press, 1996.

Troy presents an interesting commentary on the evolution of presidential campaigns. From an age when active campaigning was unthinkable to the period of active party involvement and ultimately to the modern media campaign, Troy traces the variations in the process. In response to strong criticisms of contemporary media-oriented campaigns, the author raises serious doubts about whether the nation ever experienced a golden age of positive, issue-oriented campaigning.

Whillock, Rita Kirk. *Political Empiricism: Communication Strategies in State and Regional Elections*. Westport, CT: Praeger, 1991.

Although not oriented toward campaign reform, Whillock analyzes important aspects of campaigning that raise possible questions about electoral change. The author deals with such topics as the handling of consultants, the use of persuasion techniques, political marketing and packaging of candidates, candidate image making, negative campaign strategies, the advantageous use of issues, and campaign finance.

Elections and the Political Process

Bennett, Stephen Earl. *Apathy in America, 1960–1984: Causes and Consequences of Citizen Political Indifference*. Ardsley-on-Hudson, NY: Transnational, 1986.

This study operationalizes the concept of political apathy, employing questions from the University of Michigan survey data. Bennett finds that the level of apathy remained stable over the 24-year period of the study, with a more recent decline. The consequences of apathy include low knowledge of public affairs, low voter turnout rates, and failure to engage in other forms of political participation. Bennett leaves it to others to explore the causes of apathy and low participation and hence to recommend possible ways to ameliorate the situation.

Beyle, Thad L., ed. *State Government: CQ's Guide to Current Issues and Activities, 1997–1998*. Washington, DC: Congressional Quarterly, 1997.

This collection of previously published essays touches on various issues facing state and local government. Among the topics relevant to campaigns and elections are term limits, incumbency and elections, media coverage of politics, and the impact of the initiative and referendum on state and local government. Revised editions of this work are published yearly.

Birch, Anthony H. *The Concepts and Theories of Modern Democracy.* New York: Routledge, 1993.

Birch's very helpful discussion of democracy provides a theoretical context in which to evaluate proposed election reforms and introduces comparisons among democratic nations. In a discussion of political participation, Birch examines suggestions that the United States adopt policies such as compulsory voting and create political parties with mass memberships. Other topics discussed are broader political participation at the local level and the increased use of the initiative and referendum.

Campbell, James E. *The Presidential Pulse of Congressional Elections.* Lexington: University Press of Kentucky, 1993.

Campbell presents a detailed analysis of congressional elections, especially in nonpresidential election years. He employs a modified theory of surge and decline, which interprets the outcome of a congressional election as a consequence of the previous presidential contest. The author examines the possible effects of creating four-year terms for House members, which would thus establish concurrent terms for the U.S. House of Representatives and the president.

Ceaser, James, and Andrew Busch. *Interpreting the 1996 Elections.* Lanham, MD: Rowman and Littlefield, 1997.

This analysis of the 1996 presidential and congressional elections covers a number of subjects relevant to campaign and election reform. The authors deal with such topics as divided control of the national government between the two parties, independent candidates in the presidential race, the significance of party platforms, the question of party realignment, and the campaign strategies used by the candidates.

Cook, Rhodes, and Alice V. McGillivray. *U.S. Primary Elections: President, Congress, Governors, 1995–1996.* Washington, DC: Congressional Quarterly, 1997.

This reference volume contains complete results for the 1995–1996 primary election season. The authors present county-by-county results of presidential primaries in 41 states, as well as the outcomes of caucuses in the remaining states. Similar data are provided for primaries to nominate candidates for governor, the U.S. Senate, and the U.S. House of Representatives. Cook and McGillivray have compiled a very useful set of data for those conducting research on elections.

Darcy, R., Susan Welch, and Janet Clark. *Women, Elections, and Representation*. New York: Longman, 1987.

Through an analysis of election data for local, state, and national legislative races, the authors measure the progress of female electoral candidates. They conclude that although barriers to political rights for women were overt and intentional earlier in the nation's history, women candidates no longer face significant prejudice. The authors suggest that multimember districts might increase women's chances of gaining office and urge further research to determine what electoral practices will enhance women's political fortunes without having a detrimental effect on minority representation.

Ehrenhalt, Alan. *The United States of Ambition*. New York: Times Books, 1991.

This critical study of electoral politics examines the professionalization of candidates for office. Although candidates possess the expertise to gain public office, they often fall short of the mark when it comes to formulating public policy. Ehrenhalt bases his analysis on data gathered from selected state and local political arenas.

Fenno, Richard F. *On the Campaign Trail: The Politics of Representation*. Norman: University of Oklahoma Press, 1996.

Fenno, a noted scholar of congressional politics, examines the connection between elections and representation. The author draws his data from an investigation of over 200 individuals who ran for the U.S. Senate over a 15-year period. The role played by campaigns in establishing and altering the relationship between elected officials and constituents is presented in rich detail. The book provides a good background to any discussion of campaign reform.

Ginsberg, Benjamin, and Martin Shefter. *Politics by Other Means: The Declining Importance of Elections in America.* New York: Basic Books, 1991.

The authors argue that the relevance of elections to governing has been declining in the United States. They conclude that this decline undermines the efficacy of American government and adversely affects the nation's status in the world.

Ginsberg, Benjamin, and Alan Stone, eds. *Do Elections Matter?* Second ed. Armonk, NY: M. E. Sharpe, 1991.

This series of essays answers yes to the question presented in the title, notwithstanding claims that influential elites ultimately control the actions of public officials, that special interest groups influence policy making, and that scientific and economic experts often make the final decisions. Individual essays deal with such topics as campaign advertising, the cause and amelioration of low voter turnout, and the positive effects of voting, as witnessed by the experience of black enfranchisement.

Gould, Lewis L. *Reform and Regulation: American Politics, 1900–1916.* New York: Wiley, 1978.

Gould delineates the path toward acceptance of greater government regulation during the Progressive Era. He examines the efforts of reformers such as Theodore Roosevelt, Robert LaFollette, and Woodrow Wilson, who competed for control of their respective political parties. Such electoral changes as the referendum, the initiative, and the direct primary were advocated by Progressive Era reformers. Gould includes data tracing the fall of voter turnout in northern states from just over 78 percent in 1896 to just under 60 percent in 1916.

Grady, Robert C. *Restoring Real Representation.* Urbana: University of Illinois Press, 1993.

Grady recommends fundamental reforms in the American political process in order to create an electoral system that would allow for more meaningful citizen participation. By replacing the present system of interest groups with what the author terms "democratic functional constituencies," voters would become more civic-minded, leaving them in a better position to select legislators concerned with serving the overall public interest rather than narrow special interests.

Greider, William. *Who Will Tell the People: The Betrayal of American Democracy.* New York: Simon and Schuster, 1992.

Greider presents an impassioned argument that American democracy has come under the control of privileged elite groups. The author claims that such institutions as political parties and the mass media no longer provide support for the democratic process. Confrontation is recommended as possibly the only way the disadvantaged have to return to democratic politics.

Harrigan, John J. *Politics and the American Future: Dilemmas of Democracy.* Fourth ed. New York: McGraw-Hill, 1996.

This reform-oriented book includes several topics relevant to campaigns and elections. Among the subjects discussed are a single six-year term for the president, the results of party reform (especially as reform affects the presidential primary system), campaign finance reform, and voter participation. Harrigan's major theme is that American democracy faces the dilemma of maintaining a balance between the goal of increased government efficacy and the goal of greater representativeness.

Herrnson, Paul S. *Congressional Elections: Campaigning at Home and in Washington.* Washington, DC: Congressional Quarterly, 1995.

In this study of congressional elections, Herrnson analyzes a wealth of data, including information about 10,000 candidates for the House of Representatives from 1978 to 1992; interviews with the 1992 candidates and their aides, political party leaders, and political action committee officials; and case studies of 24 candidates. The author identifies a candidate's need to win both local support as well as the backing of national politicians. The present electoral system has led to a decentralized Congress in which policy making has become difficult.

Hudson, William E. *American Democracy in Peril: Seven Challenges to America's Future.* Chatham, NJ: Chatham House, 1995.

One of Hudson's seven challenges to American democracy is trivialized elections: elections that fail to offer citizens the opportunity to make meaningful vote choices based on a reasoned consideration of issues they consider important. The decline of political parties, the rise of candidate-centered campaigns, and the increased power of political action committees have contributed to the declining importance of elections. Hudson recommends the introduction of democratic deliberation among voters and the revitalization of political parties to reverse the trend.

Jacobson, Gary C. *The Politics of Congressional Elections.* Third ed. New York: HarperCollins, 1992.

Jacobson examines major topics related to congressional elections, including the legal and institutional context in which elections occur, the candidates and the character of their campaigns, voting behavior, and the influence of elections on the behavior of elected officials. One response to dissatisfaction with the electoral process is support for term limits. Although recognizing problems, Jacobson denies that this possible reform will bring any significant improvement in congressional performance.

Key, V. O., Jr. *Southern Politics in State and Nation.* New York: Vintage, 1949.

This classic volume by an eminent political scientist provides an analysis of the political process in southern states just after World War II. Key describes an electoral system in critical need of reform. Among the topics discussed are the primary system of nomination; the conduct of general elections; campaign finance; voter turnout; and restrictions on the right to vote such as the literacy test, the poll tax, and the white primary.

Kimball, Penn. *The Disconnected.* New York: Columbia University Press, 1972.

Kimball offers a detailed description of efforts to increase voter turnout following passage of the Voting Rights Act of 1965. A concluding chapter includes recommendations for increasing participation, such as a system of universal voter enrollment in which the federal government would assume responsibility for registering every eligible citizen. This and other proposals are interesting in light of passage of the National Voter Registration Act 20 years after publication of this book.

King, Anthony. *Running Scared: The Victory of Campaigning over Governing in America.* New York: Free Press, 1997.

"Running scared" refers to the vulnerability that American public officials experience in the face of frequent elections, which require them to campaign almost constantly for reelection. As King notes, the United States has shorter terms for elected officials than any other major democracy. The author claims that this vulnerability helps to explain the inability of officials to deal effectively with major issues facing the nation.

Leduc, Lawrence, Richard G. Niemi, and Pippa Norris, eds. *Comparing Democracies: Elections and Voting in Global Perspective.* Thousand Oaks, CA: Sage, 1996.

This collection of essays examines the electoral systems of several democracies, thus providing a basis for comparing the American electoral process with other nations. Among the subjects discussed are electoral laws, campaign finance laws, the role of the mass media, and varying levels of voter turnout.

Mayhew, David R. *Congress: The Electoral Connection.* New Haven, CT: Yale University Press, 1974.

Mayhew's analysis proceeds under the basic assumption that the desire for reelection motivates much of the activities of members of Congress. Such behavior as "advertising" (creating a favorable image among constituents), "credit claiming" (taking credit for positive government action), and "position taking" (making popular judgmental statements) are associated with a desire for reelection. Mayhew touches on such reform proposals as strengthening political parties, increasing press monitoring, and regulating campaign finance but does not mention term limits as a possible reform.

McGerr, Michael E. *The Decline of Popular Politics: The American North, 1865–1928.* New York: Oxford University Press, 1986.

McGerr describes the transformation of American politics that occurred in the North after the Civil War and identifies changes as a major cause of declining voter participation in the twentieth century. The author argues that campaign advertising and a focus on personalities replaced a basically democratic culture.

Meadow, Robert G., ed. *New Communication Technologies in Politics.* Washington, DC: Annenberg School of Communications, 1985.

The essays in this volume present a generally positive perception of technological changes in the methods used to campaign for public office. Improved technology is making it easier for candidates and political causes to approach voters on a more personal basis. For instance, direct mail fund-raising has made the political process more accessible because the average citizen has greater ability to participate, at least by making campaign donations. However, more complex technology is viewed as increasing the professionalization of campaigns. An important question raised is whether political needs lead to new technologies or whether technologies reshape politics.

Miller, Arthur H., and Bruce E. Gronbeck, eds. *Presidential Campaigns and American Self Images.* Boulder, CO: Westview, 1994.

The editors contend that election campaigns play a vital role in constructing Americans' perceptions of political reality. Individual chapters deal with various aspects of campaigning, including negative campaign advertising, media influence on campaigns, candidates' strategies to affect their images in the media, candidate debates, and campaign finance. According to the editors, a more democratic electoral process depends on higher ethical standards for candidates, mass media that more effectively oversee the electoral process, and citizens who are better informed and more willing to participate.

Nelson, Michael, ed. *The Elections of 1996.* Washington, DC: Congressional Quarterly, 1997.

The authors discuss the 1996 presidential and congressional election outcomes. The essays cover such topics as the nomination campaigns, media coverage, and the role of issues in the campaign. The 1996 elections are placed in historical context to provide a perspective from which to interpret the significance of outcomes.

Parenti, Michael. *Democracy for the Few.* New York: St. Martin's, 1995.

Parenti examines the electoral process within the context of a scathing attack on the American political process. The author identifies the single-member district system, news media that ignore third-party candidates, at-large elections, voter apathy in the face of two major parties unresponsive to citizen preferences, and continued opportunities for vote fraud in computer voting systems as reasons for low voter turnout. Parenti recommends proportional representation, cumulative and limited voting systems, and the elimination of the electoral college as possible reforms.

Patterson, Kelly D. *Political Parties and the Maintenance of Liberal Democracy.* New York: Columbia University Press, 1996.

Patterson examines presidential campaigns from 1952 to 1992 and investigates their relation to the development of public policy. The author conducts a content analysis of party platforms and the promises and issue positions of presidential and congressional candidates. The importance of building a consensus for governing and the significance of campaigns to democracy are emphasized.

Pika, Joseph. *The Presidential Contest.* Fifth ed. Washington, DC: Congressional Quarterly, 1995.

Pika presents a broad analysis of the presidential selection process. In this edition, the author focuses on the 1992 campaign, comparing the George Bush and Bill Clinton campaign strategies.

Popkin, Samuel L. *The Reasoning Voter: Communication and Persuasion in Presidential Campaigns.* Chicago: University of Chicago Press, 1991.

Popkin presents a reassuring account of the American voter's ability to arrive at a rational vote decision despite the technological advances and mass media appeals of recent elections. Voters are able to use basic reasoning skills to determine candidate and party positions on issues and to evaluate government performance. The author uses case studies of three primaries (1976, 1980, and 1984) to provide evidence for his position.

Preismesberger, Jon, ed. *National Party Conventions, 1831–1992.* Washington, DC: Congressional Quarterly, 1995.

Party conventions played an important part in American politics as they evolved through a series of reforms. This volume details the events at the major, and some minor, party conventions from their beginnings to 1992. The narrative presents summaries of party platforms, especially for more recent conventions, and tables detail delegate votes for presidential hopefuls.

Reichley, James A. *Elections American Style*. Washington, DC: Brookings Institution, 1988.

This volume of essays identifies the various difficulties the American electoral system presently faces and proposes reforms that could alter electoral outcomes. Among the topics treated are the cost of campaigns and the role of political action committees in campaign finance, the mass media and voter perceptions of candidates, the influence of special interests in campaigns, declining voter turnout, political party conventions and the diminishing role of parties in the electoral process, congressional redistricting, and state laws that limit fledgling parties' access to the ballot.

Reynolds, David. *Democracy Unbound: Progressive Challenges to the Two Party System*. Boston: South End Press, 1997.

Political parties have traditionally played an important role in the American electoral process. Therefore we should expect that any alterations in the party system will result in electoral changes. Reynolds describes the efforts that third-party movements, such as the New party, the Labor party, and the Greens, are making today to challenge the dominance of the two major political parties over the electoral system.

Riordon, William L. *Plunkitt of Tammany Hall: A Series of Very Plain Talks on Very Practical Politics*. New York: E. P. Dutton, 1963 (1905).

This entertaining little book includes the common wisdom of George Washington Plunkitt, Tammany Hall leader in New York City's Fifteenth District. A party man, Plunkitt opposed the progressive reforms of the late nineteenth and early twentieth centuries. Civil service reform denied political parties the ability to reward the party faithful for campaign work, and the primary nomination system denied the party organization and leaders control over the choice of party candidates. An underlying theme is that reformers should be cautious of the unintended consequences of their proposed changes in the political process.

Rollins, Ed. *Bare Knuckles and Back Rooms: My Life in American Politics*. New York: Doubleday, 1996.

Rollins, a major political strategist, relates his personal experiences with American politics. Through descriptions of major contemporary political figures such as Richard Nixon, Ronald Reagan, George Bush, Ross Perot, and Newt Gingrich, Rollins offers insights into the more sordid aspects of the American political and electoral system.

Roth, Timothy P. *Information and Freedom: The Disenfranchised Electorate.* Lanham, MD: University Press of America, 1994.

Economist Timothy Roth focuses on the extremely difficult task of holding elected officials responsible for their promises regarding government spending. Politicians can publicly oppose larger government during election campaigns while at the same time contributing to its expansion once they gain office. The author attributes the problem to "information asymmetry" between voters and their elected representatives.

Ryden, David K. *Representation in Crisis: The Constitution, Interest Groups, and Political Parties.* Albany: State University of New York Press, 1996.

Ryden's goal is to clarify a legal theory of representation. After examining the basic nature of the concept, the author explores notions of group representation and finds them wanting because groups are "empirically impossible" to identify and weight for representation. Political parties are singled out as the institution especially equipped to provide representation.

Salmore, Barbara G., and Stephen A. Salmore. *Candidates, Parties, and Campaigns: Electoral Politics in America.* Second ed. Washington, DC: Congressional Quarterly, 1989.

As their major thesis, the authors note that significant changes have occurred in political campaigns over a 50-year period. Campaigns have come to play a more significant role in influencing election results and have become candidate-centered rather than party-centered, due in part to media and technological developments. The authors indicate that the growing costs of new technologies have increased the urgency of campaign finance reform.

Scammon, Richard M., and Alice V. McGillivary, eds. *America Votes 21: A Handbook of Contemporary American Election Statistics.* Washington, DC: Congressional Quarterly, 1995.

This series, published every two years, provides detailed data on voter registration and election results. Summary tables present voter turnout rates for presidential, gubernatorial, senatorial, and House elections, and maps indicate the most recent results of redistricting efforts in each state. The volume offers valuable background information for investigating current electoral procedures and the consequences of reform efforts.

Schlesinger, Joseph A. *Political Parties and the Winning of Office.* Ann Arbor: University of Michigan Press, 1991.

Schlesinger tackles the question of what function political parties will continue to perform in American elections. Parties play a role distinct from interest groups in that they provide less direct benefits to members. The author notes that notwithstanding an altered electoral system, voters continue to support the candidates presented to them by the parties.

Schlozman, Kay Lehman, ed. *Elections in America.* Boston: Allyn and Unwin, 1987.

The essays in this volume treat a number of electoral topics, including presidential nominating rules and their possible reform, the importance of nonvoters to the outcomes of electoral contests, the role played by the media in the 1984 presidential election, a comparison of House and Senate campaign financing, and a critical look at proposed measures for campaign finance reform.

Shienbaum, Kim Ezra. *Beyond the Electoral Connection: A Reassessment of the Role of Voting in Contemporary American Politics.* Philadelphia: University of Pennsylvania Press, 1984.

Shienbaum presents an analysis of the role of voting in America, attempting to explain why certain people vote and others do not. Alterations in the political process have made voting a largely ritualistic procedure. Increased policy-making authority held by nonelected officials has encouraged alternative forms of participation, leaving voting with symbolic functions, such as legitimizing the actions of decision makers. Those who have a limited role to play in the nonelectoral process tend to absent themselves from the election process. The author finds little immediate hope for reforming the system.

Silbey, Joel H., Allan G. Bogue, and William H. Flanigan, eds. *The History of American Electoral Behavior.* Princeton, NJ: Princeton University Press, 1978.

This collection of essays deals with various determinants of American voting behavior, including political party realignment and third-party movements. An especially important chapter provides a methodologically sophisticated analysis of the election law provisions in the southern states, such as the poll tax, the literacy test, and the grandfather clause, that led to declining turnout rates.

Teixeira, Ruy A. *Why Americans Don't Vote: Turnout Decline in the United States, 1960–1984.* Westport, CT: Greenwood, 1987.

Teixeira attempts to explain the phenomenon of declining voter participation in U.S. presidential elections from 1960 to 1980. From an analysis focusing on demographic variables, the author suggests that a decline in "rootedness," as indicated by fewer people who are married and living with their spouses and an increase in geographical mobility, can result in lower political participation. Although Teixeira's model statistically explains over 80 percent of the decline in turnout, other suggested explanations for persistent low voter turnout rates that emphasize institutional factors lead more directly to reform efforts.

―――. *The Disappearing American Voter.* Washington, DC: Brookings Institution, 1992.

Continuing his research on voting participation in presidential elections, Teixeira examines the years 1960 to 1988. Employing data from the Bureau of the Census Current Population Surveys and the American National Election Study, the author focuses on two explanations for low voter turnout: the high costs of voter registration for the individual and the perceived low benefits of participation. Concluding that voter registration reforms would increase turnout by no more than 15 percent, Teixeira concentrates on reforms to increase citizen motivation to vote, such as altering the conduct of campaigns and improving the interactions among citizens and politicians, political parties, and the media.

Wayne, Stephen J. *The Road to the White House, 1996: The Politics of Presidential Elections.* New York: St. Martin's, 1996.

Published prior to the 1996 election, this book focuses on the 1992 process and results while looking toward the coming election. Wayne treats basic election topics such as the history of presidential selection, campaign finance, delegate selection, the party conventions, the media and elections, and election outcomes. The author discusses possible reforms, including changes in political party rules, finance laws, news media coverage, and the electoral college. Low voter turnout is also confronted.

Young, Michael L. *The American Dictionary of Campaigns and Elections*. Lanham, MD: Hamilton, 1987.

This volume includes definitions for key terms relevant to campaigns and elections. Young has arranged the dictionary by topic, including the media and politics, political parties and political action committees, money and politics, and campaign processes.

Electoral Mechanics and Administration

Abbott, David W., and James P. Levine. *Wrong Winner: The Coming Debacle in the Electoral College*. Westport, CT: Praeger, 1991.

The authors consider the method of electing the president outmoded and a potential threat to the political process. They warn that the electoral college may well give the United States a president elected by a minority of the voters or leave the choice of president up to the House of Representatives, which in each case would lead to a political crisis.

Albright, Spencer D. *The American Ballot*. Washington, DC: American Council on Public Affairs, 1942.

This early treatment of ballot reform provides an excellent summary of the major concerns regarding voting procedures. Among the topics the author covers are the activities of ballot reform organizations, development of the Australian ballot, improving the format of the ballot to avoid voter confusion, the office block and the party column ballots, the nonpartisan ballot, the primary ballot, and the development of voting machines.

American Enterprise Institute for Public Policy Research. *Proposals for Revision of the Electoral College System*. Washington, DC: American Enterprise Institute for Public Policy Research, 1966.

This monograph presents the major objections to the electoral college. Proposals for revising the system include proportional distribution of electoral votes according to popular vote within each state, the distribution of votes by congressional district, the automatic plan, and direct popular election. Arguments for and against each plan are presented.

————. *Direct Election of the President*. Washington, DC: American Enterprise Institute for Public Policy Research, 1977.

A push to eliminate the electoral college occurred in the 1970s, spurred on by the principle of one person, one vote that the Supreme Court enunciated in reapportionment decisions and by the specter of a third-party candidate forcing the presidential election into the House of Representatives. This brief monograph relates the historical development of the electoral college, offers criticisms of the present system, and presents a proposal for the direct election of the president, along with possible negative consequences, including the increased influence of the mass media over the electoral process.

Amy, Douglas. *Real Choices, New Voices: The Case for Proportional Representation Elections in the United States*. New York: Columbia University Press, 1993.

Amy claims that the single-member district plurality system for electing representatives is responsible for many of the evils in the American political process, including gerrymandering, the inability of third parties to compete effectively with the two dominant parties, and low voter participation. The author argues that a system of proportional representation would significantly improve the political process by eliminating the need to gain a plurality of the votes in a district, thus encouraging parties to focus more on issues. Amy claims that proportional representation would also increase voter participation.

Bain, Henry M., Jr., and Donald S. Hecock. *Ballot Position and Voter's Choice*. Detroit, MI: Wayne State University Press, 1957.

Bain and Hecock conclude from an empirical investigation that a strong relationship exists between vote choice and the position of candidates on the ballot. The authors recommend various reforms intended to minimize this effect, including ballot rotation. Candidates would appear at each location on the ballot on an equal number of ballots. They also recommend increased voter education and reduction of the number of offices appearing on the ballot.

Balinski, Michel L., and H. Peyton Young. *Fair Representation: Meeting the Ideal of One Man, One Vote.* New Haven, CT: Yale University Press, 1982.

The system of representation now employed in the United States requires periodic, fair reapportionment of legislative districts. While the authors admit that the process demands decisions that are ultimately political and should be made by legislators, they indicate that sophisticated mathematical principles should be employed. Balinski and Young examine the history of apportionment methods and offer their own mathematically complex model.

Barber, Kathleen L. *Proportional Representation and Election Reform in Ohio.* Columbus: Ohio State University Press, 1995.

Barber presents a historical overview of proportional representation, focusing on the Progressive Era. The experience with proportional representation of five Ohio cities—Ashtabula, Cincinnati, Cleveland, Middletown, and Toledo—is presented. These case studies deal with the introduction of the single transferable vote version of proportional representation, the effects of the system on representation for minority groups, and the ultimate repeal of this alternative voting system.

Benjamin, Gerald, and Michael J. Malbin, eds. *Limiting Legislative Terms.* Washington, DC: Congressional Quarterly, 1992.

The editors present a balanced set of essays that deal with the question of legislative term limits. Individual essays focus on such topics as specific state campaigns to institute term limits, the history of legislative term limits, term limits for officials in state executive branches, and speculation about the operation of state legislatures under such provisions. In a final section, the editors allow contributors to express their own conclusions regarding term limits.

Best, Judith. *The Case against Direct Election of the President: A Defense of the Electoral College.* Ithaca, NY: Cornell University Press, 1971.

Best confronts the major arguments against the electoral college and concludes that the present system, despite minor defects, is preferable to direct popular election. The electoral college has been overwhelmingly successful in providing the nation with a president every four years, complements a two-party system and national party conventions, and supports the constitutional framework of federalism.

————. *The Choice of the People? Debating the Electoral College.* Lanham, MD: Rowman and Littlefield, 1996.

Best has collected a number of key sources in the debate over the electoral college. The book contains early documents, such as Gouverneur Morris's statement at the 1787 Constitutional Convention and sections of the Federalist Papers, as well as more recent writings, such as the 1977 Report of the Senate Judiciary Committee on the Direct Popular Election of the President and Vice President and Senator Daniel Patrick Moynihan's 1979 speech to the U.S. Senate on electoral reform. A thorough analysis of the electoral college from many viewpoints is presented, along with several suggested reforms.

Bickel, Alexander M. *Reform and Continuity: The Electoral College, the Convention, and the Party System.* New York: Harper and Row, 1971.

This brief earlier treatment of electoral college and party reform is notable for the author's extremely cautious approach to altering the political process. Bickel admits to the appeal a conservative attitude toward changes in governing structures has for him. He finds virtue in the electoral college because it helps to maintain the political party status quo. He also finds much to maintain in the party nomination process, rejecting a possible national presidential primary.

Blair, George S. *Cumulative Voting: An Effective Electoral Device in Illinois Politics.* Urbana: University of Illinois Press, 1960.

Cumulative voting has recently experienced renewed popularity among those concerned that minorities gain representation in legislative bodies. Use of the system might avoid the court challenges that majority-minority districts have faced. Blair analyzes the operation of cumulative voting in Illinois from 1872 to 1954, a period during which members of the state legislature were chosen from three-member districts in which each voter had three votes, all of which could be cast for the same candidate, or one each for three candidates, and so forth.

Bogdanor, Vernon. *What Is Proportional Representation?* Oxford: Martin Robertson, 1984.

Bogdanor propounds the thesis that the use of differing electoral systems will result in varied electoral outcomes, to the advantage of some political groups and the disadvantage of others. The author investigates alternative electoral systems in Great Britain and Germany, discusses the single transferable vote, and analyzes the consequences of proportional representation, particularly for women and minorities.

Buell, Emmett H., Jr., and Lee Sigelman, eds. *Nominating the President.* Knoxville: University of Tennessee Press, 1991.

This treatment of the 1988 presidential nominating process contains chapters that deal with various subjects important to electoral reform, including such topics as the rules employed by the Republican and Democratic parties to select convention delegates, the outcome of the Super Tuesday primary, campaign fund-raising and spending, content analysis of campaign press coverage, the historical evolution of presidential nominating conventions, and the tendency of the present nominating system to weaken political parties.

Bullock, Charles S. III, and Loch K. Johnson. *Runoff Elections in the United States.* Chapel Hill: University of North Carolina Press, 1992.

The authors investigate the origins of runoff, or "dual," primary systems, presently used in 12 states, and focus on several charges that have led to calls for their elimination. Among the claims investigated are that women and blacks tend to lose in runoff primary elections because neither can create the majorities necessary to win. On the basis of runoff results in statewide and congressional elections from 1970 to 1986, the authors conclude that women are not disadvantaged by runoff elections. However, only 50 percent of black candidates who led after the first primary went on to win the runoff.

Cain, Bruce E. *The Reapportionment Puzzle.* Berkeley: University of California Press, 1984.

Cain, who served as a reapportionment consultant in California in 1981, examines reapportionment as a political question, presenting a case study of the process. In suggesting modest reforms, the author assumes that the lengthy procedure of reapportionment will always remain political, requiring the input of many interests. Though calling for open negotiations about which the general public is kept informed, Cain notes that average citizens are uninterested in the complex details of establishing district boundaries.

Carey, John M. *Term Limits and Legislative Representation*. New York: Cambridge University Press, 1996.

In his treatment of term limits, Carey has three objectives. First, the author examines the hypothesis that legislators are motivated primarily by the desire for reelection. Second, he evaluates the debate between supporters and opponents of term limits, concluding that the opponents' arguments are better substantiated by the evidence. Finally, Carey investigates the term limit experiences of other countries, especially Costa Rica.

Carlson, Richard J., ed. *Issues of Electoral Reform*. New York: National Municipal League, 1974.

The articles in this earlier edited volume treat several topics relevant to electoral reform, including universal voter registration, the history of Voting Rights Acts, African American voter registration in the South, extension of the vote to 18-year-olds, the need for improved election administration in the states, and the role of technological change in election administration.

Commons, John R. *Proportional Representation*. New York: Augustus M. Kelley, 1967 (1907).

This early treatment of proportional representation presents a historical analysis of the subject and its possible application to the United States. A major argument for its adoption is that the district system inefficiently translates popular vote into legislative representation. Appendixes deal with application of the referendum and initiative at the national and local levels and the special need for proportional representation in the United States.

Congressional Quarterly. *National Party Conventions, 1831–1992*. Washington, DC: Congressional Quarterly, 1995.

Certainly an important part of the American electoral process is the national party nominating convention. Introduced as an electoral reform in the early nineteenth century, this institution has undergone several revisions. This book examines the candidate nomination process prior to 1831 and describes the development of the convention system from the early years to the present. Topics such as methods of selecting delegates, convention rules, and the role of the mass media are covered.

Cortner, Richard C. *The Apportionment Cases.* Knoxville: University of Tennessee Press, 1970.

In the early 1960s, cases challenging the legislative apportionment policies of the states reached the Supreme Court, resulting in major reform of state-conducted redistricting. Cortner presents a detailed study of the Tennessee and Alabama cases (*Baker v. Carr* and *Reynolds v. Sims*), analyzing the shift in the Court's position on the justiciability of such cases and identifying the loose coalitions of individuals and groups that sponsored the litigation.

Coyne, James K. *Kick the Bums Out! The Case for Term Limitations.* Washington, DC: National Press Books, 1992.

Coyne, a former congressman and head of Americans to Limit Congressional Terms, argues for term limitations and defends their constitutionality. In addition to providing reasons for term limits, including the need to control the misdeeds of members of Congress that the present system encourages, the author responds to those who oppose such limits. An appendix provides the addresses and numbers of state affiliates of his national organization.

Coyne, James K., and John H. Fund. *Cleaning House: America's Campaign for Term Limits.* Washington, DC: Regnery Gateway, 1992.

A companion to *Kick the Bums Out!*, this book takes an insider's look at members of Congress and their privileged status, the inordinate attention they give to reelection, and the overwhelming influence of lobbyists and congressional staff on the legislative process. In the context of this unflattering look at Congress, the authors argue that term limits would significantly improve the American political process.

Crotty, William J., ed. *Paths to Political Reform.* Lexington, MA: Lexington Books, 1980.

This collection of articles focuses primarily on subjects relevant to electoral reform that have continued to concern politicians and political scientists since publication of this book. Chapters cover such topics as political party reform, presidential nomination procedures, electoral college reform, voter registration and turnout, campaign finance, and changes in voting behavior.

Crotty, William, and John S. Jackson III. *Presidential Primaries and Nominations.* Washington, DC: Congressional Quarterly, 1985.

The authors categorize the presidential nomination process into three eras: prereform (prior to 1968), reform (1968–1976), and postreform (after 1976). The origins of the nominating process are investigated, along with its present operation and its strengths and weaknesses. The following areas of possible reform are examined: a national primary, a national postconvention primary, regional primaries, approval voting in which electors may vote for more than one candidate, and the adoption of more standardized rules for all states.

David, Paul T., and James W. Ceasar. *Proportional Representation in Presidential Nominating Politics.* Charlottesville: University Press of Virginia, 1980.

The authors examine the changes that occurred in the delegate selection process, particularly for the Democratic National Convention. Moving from a winner-take-all system of delegate selection in the states to a proportional system might lead to expecting a "brokered" convention in which no candidate has the necessary number of delegates to win the nomination on the first ballot. However, David and Ceasar, writing in 1980, perceive other factors, including new candidate-centered politics, that tend to foster first-ballot nominations.

Diamond, Martin. *The Electoral College and the American Idea of Democracy.* Washington, DC: American Enterprise Institute for Public Policy Research, 1977.

In defending the existing presidential election system, Diamond argues that the electoral college, far from being archaic, is a model for a modern, flexible component of a federal constitution and a "paradigm of the American idea of democracy." The author identifies three dangers of change: weakening the two-party system, undermining party politics per se, and creating an imperial presidency.

DiClerico, Robert E., and Eric M. Uslaner. *Few Are Chosen: Problems in Presidential Selection.* New York: McGraw-Hill, 1984.

The authors focus on a number of difficulties surrounding the election of the president, including decreased voter turnout, the role of money in campaigns, and the nomination process. They recommend nomination by the congressional parties in order to strengthen ties between the president and Congress and urge direct popular election of the president as a system that favors no candidate or group of voters.

Eshleman, Kenneth. *Where Should Students Vote? The Courts, the States, and Local Officials.* Lanham, MD: University Press of America, 1989.

Given the low voter turnout rates of college-age Americans, student registration becomes a significant election reform issue. Eshleman discusses the fears expressed in college communities that students may outvote the local residents if they are allowed to register where they attend school. The author observes that a majority of students are unlikely to register and vote in the college community. Uniform state residency requirements for students are recommended.

Fox, Mike. *Innovations in Election Administration 13: Simplifying Forms and Materials.* Washington, DC: Office of Election Administration, 1996.

In an effort to assist registrars of voters in increasing the proportion of eligible Americans who register, Fox presents practical suggestions for simplifying the wording and layout of registration and voting forms. Noting the U.S. Department of Education's estimate that 90 million Americans would find it difficult to read and understand complex writing, Fox urges local administrations to follow his suggestions. Sample forms, a word exchange list (simpler and more familiar for more complicated), and recommendations for testing new forms are included.

Fredman, Lionel E. *The Australian Ballot: The Story of an American Reform.* East Lansing: Michigan State University Press, 1968.

This book is an excellent brief treatment of the history of the Australian ballot in the United States. The author relates the introduction of the standardized secret ballot into Australia by British reformers and the circumstances leading to its adoption in the United States in the 1880s and 1890s. The Australian ballot reform was closely associated with other progressive reform efforts.

Garber, Marie. *Innovations in Election Administration 8: Election Document Retention in an Age of High Technology.* Washington, DC: National Clearinghouse on Election Administration, 1994.

Noting the value of document retention to resolve disputed election outcomes, Garber reviews the national legislation requiring states to maintain registration and voting records. An appendix provides detailed information regarding required and recommended retention periods for various documents. In another appendix, Craig C. Donsanto, director of the Election Crimes Branch of the U.S. Department of Justice, presents an extensive list of records to be preserved, including programmable data storage devices (PROMs) from electronic voting equipment.

———. *Innovations in Election Administration 10: Ballot Security and Accountability.* Washington, DC: National Clearinghouse on Election Administration, 1995.

Garber notes that effective security and accountability measures make it possible to "reconstruct" an election should the outcome be in doubt. Such measures also deter fraud, identify those responsible should malfeasance occur, and assure election participants that all ballots were honestly counted. Security during each step of the ballot process, from printing to storage, is discussed, along with the special case of direct recording electronic (DRE) voting machines.

Geer, John G. *Nominating Presidents.* New York: Greenwood, 1989.

Geer examines topics relevant to the presidential primary system such as the representativeness of primary voters, voter turnout rates, the levels of information upon which voters make their choices, and the effects of election rules on primary outcomes. The author criticizes the primary system for selecting candidates with narrow support in the electorate. He proposes a system of regional primaries spaced sufficiently far apart to allow for voter reflection on the results of the previous primary.

Glennon, Michael J. *When No Majority Rules: The Electoral College and Presidential Succession.* Washington, DC: Congressional Quarterly, 1993.

In this brief treatment Glennon presents a description of the constitutional mechanics established to elect the president and vice president and identifies the potential difficulties that can arise in the workings of the system. The author examines the history of the system; its relationship to political institutions and groups such as the House of Representatives, the Senate, political parties, and the courts; and current discussions about reform.

Grassmuck, George, ed. *Before Nomination: Our Primary Problems.* Washington, DC: American Enterprise Institute for Public Policy Research, 1985.

The articles in this volume, presented at a conference sponsored by the Gerald R. Ford Foundation, offer analyses of the presidential primary system, including such topics as the role of political parties, voters, and political activists; campaign financing; and the mass media. Between the extremes of returning to the former system of elite nominations of presidential candidates and suggesting progressive changes, such as a national primary, the preference of many at the conference was for moderate adjustments to the present system.

Griffith, Elmer C. *The Rise and Development of the Gerrymander.* New York: Arno Press, 1974 (1907).

According to Griffith the gerrymander is "a species of fraud, deception, and trickery which menaces the perpetuity of the Republic of the United States." The author relates the origin of the gerrymander and its use in the several states up to 1840. The gerrymander has tended to persist despite attempts by states to control the practice. Griffith notes that federal legislation in 1842 establishing the single-member district system for electing representatives failed to control gerrymandering.

Grofman, Bernard, ed. *Legislative Term Limits: Public Choice Perspectives.* Boston: Kluwer Academic Publishers, 1996.

The result of a national conference at the University of California, Irvine, in 1991, this volume presents a broad discussion of term limits. The first section deals with probable effects of limits on the legislator-constituency relationship. While some point to positive results, such as the strengthening of parties, others point to the weakening of citizen control over their representatives. The second section examines predictions of legislative turnover, and the third investigates background explanations for term limit popularity. The final section explores the historical context of limits.

Grofman, Bernard, Arend Lijphart, Robert B. McKay, and Howard A. Scarrow, eds. *Representation and Redistricting Issues*. Lexington, MA: Lexington Books, 1982.

This edited work from the early 1980s deals with many of the same issues that have recently gained the attention of the federal courts. The question in the 1960s—how nearly equal in population must legislative districts be?—was fairly easily resolved. More recently the focus has shifted to considerations other than equal population in drawing district lines. For instance, should concern for actual representation of minority groups be taken into account to allow for "affirmative gerrymandering"? Some essays suggest alternatives to the single-member district system.

Guinier, Lani. *The Tyranny of the Majority: Fundamental Fairness in Representative Democracy*. New York: Free Press, 1994.

The controversial proposals expressed in this collected group of essays led President Bill Clinton, under pressure from Congress and the media, to withdraw Guinier's 1993 nomination to head the Justice Department's Civil Rights Division. Guinier contends that although the right to vote is fundamental to democracy, the present electoral system can unfairly ensure that some groups always win and others always lose. She examines methods of remedying this situation, both with the single-member district and with alternative systems such as cumulative voting.

Hallett, George H., Jr. *Proportional Representation: The Key to Democracy*. New York: National Municipal League, 1940.

Published at a time when democratic systems were being threatened throughout the world, this book provides a clear explanation of proportional representation as an alternative to the single-member district plurality system. The deficiencies of the plurality system are presented along with the remedies that proportional representation would provide.

Hardaway, Robert M. *The Electoral College and the Constitution: The Case for Preserving Federalism.* Westport, CT: Praeger, 1994.

Hardaway provides a thorough examination of the electoral college, devoting chapters to its historical origins and evolution, its effects on presidential election outcomes, and its present operation. The author interprets the electoral college within the context of the framers' original intentions for a federal system and the subsequent adaptation process that has occurred over generations. Hardaway examines the various proposals for reform, including direct popular election, and what he considers the weaknesses of such changes.

Hardy, Leroy, Alan Heslop, and Stuart Anderson, eds. *Reapportionment Politics: The History of Redistricting in the 50 States.* Beverly Hills, CA: Sage, 1981.

The essays in this volume describe the process of reapportionment in each of the 50 states, concentrating primarily on the redrawing of state legislative districts. Far from a uniform process, reapportionment has had a widely varied history in the several states. In addition to affecting voter representation, the process alters the fortunes of politicians. The effects of court decisions in the 1960s are described.

Haskell, John. *Fundamentally Flawed: Understanding and Reforming Presidential Primaries.* Lanham, MD: Rowman and Littlefield, 1996.

Haskell provides a primer on the presidential nomination process from the perspective of public choice analysis. As the title indicates, the author concludes that the process suffers from major defects. Among the reforms suggested are establishing approval voting in early primaries and reducing their overall effect on the nomination outcome.

Heikkila, Ralph C. *Innovations in Election Administration 3: Election Signature Retrieval Systems.* Washington, DC: National Clearinghouse on Election Administration, 1992.

With the increasing use of mailed ballots and the initiative, election officials must be able to verify signatures in an efficient and timely way. Heikkila reviews the present state of signature digitization technology, which produces an image of the voter's signature by scanning a document and making an electronic copy. The stored document can then be quickly retrieved in order to validate a signature on another document. The ultimate goal is to achieve automated signature verification that is conducted entirely by computer.

————. *Innovations in Election Administration 12: The Electronic Transmission of Election Materials.* Washington, DC: National Clearinghouse on Election Administration, 1995.

The initial use of electronic transmission of voting materials occurred during Operation Desert Shield in 1990 at the encouragement of the Federal Voting Assistance Program. Heikkila discusses the potential for sending election documents by FAX or other electronic means to overseas members of the military and civilians as well as to persons with disabilities and absentee voters. Such transmission raises questions regarding potential high costs, the possibility of fraud, and the need to maintain the secret ballot.

Keech, William R. *Winner Take All: Report of the Twentieth Century Fund Task Force on Reform of the Presidential Election Process.* New York: Holmes and Meier, 1978.

Keech discusses various alternatives to the electoral college, including the automatic plan, the proportional plan, the district plan, and direct popular election. Concerned that the "right" candidate win, he also analyzes the possibility of a runoff provision should no candidate receive a majority. A proposal from the task force recommends the "national bonus plan," by which the popular vote winner receives 102 additional electoral college votes. This plan would virtually assure that the popular vote winner receives a majority in the electoral college.

Kimberling, William, and Peggy Sims. *Federal Election Law 96: A Summary of Federal Laws Pertaining to Registration, Voting, and Public Employee Participation.* Washington, DC: Office of Election Administration, 1996.

The authors present a helpful summary of federal regulations regarding registration and voting, including constitutional amendments and statutes. Among the legislation summarized are the Voting Rights Act of 1965, the Uniformed and Overseas Citizens Absentee Voting Act of 1986, and the National Voter Registration Act of 1993. A final section deals with subjects primarily within the jurisdiction of states, such as the voting rights of institutionalized persons, employees' time off for voting, election procedures (including polling hours and voting equipment), and poll worker recruitment.

Kleppner, Paul, Walter Dean Burnham, Ronald P. Formisano, Samuel P. Hays, Richard Jensen, and William G. Shade. *The Evolution of American Electoral Systems*. Westport, CT: Greenwood, 1981.

Each author contributes a chapter to this treatment of changing voting systems in the United States. Essays analyze such subjects as the Progressive movement and resulting electoral reforms of the late nineteenth century and the more recent weakening of political parties and the increasing influence of organized special interests.

Kuroda, Tadahison. *The Origins of the Twelfth Amendment: The Electoral College in the Early Republic, 1787–1804*. Westport, CT: Greenwood, 1994.

The Twelfth Amendment to the Constitution, which established the present system of presidential election, was an important step in legitimizing the political changes that occurred in the first years of the Republic. Kuroda provides a thorough account of the events leading to the amendment, describing it as a partisan Jeffersonian reform that ensured Republican victory in the 1804 election.

Lakeman, Enid, and James D. Lambert. *Voting in Democracies: A Study of Majority and Proportional Electoral Systems*. London: Faber and Faber, 1959.

Although the major focus of this early study is British politics, the authors provide a thorough investigation of contrasting electoral systems. Lakeman and Lambert explain the operation and limitations of the single-member district plurality, or "first past the post," system and examine semiproportional and proportional representation systems and the single transferable vote as possible electoral reforms.

Lee, Eugene C. *The Politics of Nonpartisanship: A Study of California City Elections.* Berkeley: University of California Press, 1960.

Nonpartisan municipal elections were one of the major electoral reforms of the Progressive Era. Lee investigates the results of nonpartisan elections in California, comparing the theory and objectives of the reform with its actual operation. Rather than generalizing to all cases, the author concludes that the circumstances in individual communities will determine the desirability of nonpartisanship.

Lijphart, Arend, and Bernard Grofman, eds. *Choosing an Electoral System: Issues and Alternatives.* New York: Praeger, 1984.

The essays in this volume examine electoral arrangements in several countries. Various systems are investigated, including plurality, majority runoff, single transferable vote, the list variant of proportional representation, and semiproportional. The authors generally conclude that the preferred system varies with such characteristics as a country's political traditions and social system.

Loevy, Robert D. *The Flawed Path to the Presidency, 1992: Unfairness and Inequality in the Presidential Selection Process.* Albany: State University of New York Press, 1995.

According to Loevy the presidential selection process is not only highly unstable but unfair because voter preferences in some states are given greater weight. The author proposes reforms, such as revising the presidential primary calendar, holding preprimary conventions, and replacing the electoral college with direct popular election.

Longley, Lawrence D., and Alan G. Brown. *The Politics of Electoral College Reform.* New Haven, CT: Yale University Press, 1972.

In this earlier critical treatment of the electoral college Longley and Brown discuss the system in the context of recent elections and the potential dangers they foresee. The electoral college is described as potentially disastrous. After presenting various possible reforms, the authors focus on direct popular election as the only presidential election method that is truly democratic.

Longley, Lawrence D., and Neal R. Peirce. *The Electoral College Primer.* New Haven, CT: Yale University Press, 1996.

Although the authors present a good account of the workings of the electoral college, their ultimate purpose is clear: abolition of the system. They detail the various undesirable consequences identified with the system, including distortion of the popular vote, distortion of candidate campaign strategies, the potential "faithless elector," victory for a candidate who received a minority of the popular vote, the possibility of deals among electors, and the prospect of the U.S. House of Representatives electing the president. The authors fear that only disaster will stimulate reform.

Lowenstein, Daniel, ed. *Election Law: Cases and Materials.* Durham, NC: Carolina Academic Press, 1995.

This edited volume includes articles by legal scholars and political scientists on such subjects as representation, districting, incumbency, and public financing. The authors deal with issues at the local, state, and national levels. Also discussed are important court decisions, including *Buckley v. Valeo* and *FEC v. National Right to Work Committee.*

Magleby, David B. *Direct Legislation: Voting on Ballot Propositions in the United States.* Baltimore: Johns Hopkins University Press, 1984.

Begun early in the twentieth century, the referendum and initiative, or "direct legislation," have become a significant part of the political process in several states. Magleby examines voter participation in these special elections and the unique problems they pose. The author concludes that referendum and initiative elections fail to accomplish their original objective—to record a citizen mandate—because voters do not represent the whole community, tend to be confused about ballot measures, and are susceptible to emotional appeals in the media.

Michener, James A. *Presidential Lottery: The Reckless Gamble in Our Electoral System.* New York: Random House, 1969.

This earlier treatment of the electoral college severely criticizes the system for electing the president, claiming that there are too many imponderables in the system to continue depending on it to elect our most powerful public figure. Arguing that the system is unfair, Michener proposes constitutional amendments to abolish the electoral college and deny the U.S. House of Representatives the authority to select the president. The author prefers an "automatic plan" with a runoff in the electoral college should no one receive a majority.

Montjoy, Robert S. *Innovations in Election Administration 6: Motor Voter Registration Programs.* Washington, DC: National Clearinghouse on Election Administration, 1992.

In 1992, prior to passage of the National Voter Registration Act, approximately half of the states had already implemented some form of voter registration at driver's license offices. Montjoy describes the systems in place at that time, comparing passive, computer-assisted, active, and combined passive and active registration procedures. Montjoy concludes that motor-voter laws can increase the proportion of citizens who are registered to vote. Appendixes include sample registration forms and data indicating the success of motor-voter provisions.

————. *Innovations in Election Administration 7: Mail Voter Registration Programs.* Washington, DC: National Clearinghouse on Election Administration, 1994.

Montjoy examines the experiences of local jurisdictions with mail registration procedures prior to the National Vote Registration Act, although the monograph is written in the context of the changes in registration procedures mandated by the act. The author discusses such topics as acceptable methods of purging registration roles, distribution and receipt of mail applications, and maintenance of the integrity of the system against fraudulent and frivolous registrations. An appendix includes sample registration forms from several states.

Mullins, Charlotte G. *Innovations in Election Administration 4: Using NCOA Files for Verifying Voter Registration Lists.* Washington, DC: National Clearinghouse on Election Administration, 1992.

States wish to maintain accurate lists of eligible voters without excluding legitimately registered individuals. Mullins discusses the results of a nationwide survey conducted to determine the use of the U.S. Postal Service's National Change of Address (NCOA) system to confirm the eligibility of voters. Kentucky's experience with using the system is described in detail.

Norrander, Barbara. *Super Tuesday: Regional Politics and Presidential Primaries.* Lexington: University of Kentucky Press, 1992.

Norrander analyzes the results of Super Tuesday, March 8, 1988, a day when 16 states held primaries and another 8 states conducted caucuses to choose delegates to the presidential nominating conventions. The author, employing data derived from campaign spending reports, public opinion polls, and election statistics, concludes that Super Tuesday, on which more delegates were chosen than on any previous presidential primary day, failed to meet the expectations of Democratic party leaders who wished to alter the nomination process in favor of a moderate candidate.

Oberholtzer, Ellis Paxson. *The Referendum in America, Together with Some Chapters on the Initiative and the Recall.* New York: Charles Scribner's Sons, 1912.

At the time this book was published the referendum, initiative, and recall were increasingly popular instruments of direct democracy in many states. Oberholtzer presents the historical background to these election systems and describes their varied forms. A concluding chapter examines the relative merits of referendum versus representative systems.

Parris, Judith H. *The Convention Problem: Issues in Reform of Presidential Nominating Procedures.* Washington, DC: Brookings Institution, 1972.

Parris examines the need for reform in the presidential nominating convention. Although concerned about questions regarding the democratic nature of the system, the author examines reformers' objectives of the early 1970s, keeping in mind the need for a convention to perform effectively and efficiently its nominating role. Among topics covered are the delegate selection process, management of the conventions, platform writing, and the increased role of the media.

Peirce, Neal R. *The People's President*. Revised ed. New Haven, CT: Yale University Press, 1981.

Peirce can find little virtue in the electoral college, claiming that the system might lead to the election of a minority president. The author recommends replacing what he considers an outdated and undemocratic process with direct popular election.

Peterson, Paul E., ed. *Classifying by Race*. Princeton, NJ: Princeton University Press, 1995.

This edited work deals with various aspects of race in American politics. Of greatest significance is a group of articles analyzing race and representation. For example, Lani Guinier examines the representation of minority interests, referring to "proportionate interest representation." To achieve fairness in the electoral process, Guinier suggests moving away from a majoritarian model and toward a system of proportional representation so that government officials will more closely reflect the characteristics of a diverse population.

Peverill, Squire, ed. *Iowa Caucuses and the Presidential Nominating Process*. Boulder, CO: Westview, 1989.

Although the Iowa caucuses, as the first test of presidential candidates, have declined somewhat in importance since the publication of this book, they still remain a potentially significant factor in the race for the presidency. The essays discuss such topics as the representativeness of the caucuses, voter turnout, momentum in the race for the nomination, and the role of the media. One of the contributors admits that although the system is flawed, such reforms as regional primaries or a single national primary do not represent plausible improvements.

Phillips, Kevin P., and Paul H. Blackman. *Electoral Reform and Voter Participation; Federal Registration: A False Remedy for Voter Apathy*. Washington, DC: American Enterprise Institute for Public Policy Research, 1975.

Long before passage of the National Voter Registration Act, which is geared to increase voter turnout, Phillips and Blackman raise doubts about the efficacy of such a reform. The authors conclude that without extensive organized efforts to get people to the polls, national voter registration legislation will not have a significant impact on turnout, especially among those with low income.

Polinard, J. L., Robert D. Wrinkle, Tomas Longoria, and Norman E. Binder. *Electoral Structure and Urban Policy: The Impact on Mexican American Communities.* Armonk, NY: M. E. Sharpe, 1994.

Employing quantitative analyses and case studies, the authors investigate the political and policy changes that occur when electoral systems are altered. They focus on the effects the Voting Rights Act has had on Hispanic American politics in Texas, examining representation on city councils and school boards and assessing different policy outcomes. In order to increase minority representation, the authors recommend district elections but suggest alternatives such as cumulative voting in areas where minority populations are dispersed.

Polsby, Nelson W. *Consequences of Party Reform.* New York: Oxford University Press, 1983.

Polsby, one of the most noted students of political party organization, investigates the consequences of reforms initiated by American political parties after 1968. He describes changes in the presidential nominating process and their effects on the organizations of the major parties.

Rose, Gary L., ed. *Controversial Issues in Presidential Selection.* Second ed. Albany: State University of New York Press, 1994.

Rose begins with the premise that the presidential selection process faces a major crisis. Each chapter focuses on a particular problem, offering the opinion of two contributors, one supporting and the other opposing reform. The chapters cover such topics as reforming the nominating process, regulation of campaign commercials, public financing of presidential campaigns, presidential debates, abolishing the electoral college, and the motor-voter bill.

Rosenfield, Margaret. *Innovations in Election Administration 5: Agency Voter Registration Programs.* Washington, DC: National Clearinghouse on Election Administration, 1992.

Rosenfield reviews active and passive agency voter registration in the states prior to passage of the National Voter Registration

Act. For over 20 years some states have offered citizens the opportunity to register at government offices. Appendixes include sample state statutes and executive orders, instructions to officials, sample forms, and assistance in planning for agency registration.

———. *Innovations in Election Administration 9: Early Voting.* Washington, DC: National Clearinghouse on Election Administration, 1994.

Rosenfield describes the system of early voting, a procedure that allows voters to cast their ballots during a set period before election day. Supporters of the system, which originated in Texas and is now used in other states, argue that it provides an important service to citizens. However, opponents claim that early voting increases the costs of elections and opens the way for possible election fraud. The consensus among election officials is that voters like early voting and hence it is a practice that is here to stay.

———. *Innovations in Election Administration 11: All-Mail-Ballot Elections.* Washington, DC: National Clearinghouse on Election Administration, 1995.

Rosenfield investigates the experience of those states that at the time of publication had conducted all-mail-ballot elections. She notes that the major benefits of voting by mail reported by local jurisdictions are increased turnout and greater administrative efficiency. Possible vote fraud and threats to the secret ballot remain concerns. Extensive appendixes provide documents from states and localities allowing for an all-mail ballot in at least some elections.

Rossetti, Barbara. *Innovations in Election Administration 2: Optical Scanning Technology for Purposes Other Than Ballot Counting.* Washington, DC: National Clearinghouse on Election Administration, 1992.

Optical scanning technology includes bar coding, optical character recognition, and magnetic ink character recognition (MICR). Rossetti discusses their use in various aspects of election administration such as processing absentee ballots, updating voter history, and delivering election supplies. The technology can be used to increase security. An appendix lists those jurisdictions employing optical scanning technology at the time this monograph was published.

Rush, Mark E. *Does Redistricting Make a Difference? Partisan Representation and Electoral Behavior.* Baltimore: Johns Hopkins University Press, 1993.

Basing his empirical analysis on congressional, gubernatorial, and state senate election results in Connecticut and Massachusetts from 1972 to 1986, Rush argues that the effectiveness of the partisan gerrymander has not been substantiated by research. He identifies shifts in partisan support within districts from election to election as an explanation for the failure of attempted gerrymanders. Rush suggests that the courts should remove themselves from questions of partisan gerrymandering. The limited scope of the study ignores examples of apparently successful gerrymanders.

Sayre, Wallace S., and Judith H. Parris. *Voting for President: The Electoral College and the American Political System.* Washington, DC: Brookings Institution, 1970.

The authors examine the virtues and limitations of the electoral college and investigate suggested alternative election systems. Sayre and Parris argue that under the electoral college, at least in the late 1960s, urban areas have a significant voice in the presidential election process. For that reason the authors recommend maintaining the electoral college.

Schwab, Larry M. *The Impact of Congressional Reapportionment and Redistricting.* Lanham, MD: University Press of America, 1988.

Schwab investigates the effects of congressional redistricting following court decisions ordering state legislatures to reapportion seats in Congress. The author discusses population trends and the politics of redistricting, analyzing their effects on the relative strength of the two major political parties, the reelection prospects of incumbents, and the leadership structure in the U.S. House of Representatives.

Szekely, Kalman S. *Electoral College: A Selective Annotated Bibliography.* Littleton, CO: Libraries Unlimited, 1970.

This volume traces the longtime concern for the method of electing the president. Szekely includes over 750 annotated citations of various works dealing with the electoral college, including books, periodicals, and government documents. The materials cited deal with such topics as the history of the system, arguments for its preservation, and recommendations for reform.

Taapera, Rein, and Matthew Soberg Shugart. *Seats and Votes: The Effects and Determinants of Electoral Systems.* New Haven, CT: Yale University Press, 1989.

This comparative study of representation focuses on the relationship between voting and the acquisition of legislative seats. The authors examine the characteristics of election systems that affect the translation of voter preferences into representation. A theoretically sophisticated and empirically detailed study, this book offers a good background understanding of election systems for those interested in electoral reform.

Tallian, Laura. *Direct Democracy: An Historical Analysis of the Initiative, Referendum, and Recall Process.* Los Angeles: People's Lobby, 1977.

Tallian calls for the broad establishment of the initiative, referendum, and recall at all levels of government so that citizens might initiate legislation that representatives fail to enact, reject legislation that they do not want, and remove from office representatives who have violated their public trust. One chapter presents advice for anyone wishing to begin an initiative, and an appendix lists and describes California initiatives from 1912 to 1976.

Wachtel, Ted. *The Electronic Congress: A Blueprint for Participatory Democracy.* Pipersville, PA: Piper's Press, 1992.

After witnessing the political events of the 1970s and 1980s and observing their disillusioning effects on citizens, Wachtel suggests a major alteration in the electoral process. He recommends a constitutional amendment that would allow each house of Congress to delegate to all citizens the role of legislator, granting them the right to vote on certain legislation. The vote outcomes in a national referendum would be considered voting instructions to members of the House and Senate.

Welch, Susan, and Timothy Bledsoe. *Urban Reform and Its Consequences: A Study in Representation.* Chicago: University of Chicago Press, 1988.

The authors conducted an analysis of data from municipalities nationwide in order to determine differences in representation between district and at-large systems and between partisan and nonpartisan systems. With district systems, more diverse councils are chosen, although the differences from at-large systems are modest. The authors suggest proportional systems as a way of further increasing representational diversity on city councils.

Will, George F. *Restoration: Congress, Term Limits, and the Recovery of Deliberative Democracy.* New York: Free Press, 1992.

Will defends proposed term limits for members of Congress, arguing that many of the problems the federal government presently faces, such as pork-barrel spending, would be ameliorated. Legislators who legally could not seek reelection would no longer concentrate their efforts on satisfying special interests in order to win the next election but supposedly would act according to a broader conception of the public good.

Zeidenstein, Harvey G. *Direct Election of the President.* Lexington, MA: Lexington Books, 1973.

This earlier treatment of the electoral college provides standard arguments against the constitutional method of electing the president. The author's unsurprising conclusion is that the electoral college should be replaced with a system of direct election.

Media and Elections

Alvarez, Michael R. *Information and Elections.* Ann Arbor: University of Michigan Press, 1996.

This book presents a statistically sophisticated examination of voting behavior in presidential elections. Alvarez notes that voters have little motivation to become informed about the candidates and that candidates often have an interest in providing unclear information about their issue positions. However, recent criticism of the mass media notwithstanding, the author concludes that the media provide considerable coverage of campaign issues.

Ansolabehere, Stephen, Roy Behr, and Shanto Iyengar. *The Media Game: American Politics in the Television Age.* New York: Macmillan, 1993.

The authors describe the advent of the broadcasting media and the government response of instituting such regulations as the equal time rule and the fairness doctrine. A chapter treats the significance of television to political campaigning. In a section on evaluating the media, the authors suggest that the mass media can serve as an educator of citizens and a monitor of political activists, thus improving the quality of campaigns.

Ansolabehere, Stephen, and Shanto Iyengar. *Going Negative: How Attack Ads Shrink and Polarize the Electorate.* New York: Free Press, 1995.

Although the authors conclude that the most serious charges against media advertising are largely untrue, they believe there remains considerable reason for concern. They focus their examination on questions of advertising distortion and manipulation. The most serious problem they attribute to media advertising is the decline in voter turnout. Although the watchdog role of the news media has been ineffective and perhaps actually increases voter disaffection, the authors believe that the antidemocratic effects of negative ads deserve serious media consideration. They see stronger political parties as a step in the right direction.

Armstrong, Richard. *The Next Hurrah: The Communications Revolution in American Politics.* New York: Beech Tree, 1988.

In this highly critical account of the use of communications technology in American politics, Armstrong deals with such subjects as telemarketing, the use of computers, direct mailings, and the effects of each on elections. Armstrong highlights the less-than-savory uses to which contemporary information technologies have been put in order to package candidates. He recounts his own political experiences and those of others derived from interviews.

Bennett, W. Lance. *The Governing Crisis: Media, Money, and Marketing in American Politics.* New York: St. Martin's, 1992.

Bennett presents a critical view of the contemporary electoral process in the United States, pointing to the influence of special interest money and the media marketing of candidates. The unsatisfactory elements of the system lead to the selection of public officials who fail to deal effectively with the nation's problems. The author suggests such reforms as regulation of media advertising and campaign finance, improved media coverage of campaigns, and the introduction of a proportional representation system.

Buchanan, Bruce. *Electing a President: The Markle Commission Research on Campaign '88*. Austin: University of Texas Press, 1991.

This report concentrates primarily on the level of information possessed by voters at various stages of the 1988 campaign and on what information the media provided to citizens. The book concludes with a number of recommendations for reform, including creating a national program to educate citizens about the political process, eliciting candidate pledges to conduct clean campaigns, making presidential debates permanent, offering free air time to presidential candidates, establishing the same poll hours nationwide, and simplifying voter registration.

————. *Renewing Presidential Politics: Campaigns, Media, and the Public Interest*. Lanham, MD: Rowman and Littlefield, 1996.

Examining the 1988, 1992, and 1996 presidential campaigns, Buchanan argues in favor of election campaigns that include greater media attention on the issues and campaign advertisements that avoid negative attacks. A campaign that takes the high road improves the level of citizen participation in both quantity and quality. The author anticipates improved election campaigns in which citizens have become avid participants in the political process.

Denton, Robert E., Jr., ed. *Ethical Dimensions of Political Communication*. New York: Praeger, 1991.

This volume on political communication contains essays dealing with the presidential campaign and political advertising. In her essay on advertising, Lynda Lee Kaid recommends only limited reforms, preferring to maintain a free marketplace with minimal government intervention. However, she does recommend free broadcast time to "qualified candidates" for major office, stricter state laws against corrupt campaign practices, and establishment of a federal campaign commission to hear complaints about alleged campaign advertising abuses.

Frantzich, Stephen, and John Sullivan. *The C-SPAN Revolution*. Norman: University of Oklahoma Press, 1996.

C-SPAN, the Cable-Satellite Public Affairs Network, has truly contributed to a major change in public affairs programming. The authors recount Congress's cautious acceptance of the idea of broadcasting legislative proceedings. The network has grown to include interviews with public officials, forums for public policy debates, and call-in programs for viewers. C-SPAN represents an important campaign and election reform, providing Americans with extensive coverage of the political process.

Hart, Roderick P. *Seducing America: How Television Charms the Modern Voter.* New York: Oxford University Press, 1994.

Hart holds television responsible for major changes that have occurred in the electoral process and American politics generally over the last three decades. According to the author, television is to blame for declining voter turnout and the erosion of trust in government because of the medium's tendency to personalize politics. Although any attempts to reform television broadcasting are rejected as impractical, Hart suggests the development of a more community-oriented perspective to alter the personalistic political perspective he attributes to television.

Jamieson, Kathleen Hall. *Eloquence in the Electronic Age: The Transformation of Political Speechmaking.* New York: Oxford University Press, 1988.

Speech making has played a crucial role in politics and election campaigns throughout American history. Jamieson argues that today speeches fail to confront significant substantive issues. Perhaps due to television, Americans no longer tolerate anything but the briefest discourse and find little of interest in public affairs, a condition ultimately detrimental to democracy.

———. *Packaging the Presidency: A History and Criticism of Presidential Campaign Advertising.* Third ed. New York: Oxford University Press, 1994.

In an expanded edition, Jamieson chronicles media campaigns in presidential elections from the beginning of the American republic to the 1992 election and describes the technological advances in advertising from the early use of the handbill and the political cartoon to the contemporary use of radio and television. Although noting the misuse of media advertising and the employment of dishonest advertising tactics, Jamieson concludes that campaign advertising remains an important part of American election campaigns, informing voters of the candidate choices.

Jamieson, Kathleen Hall, and David S. Birdsell. *Presidential Debates: The Challenge of Creating an Informed Electorate.* New York: Oxford University Press, 1988.

The authors place the phenomenon of contemporary presidential debates within a cultural and historical context. They trace the development of the debates from the eighteenth century and make suggestions for improving a practice that has become a major part of the quadrennial campaign for the White House.

Kaid, Lynda Lee, and Christina Holtz-Bacha, eds. *Political Advertising in Western Democracies: Parties and Candidates on Television.* Thousand Oaks, CA: Sage, 1995.

As political advertising has become increasingly important in the United States, politicians and parties in other democracies have introduced modern media techniques. The contributors to this volume describe television advertising and its effects in other countries as well as the United States. The legal limitations on television advertising in other countries provide at least a basis for discussing the potential problems of media politics in the United States. For instance, Italy in 1994 banned political advertising a month prior to the election campaign, and Israel forbids news programs to show images of candidates in the final weeks of the campaign.

Kaid, Lynda Lee, and Anne Johnston Wadsworth. *Political Campaign Communication: A Bibliography and Guide to the Literature, 1973–1982.* Metuchen, NJ: Scarecrow Press, 1985.

This extensive bibliography contains a variety of earlier sources on such topics as political campaigns, the use of the mass media, the effects of debating, and campaign finance. The bibliography includes several citations dealing with such campaign and election reform topics as campaign finance regulation, the broadcast media, and presidential election procedures.

Kern, Montague. *30-Second Politics: Political Advertising in the Eighties.* New York: Praeger, 1989.

Kern examines the changes in political advertising during the 1980s, noting the increase in mistrust of political institutions and candidates. Although voter participation has declined as the media have gained influence, the author claims no direct relation. The various aspects of campaign advertising are analyzed and lessons are drawn from actual campaigns. Not recommending any specific reforms, Kern does suggest that researchers investigate how the news industry can cope with the increasing importance of political advertising.

Lemert, James B., William R. Elliott, William L. Rosebert, and James M. Bernstein. *The Politics of Disenchantment: Bush, Clinton, Perot, and the Press.* Cresskill, NJ: Hampton, 1996.

The authors view the 1992 presidential campaign as introducing a potentially significant shift in campaign tactics. Within the context of Americans' disaffection with the news media, candidates bypassed traditional modes of mass communication and experimented with new ones, such as the talk shows and news channels. The authors investigate the effects of the three-way debates among George Bush, Ross Perot, and Bill Clinton and examine possible reforms in the debate system.

Litchter, S. Robert, and Richard Noyes. *Good Intentions Make Bad News: Why Americans Hate Campaign Journalism.* Lanham, MD: Rowman and Littlefield, 1995.

The authors examine the recent trends in campaign journalism, based on content analysis of media reporting, and conclude that bias and error have influenced election outcomes. They contend that slanted media reporting tends to deemphasize important issues and restricts political debate. Alternative modes of political communication are broached and suggestions made for future elections.

McCubbins, Mathew D., ed. *Under the Watchful Eye: Managing Presidential Campaigns in the Television Era.* Washington, DC: Congressional Quarterly, 1992.

This group of essays originated in a symposium on Campaigning for the Presidency held in 1991. The discussions came to revolve around the role of television in bringing about changes in the campaign process as the new medium interacted with other changes such as the Democratic party reforms of the 1970s and state electoral law reforms that helped to bring about the downfall of political machines.

Mickelson, Sig. *From Whistle Stop to Sound Bite: Four Decades of Politics and Television.* New York: Praeger, 1989.

Mickelson recounts the multifaceted effects television has had on political campaigns, from weakening political parties to vastly increasing the costs of campaigning. Although television has not by itself introduced troubling changes that have led many to call for reform, it continues to gain the attention and concern of analysts such as Mickelson. The author doubts that media coverage can improve sufficiently to bring about a more informed electorate.

Morreale, Joanne. *A New Beginning: A Textual Frame Analysis of the Political Campaign Film.* Albany: State University of New York Press, 1991.

In this brief work, Morreale presents a case study of a 1984 Republican campaign film *A New Beginning.* The 18-minute film became controversial when the Republicans used it as a replacement for a Ronald Reagan nominating speech and the networks, providing limited convention coverage, decided to drop the film from their broadcasts. Morreale contends that *A New Beginning* places the short film at the center of the election campaign. The author employs "textual frame analysis" to examine the film. In a critique, Morreale claims that the film concealed reality, widened the gap between the campaign and the people, and employed an exploitative ideology encouraged by television.

————. *The Presidential Campaign Film: A Critical History.* Westport, CT: Praeger, 1993.

Instead of the brief television campaign ads that proliferate during campaigns, Morreale focuses on the longer (about 30-minute) campaign films that offer a greater opportunity for the campaign staff to present a positive image of their candidate. The author investigates the origins and development of such films, examines their content, and identifies more recent changes. Though recognizing ethical problems, especially the uneasy partnership between television and democracy, Morreale can only suggest the use of additional media images to counter offending presentations.

Seib, Philip. *Who's in Charge? How the Media Shape News and Politicians Win Votes.* Dallas, TX: Taylor, 1987.

Seib portrays the uneasy balance between the press and politicians, indicating that the media have exerted significant influence over campaigns and elections. The author recommends a set of standards for the press, including fair treatment of competing candidates, consideration for candidates' privacy, and avoidance of sensational stories. The press also should monitor the honesty of candidates' media campaigns.

Swerdlow, Joel L., ed. *Media Technology and the Vote.* Washington, DC: Annenberg Washington Program, 1988.

This volume contains a wide variety of essays, many previously published, on the convergence of mass media innovations and political campaign techniques. It includes several presentations at a 1988 colloquium sponsored by the Annenberg Washington Program, including discussions of a presidential campaign hotline, candidate-controlled satellite feeds, and the use of computer software. Other contributions investigate the relationship between the media and political parties, the role of campaign consultants, and the importance of C-SPAN to election campaigns and the prospects of reform.

Twentieth Century Fund. *Report of the Task Force on Television and the Campaign of 1992: 1-800-PRESIDENT.* New York: Twentieth Century Fund Press, 1993.

This examination of television in the 1992 presidential campaign includes essays by Kathleen Hall Jamieson, Ken Auletta, and Thomas E. Patterson. Acknowledging the declining regard Americans have for politics, due partially to negative politics, attack advertising, and confrontational press reporting, the authors note such reform proposals as the provision of free television time for candidates and a more rigorous news media investigation of the truthfulness of campaign advertising. The National Association of Broadcasters, Jamieson notes, recommends that stations reject unfair or untruthful ads.

Vermeer, Jan Pons, ed. *Campaigns in the News: Mass Media and Congressional Elections.* Westport, CT: Greenwood, 1987.

This volume of essays deals with various aspects of the media's role in congressional election campaigns. Among the topics covered are the content of reporting, the level of information provided voters in different districts, the mass media and senatorial elections, national media exposure for congressional candidates, and the ethics of campaign reporting.

West, Darrell M. *Air Wars: Television Advertising in Election Campaigns, 1952–1992.* Washington, DC: Congressional Quarterly, 1993.

Any discussion of campaign reform must acknowledge the influence of television on changing campaign strategies in recent decades. West provides a good summary and integration of past research on the role of television advertising in election campaigns, thus portraying the evolution of the medium. The author identifies the types of ads most likely to be employed, focuses on the effects that campaign ads have on viewers, and considers whether these effects constitute an alteration of the political process.

Woodward, Gary C. *Perspectives on American Political Media.* Needham Heights, MA: Allyn and Bacon, 1997.

Woodward analyzes the presentation of political issues and public figures in the mass media and the role the media play in a modern democracy. The author examines the ways in which public officials use the media in their attempts to activate politically a public grown less interested in the electoral process and increasingly alienated from politics in general. Interesting case studies are presented.

Voting Rights

Adams, Mildred. *The Right to Be People.* Philadelphia: J. B. Lippincott, 1967.

Adams presents an overview of the struggle for woman suffrage, beginning with the Declaration of Independence and proceeding to the national victory in 1920. By then 17 states had already granted women the right to vote. The author continues the story of woman suffrage, describing the early experience of women with the newly granted political role.

Aikin, Charles, ed. *The Negro Votes.* San Francisco: Chandler, 1962.

Published prior to passage of the 1965 Voting Rights Act, this volume includes documents crucial to establishing the right to vote for African Americans. Along with constitutional provisions, legal decisions are presented, including those dealing with the grandfather clause (*Guinn and Beal v. United States*, 1915, and *Lane v. Wilson*, 1939) and the gerrymander (for instance, *Colegrove v. Green et al.*, 1946).

Andersen, Kristi. *After Suffrage: Women in Partisan and Electoral Politics before the New Deal*. Chicago: University of Chicago Press, 1996.

Andersen investigates the initial experiences of women with the right to vote during the first decade after passage of the Nineteenth Amendment. The author reflects on the resulting alterations in the political process and the changing roles of women in American society.

Arrington, Karen McGill, and William L. Taylor, eds. *Voting Rights in America: Continuing the Quest for Full Participation*. Washington, DC: Leadership Conference Education Fund/Joint Center for Political and Economic Studies, 1992.

The essays included in this volume focus on expanding the right of minorities to vote. Chapters cover such topics as the long history of enfranchisement, voting rights and political power, the Civil War amendments, the 1982 amendments to the Voting Rights Act, and the political participation of Native Americans. Bill Clinton contributed an essay on state initiatives to increase voting participation.

Ball, Howard, Dale Drane, and Thomas P. Lauth. *Compromised Compliance: Implementation of the 1965 Voting Rights Act*. Westport, CT: Greenwood, 1982.

The authors investigate the implementation of the 1965 Voting Rights Act. They provide a story of the very difficult process of making the promises of the act a reality for minority Americans, detailing the activities of subsequent federal courts and the complexities of federal, state, and local government interaction. Appendixes include a pre-1965 Alabama literacy test and a chart of the number of changes to voting regulations submitted by states covered by the act from 1965 to 1980.

Beeton, Beverly. *Women in the West: The Woman Suffrage Movement, 1869–1896*. New York: Garland, 1986.

Beeton examines the introduction of woman suffrage in four western states—Wyoming, Utah, Colorado, and Idaho—in the late nineteenth century. By 1896 women had achieved full voting rights in each of these states. Why did woman suffrage succeed in the West more than 20 years before ratification of the Nineteenth Amendment? Beeton suggests a number of reasons, including the desire to attract settlers, the belief that suffrage would win eastern support for statehood, and the lack of organized opposition in the West.

Belknap, Michal R., ed. *Voting Rights.* New York: Garland, 1996.

This fifteenth volume in the series *Civil Rights, the White House, and the Justice Department, 1945–1968* documents the role of the federal government in the guarantee of voting rights. Various papers from the executive branch, Congress, and the Supreme Court are included. Belknap provides an introductory essay that integrates the materials.

Buhle, Mari Jo, and Paul Buhle, eds. *The Concise History of Woman Suffrage: Selections from the Classic Work of Stanton, Anthony, Gage, and Harper.* Urbana: University of Illinois Press, 1978.

The editors offer a digest of the more significant documents from *History of Woman Suffrage.* Selections cover such topics as the anti-slavery origins of the movement, the role of the temperance movement, National American Woman Suffrage Association conventions, suffrage campaigns in the states, and the final push for the woman suffrage amendment.

Burnett, Constance Buel. *Five for Freedom.* New York: Abelard, 1953.

Any reform movement requires strong and inspiring leadership. Burnett relates the contributions Lucretia Mott, Elizabeth Cady Stanton, Lucy Stone, Susan B. Anthony, and Carrie Chapman Catt made to the woman suffrage movement. While Mott, Stanton, Stone, and Anthony laid the foundation for women's struggle for equal rights, Catt contributed her exceptional organizational abilities to win the final victory for woman suffrage.

Camli, Jane Jerome. *Women against Women: American Anti-Suffragism, 1880–1920.* Brooklyn, NY: Carlson, 1994.

Camli discusses the opposition of women to the idea of woman suffrage. The antisuffrage movement began in the 1880s and reached its maximum influence between 1895 and 1907. The antisuffrage forces became well organized in 25 states and were spurred on by the fear that women in public life would lead to the undoing of women and society in general. Camli's book provides a good example of the way reform movements can generate strong opposition.

Catt, Carrie Chapman, and Nettie Rogers Shuler. *Woman Suffrage and Politics: The Inner Story of the Suffrage Movement.* Seattle: University of Washington Press, 1923.

Catt and Shuler provide a retrospective on the Nineteenth Amendment soon after its ratification. They outline the long history of this vital election reform, describe the suffrage movement's relation to American politics in general, and identify the significant sources of opposition to woman suffrage. The book is an interesting treatment of an important movement written by individuals actively involved in the cause.

Cultice, Wendell W. *Youth's Battle for the Ballot: A History of Voting Age in America.* Westport, CT: Greenwood, 1992.

Cultice's broad history of the right of young people to participate in elections indicates that the question was by no means a new one in the 1970s. He notes the tendency, going back to ancient Athens, to grant the right to vote to those youth serving in the military. After outlining the struggle for the franchise, the author assesses the disappointing turnout rates of 18-to-20-year-olds in the two decades since passage of the Twenty-sixth Amendment.

Davidson, Chandler, ed. *Minority Vote Dilution.* Washington, DC: Howard University Press, 1984.

The editor defines vote dilution as any procedure involving election laws, electoral practices, and bloc voting used by one group to lessen the vote strength of another. Individual articles deal with such topics as the history of vote dilution during the Reconstruction era following the Civil War, Progressive reforms such as at-large elections and multimember districts that have discriminatory intent, the development of an effects test to determine violation of minority voting rights, and difficulties with provisions of the 1965 Voting Rights Act.

Davidson, Chandler, and Bernard Grofman, eds. *Quiet Revolution in the South: The Impact of the Voting Rights Act, 1965–1990.* Princeton, NJ: Princeton University Press, 1994.

The authors of the essays in this collection investigate the effects of the Voting Rights Act on voting and representation in southern states. Employing sophisticated statistical analysis, the authors demonstrate the consequences of electoral reform for minority group representation. Articles focus on the creation of majority-minority districts, which have assured the election of many African American officials.

Dinkin, Robert J. *Before Equal Suffrage: Women in Partisan Politics from Colonial Times to 1920.* Westport, CT: Greenwood, 1995.

Dinkin discusses the participation of women in American politics during the generations preceding adoption of the Nineteenth Amendment. Women gradually increased their participation from attending rallies and supporting party tickets to speaking at party meetings and becoming involved in women's groups that canvassed to get out the vote. As a few states, particularly in the West, adopted woman suffrage, women not only voted in ever-greater numbers but began to hold public office.

DuBois, Ellen Carol. *Feminism and Suffrage: The Emergence of an Independent Women's Movement in America, 1848–1869.* Ithaca, NY: Cornell University Press, 1978.

DuBois observes that the woman suffrage movement along with the abolition of slavery and the labor movement constitute the three major reform ventures in the United States. The author traces the women's movement from the Seneca Falls Convention in 1848 to Congress's proposal of the Fifteenth Amendment in 1869, which ensured the right to vote to former male slaves but neglected any mention of women. DuBois's narrative focuses on the efforts of Elizabeth Cady Stanton and Susan B. Anthony.

Foster, Lorn S., ed. *The Voting Rights Act: Consequences and Implications.* New York: Praeger, 1985.

The essays in this volume investigate the ways in which the reforms instituted by the Voting Rights Act of 1965 have altered the

American political process. Individual articles deal with such topics as the extended historical background to the passage of the act, the development of legal standards to guide litigation concerning vote dilution, political maneuvering involved in passage of the 1982 amendments to the act, techniques of administrative enforcement, and the act's influence on voting behavior.

Gillette, William. *The Right to Vote: Politics and Passage of the Fifteenth Amendment.* Baltimore: Johns Hopkins University Press, 1965.

The Fifteenth Amendment guaranteed the right to vote to former slaves. Ratified in 1870, it was an important ingredient in the constitutional revolution that occurred following the Civil War. Gillette focuses on the efforts in Congress to propose the amendment and the ratification procedure in the various states and sections of the country. The author does not investigate the actual minority voting trends in the post–Civil War South.

Glaser, James M. *Race, Campaign Politics, and the Realignment in the South.* New Haven, CT: Yale University Press, 1996.

Following passage of the 1965 Voting Rights Act, Republicans in southern states gained an increasing electoral advantage, especially in presidential contests. However, Glaser identifies an interesting result of electoral reform: the formation of biracial coalitions that have helped Democratic congressional candidates win election. The author bases his findings on interviews with candidates, party officials, black leaders, and other political activists.

Gluck, Sherna, ed. *From Parlor to Prison: Five American Suffragists Talk about Their Lives.* New York: Vintage, 1976.

Gluck presents a history of the woman suffrage movement through the remembrances of five unheralded members of the cause: Sylvie Thygeson, Jessie Haver Butler, Miriam Allen de-Ford, Laura Ellsworth Seiler, and Ernestine Hara Kettler. These women, members of the rank and file, inherited the cause from a previous generation of suffragists. They discuss the formation and implementation of strategies, including the willingness to be imprisoned.

Graham, Sara Hunter. *Woman Suffrage and the New Democracy.* New Haven, CT: Yale University Press, 1996.

Graham examines the establishment of a well-organized campaign for woman suffrage in the late nineteenth and early twentieth centuries. The author relates the goals and strategies of the National American Woman Suffrage Association, whose members proved to be highly effective in their political lobbying efforts.

Grofman, Bernard, and Chandler Davidson, eds. *Controversies in Minority Voting: The Voting Rights Act in Perspective.* Washington, DC: Brookings Institution, 1992.

The essays composing this volume originated in a conference at the Brooking Institution on the twenty-fifth anniversary of the Voting Rights Act. Individual chapters discuss the original goals and subsequent results of the act. Attention is given to the 1982 amendments, which some argue went beyond the original intent of guaranteeing minorities the right to vote and instead guaranteed legislative representation for minority groups. Individual essays deal with such topics as the historical background to passage, the act's influence on political parties, the use of expert witnesses in litigation, and assessments of the overall success of the act.

Grofman, Bernard, Lisa Handley, and Richard Niemi. *Minority Representation and the Quest for Voting Equality.* New York: Cambridge University Press, 1992.

The authors provide a concise history of the progress that minorities have made in achieving the right to vote and discuss the problem of vote dilution. The book's basic premise is that the 1965 Voting Rights Act, in addition to guaranteeing the right to vote, was intended to provide minorities with actual representation. In order to achieve this goal, it is suggested that minorities should receive representation in proportion to their numbers in the population. The book describes the complex statistical methods employed in court cases dealing with voting rights during the 1980s.

Gurko, Miriam. *The Ladies of Seneca Falls: The Birth of the Woman's Rights Movement.* New York: Macmillan, 1974.

Like many reform movements, the struggle for woman suffrage and women's rights in general has a definite starting point in historical lore. The Seneca Falls Convention began with five women: Lucretia Mott, Martha Wright, Jane Hunt, Mary Ann McClintock, and Elizabeth Cady Stanton. Gurko recounts the beginning of the movement that would enlist the services of other exceptional women, including Susan B. Anthony and Lucy Stone.

Hamilton, Charles V. *The Bench and the Ballot: Southern Federal Judges and Black Voters.* New York: Oxford University Press, 1973.

Hamilton examines the role of the federal judiciary in advancing minority voting rights during the eight years preceding the 1965 Voting Rights Act. The author discusses cases in Alabama, Mississippi, Louisiana, and Tennessee and examines the historical background to the cases, the civil rights acts of 1957 and 1960, and the reaction of the executive branch to the legislation and court cases.

Hine, Darlene Clark. *Black Victory: The Rise and Fall of the White Primary in Texas.* Millwood, NY: KTO Press, 1979.

In 1944 the U.S. Supreme Court brought about significant electoral reform in the *Smith v. Allwright* decision, declaring the white primary unconstitutional. Hine presents the history of the legal case that successfully challenged the policy of the Democratic party in Texas to exclude African Americans from participation in the party primary.

Johnsen, Julia E., ed. *Lowering the Voting Age.* New York: H. W. Wilson, 1944.

This interesting little book was prepared in the context of World War II and the sentiment of many that a person old enough to fight is old enough to vote. Several unsuccessful measures to lower the voting age were introduced in Congress during the war years. Johnsen compiles a series of previously published articles, both favoring and opposing the lowering of the voting age.

Kraditor, Aileen S. *The Ideas of the Woman Suffrage Movement, 1890–1920.* New York: Columbia University Press, 1965.

Kraditor focuses her investigation primarily on the national leadership of the National American Woman Suffrage Association. Employing published works supported by the association, testimony before congressional committees, and proceedings of the association, the author constructs a suffragist ideology. Kraditor notes that throughout its history, the movement was dominated by white, native-born, middle-class women who generally accepted the existing social and political structure.

Lutz, Alma. *Susan B. Anthony: Rebel, Crusader, Humanitarian.* Boston: Beacon Press, 1959.

Any account of the woman suffrage movement must take note of Susan B. Anthony, one of its founders and major figures. A longtime advocate of temperance and abolition, she helped form the National Woman Suffrage Association in 1869. After formation of the National American Association, Anthony served as its president from 1892 to 1900. Although Anthony did not live to see ratification of the Nineteenth Amendment, she played a crucial role in the success of the woman suffrage movement.

McGovney, Dudley O. *The American Suffrage Medley: The Need for a National Uniform Suffrage.* Chicago: University of Chicago Press, 1949.

Writing at a time when voting rights in the United States were far from universal, McGovney recommends the establishment of a uniform, affirmative right to vote through a constitutional amendment establishing national voting qualifications. The author reviews the varying qualifications then existing in the several states and singles out the poll tax for detailed commentary.

National American Woman Suffrage Association. *Victory, How Women Won It: A Centennial Symposium, 1840–1940.* New York: H. W. Wilson, 1940.

Several women who were active in the woman suffrage movement collaborated to write chapters in this volume. Among the contributors are Carrie Chapman Catt, Maud Wood Park, Penelope P. B. Huse, and Mary Gray Peck. Individual chapters discuss the early history of the movement, the state-by-state strategy for attaining suffrage, appeals to the U.S. Congress for a constitutional amendment, and final victory.

Olbrich, Emil. *The Development of Sentiment on Negro Suffrage to 1860.* Freeport, NY: Books for Libraries, 1971 (1912).

Olbrich describes a little-known movement prior to the Civil War to grant blacks in northern states the right to vote. Although the constitutions and statutes of states and territories often contained provisions limiting suffrage to white males, there were significant minorities favoring the right of black men to vote. Olbrich discusses the debates over the issue in the several states.

Paradigm Design Group/Paralyzed Veterans of America. *Innovations in Election Administration 15: Ensuring Accessibility of the Election Process.* Washington, DC: Office of Election Administration, 1996.

This monograph provides guidelines for assuring voting rights for those with such disabilities as impaired vision, mobility, communication, and dexterity. Applicable federal laws and standards are summarized and detailed guidelines for providing access are presented. Americans who once found it extremely difficult to exercise their right to vote are now finding the polling place physically more accessible.

Park, Maud Wood. *Front Door Lobby.* Boston: Beacon Press, 1960.

The Front Door Lobby was the National American Woman Suffrage Association's congressional committee that lobbied effectively in Washington for a woman suffrage amendment. Park, who worked as the committee's chair from 1917 to 1920, relates the committee's strategies for persuading Congress to propose a woman suffrage amendment.

Piven, Frances Fox, and Richard A. Cloward. *Why Americans Don't Vote.* New York: Pantheon, 1988.

Piven and Cloward provide a class-based explanation for low voter turnout, arguing that the American political process favors the interests of affluent elites at the expense of the disadvantaged. Written before passage of the Motor-Voter Bill, the volume claims that strict registration requirements significantly dampen voter turnout. Piven and Cloward describe the efforts of Human SERVE, an organization dedicated to registering poorer and minority Americans. The authors claim that reforms to bring about greater participation will lead to public policy more concerned with the interests of less-affluent Americans.

Porter, Kirk H. *A History of Suffrage in the United States.* Westport, CT: Greenwood, 1977 (1918).

This excellent little book provides a history of the expansion of suffrage to the period just before women received the right to vote. Beginning with attitudes toward suffrage expressed at the first state constitutional conventions, Porter relates the sometimes halting process of suffrage expansion. The states and new territories struggled with questions of property qualifications and the political rights of aliens. One chapter recounts the disfranchisement of African Americans following reconstruction, and another summarizes the progress toward woman suffrage at the time of publication.

Rembaugh, Bertha. *The Political Status of Women in the United States: A Digest of the Laws Concerning Women in the Various States and Territories.* New York: G. P. Putnam's Sons, 1911.

This volume, published before ratification of the Nineteenth Amendment, presents a summary of state and territorial provisions with regard to woman suffrage and the right to hold public office. At the time of publication five states—Washington, Idaho, Wyoming, Utah, and Colorado—had established equal voting rights for women, and several other states granted limited woman suffrage. Published in cooperation with the Women's Political Union, the book takes a strong stand in favor of suffrage.

Scher, Richard K., John Hotaling, and Jon L. Mills. *Voting Rights and Democracy: The Law and Politics of Districting.* Chicago: Nelson-Hall, 1996.

The authors—a political scientist, a professional politician, and a law professor—examine legal and political trends in voting rights over the last three decades. They investigate the development of the racial fairness standard and its consequences and suggest options other than race-based districting for assuring voting rights for minorities.

Sheppard, Alice. *Cartooning for Suffrage.* Albuquerque: University of New Mexico Press, 1994.

In the nineteenth century many newspaper cartoons portrayed the struggle for woman suffrage in a negative light. In the early twentieth century, however, women began to use the cartoon to their advantage in the campaign for the right to vote. This fascinating volume includes a wealth of drawings from this era, along with Sheppard's commentary. The book emphasizes the importance of altering public opinion through positive images when striving for political reform.

Stanley, Harold W. *Voter Mobilization and the Politics of Race: The South and Universal Suffrage, 1952–1984.* New York: Praeger, 1987.

Stanley bases his analysis on the fundamental observation that black voter registration rose by 33 percent in the 1960s, an increase attributed to passage of the Voting Rights Act of 1965. The author examines a rise in the southern white as well as the black electorate during a period in which national turnout rates were declining and identifies a number of variables, including changing political attitudes and easier registration requirements, to explain the differential increase. Stanley rejects the hypothesis that racial attitudes led to white countermobilization efforts.

Stanton, Elizabeth Cady, Susan B. Anthony, and Matilda Joslyn Gage, eds. *History of Woman Suffrage.* Six vols. New York: Arno and the New York Times, 1969.

This multivolume history of woman suffrage was edited by the most noted nineteenth-century advocates of the cause. The first volume recounts the beginning of the suffrage movement at a meeting held in Seneca Falls, New York, in July 1848 and traces its development to the Civil War. Succeeding volumes continue the movement's progress to final victory with ratification of the Nineteenth Amendment in 1920. Anthony and Ida Husted Harper edited the fourth volume, and Harper alone prepared the final two volumes.

Stevens, Doris. *Jailed for Freedom.* Freeport, NY: Books for Libraries, 1920.

Published the year the Nineteenth Amendment was ratified, this book reflects the passion of the woman suffrage movement. Stevens documents a shift in the movement's strategy toward greater militancy, which she associates with martyrdom for the cause in the face of a "ruthless" administration. Stevens's detailed account demonstrates that the path of reform can be extremely difficult and frustrating.

Strong, Donald S. *Negroes, Ballots, and Judges: National Voting Rights Legislation in the Federal Courts.* University: University of Alabama Press, 1968.

Strong offers a brief commentary on the modest election reform provisions of the 1957 and 1960 civil rights acts. The legislation had little effect on increasing the total number of African Americans registered to vote in southern states. Focusing his attention on Louisiana, Mississippi, and Alabama, the author describes the ways in which the legislatures of these states attempted to circumvent the federal legislation.

Swain, Carol M. *Black Faces, Black Interests: The Representation of African Americans in Congress.* Cambridge, MA: Harvard University Press, 1993.

Swain has conducted an empirical study of African American representatives in Congress who were elected from differing districts: historically black, newly black, mixed white and black, and majority white. The author concludes that black representation is complex, with white members of Congress capable of representing black interests. Swain concludes that the creation of more majority-minority districts is not the most efficient means to improve representation of black interests.

Taper, Bernard. Gomillion versus Lightfoot: *The Tuskegee Gerrymander Case.* New York: McGraw-Hill, 1962.

Taper presents an interesting personal account of the landmark decision in which the Supreme Court ruled that the exclusion of African Americans from city elections in Tuskegee, Alabama, through a racial gerrymandering scheme violated the Fifteenth Amendment.

Thernstrom, Abigail M. *Whose Votes Count? Affirmative Action and Minority Voting Rights.* Cambridge, MA: Harvard University Press, 1987.

Thernstrom investigates the effects of the 1965 Voting Rights Act and its subsequent amendments. In addition to recounting the history of the Voting Rights Act and its revisions, the author raises the issue of whether Congress and the courts have gone beyond the original intent of the law in providing for minority voting rights. Thernstrom argues that originally the act was intended to guarantee the equal right to vote rather than a particular outcome in terms of the proportion of government representation held by minorities. Instead of the encouragement of distinct minority representation, the author recommends coalitions across racial and ethnic lines.

Wheeler, Marjorie Spruill. *Votes for Women! The Woman Suffrage Movement in Tennessee, the South, and the Nation.* Knoxville: University of Tennessee Press, 1995.

The first part of this excellent treatment of the woman suffrage question includes a series of essays analyzing the strategies of both sides of the issue, especially in Tennessee, the state that finally brought ratification of the Nineteenth Amendment. The second part contains several documents written around the time of the final push for ratification. The last section includes published materials and political cartoons for and against woman suffrage that were published in the popular press prior to ratification.

Williamson, Chilton. *American Suffrage: From Property to Democracy, 1760–1860.* Princeton, NJ: Princeton University Press, 1960.

Williamson investigates the achievement of universal white male suffrage during the period between the Revolution and the beginning of the Civil War. He examines the nature of voting during the colonial period, when property qualifications for voting existed in all the future states, and identifies the political groups that campaigned for vote reform during the first half of the nineteenth century. Because suffrage expansion never divided the nation as did movements like abolition, each state could pursue suffrage reform separately. Therefore Williamson focuses on the history of individual states.

Periodicals

Some of the following periodicals and journals are devoted almost exclusively to an issue related to campaign and election reform, while others are more general publications that regularly include topics on election reform. Many of these publications must be acquired directly from the sponsoring association.

America Votes
Elections Research Center
1619 Massachusetts Avenue NW
Washington, DC 20036

Published every two years following the general election, *America Votes* contains a wealth of information about elections. Included are vote breakdowns in the presidential, congressional, and gubernatorial elections and maps indicating the results of the most recent reapportionment plans in each state.

American Journal of Political Science
Journals Division, University of Wisconsin Press
114 North Murray Street
Madison, WI 53715
Quarterly. $30.

This scholarly journal regularly contains articles on subjects relevant to campaign and election reform such as electoral dynamics, the mass media and voters' attitudes, the single transferable vote, the relationship between electoral institutions and the number of political parties, and the legislative effects of single-member versus multimember districts.

American Politics Quarterly
Sage Publications, Inc.
2455 Teller Road
Thousand Oaks, CA 91320
Quarterly. $52.

This scholarly publication contains articles dealing with the various aspects of American politics. Issues often include essays relevant to campaign and election reform, including such topics as legislative redistricting, majority-minority districts and the influence of racial composition on legislators' behavior, the impact of electronic voting machines, and registration reform and its effects on voter turnout.

American Prospect
New Prospect, Inc.
146 Auburn Street
Cambridge, MA 02138
Quarterly. $25.

This quarterly political journal includes articles by renowned journalists and social scientists that focus on major political issues, including campaign and election reform.

Ballot Access News
Coalition for Free and Open Elections
P.O. Box 20263
London Terrace Station
New York, NY 10011
Monthly. $7 for nonmembers.

This periodical supplies information about legislative and judicial decisions regarding the conduct of elections.

Campaign Finance Law: A Summary of State Campaign Finance Laws
Superintendent of Documents
P.O. Box 371954
Pittsburgh, PA 15250-7954
Yearly. $40.

This publication offers current information about state campaign finance laws. It includes useful charts and references to the legal codes of each state.

Campaigns & Elections
1511 K Street NW
Washington, DC 20005-1450
Ten issues per year. $39.95.

This magazine presents articles and news about campaign strategies and the personalities involved in politics. Although the magazine focuses primarily on providing political activists and prospective candidates with inside information about the political process and advice for running campaigns, such reform topics as the limitations of the electoral college and the prospects for vote-by-mail elections are treated.

Cincinnatus News Service
Precinct Project Institute
P.O. Box 11339
Cincinnati, OH 45211
Monthly. Free on request.

This newsletter, edited by James J. Condit, Jr., focuses on current instances of vote fraud. Mechanical and computer vote counting systems receive severe criticism and the traditional paper ballot is praised. Recent issues contain the claim that computerized direct recording voting machines are accessible through remote cell phones.

Common Cause Magazine
Common Cause
2030 M Street NW
Washington, DC 20036-3380
Quarterly. $20.

This publication focuses on a variety of government reform issues, including campaigns and elections. Recent issues contain articles on soft money contributions, campaign reform measures in the states, term limits, and special interest campaign donations.

Congressional Digest
Congressional Digest Corporation
3231 P Street NW
Washington, DC 20007-2772
Ten issues per year. $39.

This publication provides summaries of proposed legislation currently before Congress, commentary on testimony presented before congressional committees, and selected debates in congressional committees. The *Digest* can serve as a valuable source of information about recent proposals for campaign finance reform.

County News Magazine
National Association of Counties
440 1st Street NW, Eighth Floor
Washington, DC 20001-2080
Bimonthly. $25.

Counties have generally been given the responsibility for election administration. This publication for county officials contains articles dealing with various aspects of county management, including election regulations. Innovations and model programs are often discussed.

Election Center Reports
Election Center
444 North Capitol Street NW, Suite 349
Washington, DC 20001
Monthly.

This publication provides information about developments in registration and election practices and reports on Congress's consideration of legislation concerned with elections.

Electoral Studies
Butterworth Legal Publishers
8 Industrial Way, No. C
Salem, NH 03079-2837
Quarterly. $150.

This international journal, published in Great Britain, includes scholarly articles on election administration around the world. Among the topics covered in recent issues are campaign spending, proportional representation systems, the effects of mandatory voting, and measurement of electoral inequality. The articles tend to be methodologically sophisticated.

Governing
Congressional Quarterly
2300 N Street, Suite 760
Washington, DC 20037-1096
Monthly. $39.95.

This magazine reports on current public policy initiatives and government operations at the state and national levels, including issues related to campaigns and elections.

Grass Roots Campaigning
Campaign Consultants
P.O. Box 7281
Little Rock, AR 72217-7281
Monthly. $36.

This magazine, which contains articles on the very practical aspects of political campaign techniques at the local, state, and national levels, provides an insightful look at the contemporary campaign process.

The Guardian
Center for Governmental Studies
1091 West Pico Boulevard, Suite 120
Los Angeles, CA 90064-2126
Quarterly. $60.

Supported by the Council on Governmental Ethics Laws (COGEL), this publication reports on various issues related to governmental ethics. *The Guardian* has treated such election-related topics as campaign financing, the National Voter Registration Act and its consequences, negative campaigning, and low voter turnout.

Journal of Democracy
Johns Hopkins University Press
2715 North Charles Street
Baltimore, MD 21218-4363
Quarterly. $25.

This journal includes articles that cover various topics relevant to the nature of democracy and strategies for improving the democratic process.

Journal of Election Administration
U.S. Federal Election Commission
Office of Election Administration
999 E Street NW
Washington, DC 20463
Annual. Free on request.

Originally published semiannually by the Federal Election Commission, this journal ceased publication for several years before being resurrected in 1996 as an annual publication. The *Journal* has included many informative articles on election reform, including such topics as computer security, voter registration for the homeless, voting rights for college students, the federal role in prosecuting vote fraud, and all-mail-ballot elections.

Legislative Studies Quarterly
Comparative Legislative Research Center
307 Seashore Hall
University of Iowa
Iowa City, IA 52242
Quarterly. $38.

This scholarly journal frequently contains articles that deal with the election of representatives to Congress and state legislatures. Among the topics covered are the influence of PACs, the advantages of incumbency, the role of money in congressional campaigns, and the effects of term limits.

National Civic Review
National Civic League
1445 Market Street, Suite 300
Denver, CO 80202-1728
Bimonthly. $30.

A periodical for civic leaders and students of politics, the *Civic Review* contains general information about public affairs, including issues related to elections and electoral reform.

National Journal
1501 M Street NW, Suite 300
Washington, DC 20005-1700
Weekly. $939.

This periodical offers coverage and analysis of important issues facing the nation, including campaign and election reform.

National Voter
League of Women Voters of the U.S.
1730 M Street NW, Suite 1000
Washington, DC 20036-4587
Quarterly. $12.

This publication provides articles on a number of topics, including social policy, the environment, international relations, the governing structure, and the electoral process.

Political Fund Raising Report
12500 Fair Lakes Circle, Suite 155
Fairfax, VA 22033
Biweekly. $396.

This newsletter, published by Richard Viguerie, provides timely information on fund-raising methods. Appealing to Democrats and Republicans, conservatives and liberals, the *Report* details such media techniques as infomercials, direct mail, the Internet, and telemarketing.

Political Moneyline
Citizens' Research Foundation
University of Southern California
3716 South Hope Street
Los Angeles, CA 90007
Quarterly. $10.

This newsletter includes presentations on campaign finance and proposed political reforms. Also included are reports on campaign spending in specific elections and reviews of recent publications on campaign finance reform.

PS: Political Science and Politics
American Political Science Association
1527 New Hampshire Avenue NW
Washington, DC 20036
Quarterly. $5 for members of the organization, $10 per issue for nonmembers.

This publication of the American Political Science Association offers articles by professional political scientists that often treat contemporary issues, including election reform. Among the subjects of recent articles are the National Voter Registration Act, congressional term limits, alternative voting systems, and U.S. Supreme Court decisions regarding majority-minority districts.

Public Opinion Quarterly
Journals Division
University of Chicago Press
Box 37005
Chicago, IL 60637
Quarterly. $23.

This well-established journal contains articles dealing with the measurement and analysis of public opinion. The journal includes articles relevant to campaign and election reform such as the effects of campaign ads and presidential debates on opinion, the level of support for legislative term limits, and the influence that polling as a contemporary part of the campaign and election process has on political attitudes.

The Voluntaryist
Voluntaryists
P.O. Box 1275
Gramling, SC 29348-0275
Bimonthly. $18.

This periodical describes the activities of the Voluntaryist movement, which, in calling for nonpolitical means to achieve freedom, rejects electoral politics as a viable strategy to achieve its ends.

Voting and Democracy Review
6905 Fifth Street NW, Suite 200
Washington, DC 20012
Quarterly. $15.

Issued by the Center for Voting and Democracy, this quarterly publication provides information about the organization's activities in support of election reform, particularly the introduction of proportional representation. Lobbying efforts across the nation in favor of proportional representation receive attention.

Voting Rights Review
Southern Regional Council
134 Peachtree Street NW, Suite 1900
Atlanta, GA 30303-1825
Three issues per year. $3 per issue.

This publication updates recent efforts to maintain and advance voting rights for all citizens.

Selected Nonprint Resources

This chapter presents a variety of nonprint resources on campaign finance reform, including audio- and videotapes, films, computer software, databases, and Internet sites. These resources focus on issues relevant to campaign finance and electoral reform at the state and federal levels.

Audio and Video Tapes and Films

The Best Campaign Money Can Buy
Type: 1/2" videocassette (VHS format)
Length: 60 min.
Cost: $69.95
Date: 1992
Source: PBS Video
             Public Broadcasting Service
             1320 Braddock Place
             Alexandria, VA 22314-1698

Asking the question "Does big money control our elections?" this video indicates that the three most important issues in the 1992 presidential election were "money, money, and money." Frontline takes viewers behind the scenes of the large contributors and

257

fund-raising machines that amass huge amounts of money for candidates (for instance, $9 million in just one night for George Bush).

Campaign American Style
Type: 16 mm film
Length: 39 min.
Cost: $15 (rental)
Date: 1968
Source: Audio-Visual Services
Special Services Building
Pennsylvania State University
University Park, PA 16802

Based on the campaign of a county official on Long Island, New York, this film explores the "Madison Avenue" approach to politics prevalent in the United States. Although this Republican candidate hires pollsters and political consultants and spends campaign funds on advertising, he still loses the election.

Campaigning for the Presidency
Type: 1/2" videocassette (VHS format)
Length: 60 min.
Cost: $69.95
Date: 1992
Source: PBS Video
Public Broadcasting Service
1320 Braddock Place
Alexandria, VA 22314-1698

In this video campaign managers and key political advisers to Republican and Democratic candidates from 1968 to 1988 examine various aspects of the election process. The discussion includes such issues as the use of polling technology, fund-raising techniques, negative advertising, and effective relations with the media.

Campaigning on Cue: The Presidential Election of 1984—Debates and Political Advertising
Type: 1/2" videocassette (VHS format)
Length: 58 min.
Cost: $16.50 (rental)

Date: 1985
Source: Audio-Visual Services
           Special Services Building
           Pennsylvania State University
           University Park, PA 16802

Using the presidential election of 1984 as a case study, the participants in this video discuss the impact of debate, fund-raising, and political advertising on the modern presidential election.

The Candidate
Type: 1/2" videocassette (VHS format)
Length: 109 min.
Cost: $19.95
Date: 1972
Source: Movies Unlimited
           6736 Castor Avenue
           Philadelphia, PA 19149-2184

This true-to-life political satire starring Robert Redford follows an idealistic candidate for the U.S. Senate from his initial decision to seek office to his electoral victory.

Charisma, Personality, and Power
Type: 1/2" videocassette (VHS format)
Length: 47 min.
Cost: $89.95
Date: 1993
Source: Films for the Humanities and Sciences
           P.O. Box 2053
           Princeton, NJ 08543-2053

This program with Bill Moyers examines the 1992 presidential election and includes interviews with Abraham Zalenik, author of *Learning Leadership;* Fernando Moreno, editor of *El Diario;* and Kathleen Hall Jamieson, dean of the Annenberg School of Communications.

Computer Votefraud and the 1996 Elections
Type: Audiocassette
Length: 45 min.
Cost: Free on request

Date: 1996
Source: Cincinnatus
P.O. Box 11339
Cincinnati, OH 45211

James Condit presents evidence of alleged vote fraud in recent elections, pointing a finger at computerized vote counting and exit polls. He encourages listeners to support a return to the printed ballot.

Congress, We the People, 5: Congressional Elections
Type: 1/2" videocassette (VHS format)
Length: 30 min.
Cost: $8 (rental)
Date: 1983
Source: Audio-Visual Services
Special Services Building
Pennsylvania State University
University Park, PA 16802

This video considers how the many congressional elections of both houses resemble and differ from each other and in what ways they are undergoing change.

The Constitution, That Delicate Balance, 7:
Campaign Spending; Money, and Media
Type: 1/2" videocassette (VHS format) or 3/4 U-mat
Length: 56 min.
Cost: $6.50 (rental)
Date: 1984
Source: Audio-Visual Services
Special Services Building
Pennsylvania State University
University Park, PA 16802

Examining government regulation of the electoral process, this program highlights the importance of money and media in national elections. It focuses on efforts to reform campaign financing.

Crisis of Democracy
Type: 1/2" videocassette (VHS format)
Length: 80 min.

Cost: $99
Date: 1996
Source: Films for the Humanities and Sciences
           P.O. Box 2053
           Princeton, NJ 08543-2053

Bill Moyers moderates a discussion with Noam Chomsky, Tom Wolfe, and other noted authors about big government, the control of political parties by a power elite, government deceit, and mounting disillusionment with the democratic process. Joseph Heller, author of *Catch-22*, suggests that media-dominated political campaigns have turned democracy into a spectator sport.

The Decline of Politics: The Superficial Democracy
Type: 1/2" videocassette (VHS format)
Length: 29 min.
Cost: $89.95
Date: 1996
Source: Films for the Humanities and Sciences
           P.O. Box 2053
           Princeton, NJ 08543-2053

Featuring David Broder, Gary Hart, Mark Shields, and former senator Warren Rudman, this program focuses on the implications of an electoral system that favors slogans, personal attacks, and orchestrated appearances over a serious discussion of issues, problems, and ideas. The primary focus is how to put substance back into American politics.

Democracy and the Nature of Power
Type: 1/2" videocassette (VHS format)
Length: 30 min.
Cost: $99
Date: 1996
Source: Films for the Humanities and Sciences
           P.O. Box 2053
           Princeton, NJ 08543-2053

Political philosopher Sheldon Wolin, along with Bill Moyers, explores the meaning of democracy, the nature of power, and the role of the state by drawing on Wolin's scholarship. The video also records the views of people on the street.

Democracy in a Different Voice: Lani Guinier
Type: 1/2" videocassette (VHS format)
Length: 54 min.
Cost: $219
Date: 1995
Source: Insight Media
           2162 Broadway
           New York, NY 10024-6620

In this video Lani Guinier outlines her views on democracy and voting, discussing the meaning of democracy in a diverse society. She suggests ways to make democracy work for everyone while avoiding the "tyranny of the majority."

Electing a President
Type: 1/2" videocassette (VHS format)
Length: 45 min.
Cost: $119
Date: 1995
Source: Insight Media
           2162 Broadway
           New York, NY 10024-6620

In examining the electoral process this video focuses on the presidency and the growth of the party system. The roles of primaries, caucuses, conventions, and the electoral college are discussed, and the activities of lobbyists and the involvement of the media in the political process are explored.

Electing the President
Type: 1/2" videocassette (VHS format)
Length: 29 min.
Cost: $27.50 (rental)
Date: 1983
Source: Audio-Visual Services
           Special Services Building
           Pennsylvania State University
           University Park, PA 16802

This video describes the development of the American electoral process from George Washington to Ronald Reagan. The role of primaries as vehicles for testing candidate abilities is also investigated.

Electing the President: An American Government Series
Type: 1/2" videocassette (VHS format)
Length: Five 60 min. programs
Cost: $200
Date: 1996
Source: PBS Video
Public Broadcasting Service
1320 Braddock Place
Alexandria, VA 22314-1698

These five programs explore how presidents are elected. Program topics include an examination of the relationship between the press and politicians, the effects of public opinion polling on presidential elections, efforts to reform the electoral process, and the linkage between elections and better governance.

Electing the President: Six Steps to the Summit
Type: 1/2" videocassette (VHS format)
Length: 45 min.
Cost: $139
Date: 1995
Source: Insight Media
2162 Broadway
New York, NY 10024-6620

Using footage of presidents and former presidential candidates, this program examines how early caucuses and primaries affect the national conventions and campaigns. It also discusses the role of the electoral college and the party system.

Elizabeth Cady Stanton and Susan B. Anthony
Type: 1/2" videocassette (VHS format)
Length: 24 min.
Cost: $89.95
Date: 1988
Source: Films for the Humanities and Sciences
P.O. Box 2053
Princeton, NJ 08543-2053

This video explores the emergence of the National Woman Suffrage Association. From the first women's rights convention in Seneca Falls, New York, before the Civil War to the joining of forces of Elizabeth Cady Stanton, Susan B. Anthony, and Lucretia

Mott, this film provides a historical overview of the beginnings of the women's rights movement.

Gang Power
Type: 1/2" videocassette (VHS format)
Length: 18 min.
Cost: ⸺
Date: 1994
Source: American Broadcasting Company
             1330 Avenue of the Americas
             New York, NY 10019

Anchor Peter Jennings reports on how a Chicago street gang that is making money selling drugs begins to organize a political action committee to expand its power base and influence in Chicago, Illinois.

Getting Out the Vote
Type: 1/2" videocassette (VHS format)
Length: 30 min.
Cost: $89.95
Source: Films for the Humanities and Sciences
             P.O. Box 2053
             Princeton, NJ 08543-2053

This program features Bill Moyers, who interviews Americans, asking them to explain why they do not vote. Moyers explores what can be done to increase voter turnout.

Illusions of News
Type: 1/2" videocassette (VHS format)
Length: 60 min.
Cost: $89.95
Date: 1996
Source: Films for the Humanities and Sciences
             P.O. Box 2053
             Princeton, NJ 28543-2053

This program with Bill Moyers investigates the effect of visual images on news, politics, presidential elections, and the governing process. It analyzes the rise of news manipulation by candidates of the news media.

Lawmakers

Type:	1/2" videocassette (VHS format)
Length:	20 min.
Cost:	$89.95
Date:	1996
Source:	Films for the Humanities and Sciences
	P.O. Box 2053
	Princeton, NJ 28543-2053

While examining why people seek election to state legislatures, this video also discusses the "campaign as continuous process" phenomenon.

The Making of the President, 1964

Type:	16 mm film
Length:	79 min.
Cost:	$27.50 (rental)
Date:	1965
Source:	Audio-Visual Services
	Special Services Building
	Pennsylvania State University
	University Park, PA 16802

Based on Theodore White's book *The Making of the President, 1964,* this video covers the 1964 presidential campaign process from John F. Kennedy's assassination to Lyndon Johnson's election. This video offers behind-the-scenes footage of the candidates and their campaigns in the California and New Hampshire primaries.

Media in Politics

Type:	1/2" videocassette (VHS format)
Length:	90 min.
Cost:	$149
Date:	1996
Source:	Insight Media
	2162 Broadway
	New York, NY 10024-6642

Tony Schwartz, a political consultant, demonstrates how he has successfully employed concepts and techniques to advance political candidates and officeholders' causes, with a focus on how to manipulate the media.

Modern Campaign Techniques
Type: 1/2" videocassette (VHS format)
Length: 25 min.
Cost: $119
Date: 1993
Source: Insight Media
2162 Broadway
New York, NY 10024-6642

In addition to an examination of technology's impact on political campaigning, this video discusses the role of political consultants and how candidates manage the news. It also explores the role of money in campaigns.

Modern Presidential Campaigns
Type: 1/2" videocassette (VHS format)
Length: 2 volumes: 1924–1960, 132 min.
2 volumes: 1964–1992, 167 min.
Cost: $189 for each 2-volume set
Date: 1993
Source: Insight Media
2162 Broadway
New York, NY 10024-6642

Bringing to life the presidential campaigns since 1920, these tapes present debates, speeches, commercials, and moments from nominating conventions. Unusual events that affected election outcomes and candidates' foibles are highlighted.

Money Talks: The Influence of Money in American Politics
Type: 1/2" videocassette (VHS format)
Length: 60 min.
Cost: $89.95
Date: 1993
Source: Films for the Humanities and Sciences
P.O. Box 2053
Princeton, NJ 28543-2053

Focusing on the first days of the Clinton administration, Bill Moyers investigates the influence of corporate and special interests. Questions are raised about the role of money, power, and privilege in policy making and about the effectiveness of campaign finance reform.

Peanuts to the Presidency: The Jimmy Carter Campaign
Type: 16 mm film
Length: 29 min.
Cost: $19.50 (rental)
Date: 1977
Source: Audio-Visual Services
             Special Services Building
             Pennsylvania State University
             University Park, PA 16802

Focusing on Jimmy Carter's campaign, this film offers insights into the electoral process and the arduous type of campaign that a presidential candidate must conduct. It examines the primaries, the conventions, political commercials, the Ford-Carter debates, the election results, and Jimmy Carter's personal life.

The People and the Power Game, Part 1: The Unelected:
The Lobbies and the Media
Type: 1/2" videocassette (VHS format)
Length: 60 min.
Cost: $55.95
Date: 1996
Source: PBS Video
             Public Broadcasting Service
             1320 Braddock Place
             Alexandria, VA 22314-1698

This first part of the Power Game series describes the growth of the media and lobbies into a shadow government with great influence over American democracy.

The People and the Power Game, Part 2: The Elected: The
Presidency and Congress
Type: 1/2" videocassette (VHS format)
Length: 60 min.
Cost: $55.95
Date: 1996
Source: PBS Video
             Public Broadcasting Service
             1320 Braddock Place
             Alexandria, VA 22314-1698

The second part of the Power Game series explores the epic power struggle between Speaker of the House Newt Gingrich and President Bill Clinton over the federal budget, which influenced the 1996 election outcomes.

Political Participation vs. Serving the People
Type: 1/2" videocassette (VHS format)
Length: 28 min.
Cost: $89.95
Date: 1997
Source: Insight Media
             2162 Broadway
             New York, NY 10024-6642

Noting that Congress forms the basis of American representative democracy, this video explores the role of Congress in serving as an efficient mechanism for determining the will of the people. It examines congressional gridlock and the place of partisanship in attempts to improve government operation.

The Power Game Series: The Congress
Type: 1/2" videocassette (VHS format)
Length: 60 min.
Cost: $69.95
Date: 1988
Source: PBS Video
             Public Broadcasting Service
             1320 Braddock Place
             Alexandria, VA 22314-1698

The events of the Vietnam War and Watergate provoked the election of reform-minded members of Congress in 1974 who took office believing there was a mandate for change. This documentary details the political style of this new breed of legislator, who is distinguished by the use of political action committee funds, the 30-second campaign ad, and a three-day work week in Washington. This video also examines the role of congressional staff and the influence they have on elected officials.

The Price of Power: Money in Politics
Type: 1/2" videocassette (VHS format)
Length: 25 min.
Cost: $119

Date: 1993
Source: Insight Media
             2162 Broadway
             New York, NY 10024-6642

This video examines the relative levels of political participation of wealthy and ordinary citizens. It explores the financial resources that candidates need for media advertising and how this influences election results. The video also investigates the source of candidates' campaign funds and how money affects local and national campaigns.

The Rage for Democracy
Type: 1/2" videocassette (VHS format)
Length: 60 min.
Cost: $69.95
Date: 1992
Source: PBS Video
             Public Broadcasting Service
             1320 Braddock Place
             Alexandria, VA 22314-1698

Host Anthony Lewis of the *New York Times* presents four stories that test the ideal of democracy against the reality of everyday life and investigates the influence of race, income, and education on citizen activism.

Resurrecting Party Loyalty
Type: 1/2" videocassette (VHS)
Length: 30 min.
Cost: $89.95
Date: 1996
Source: Films for the Humanities and Sciences
             P.O. Box 2053
             Princeton, NJ 08543-2053

In an interview with James MacGregor Burns, Bill Moyers examines the importance of resurrecting party loyalty. Burns believes that the decline in party loyalty leads to excessive compromise and deadlock and also undermines leadership accountability.

So You Want to Buy a President?
Type: 1/2" videocassette (VHS format)
Length: 60 min.
Cost: $55.95
Date: 1996
Source: PBS Video
             Public Broadcasting Service
             1320 Braddock Place
             Alexandria, VA 22314-1698

Correspondent Robert Krulwich investigates campaign finance in presidential elections and finds that big donors have expectations of future influence associated with their campaign contributions.

A Third Choice
Type: 1/2" videocassette (VHS format)
Length: 60 min.
Cost: $75
Date: 1996
Source: PBS Video
             Public Broadcasting Service
             1320 Braddock Place
             Alexandria, VA 22314-1698

This video examines the role of third parties in shaping American politics and investigates the changing political landscape in light of independent candidates and our national experience with third parties.

Third Parties in American Politics
Type: 1/2" videocassette (VHS format)
Length: 26 min.
Cost: $89.95
Date: 1996
Source: PBS Video
             Public Broadcasting Service
             1320 Braddock Place
             Alexandria, VA 22314-1698

This program features several political experts discussing the pros and cons of a third party in the 1996 presidential contest.

Visions of America: Campaign Finance
Type: 1/2" videocassette (VHS format)
Length: 60 min.
Cost: ———
Date: 1994
Source: PBS Video
             Public Broadcasting Service
             1320 Braddock Place
             Alexandria, VA 22314-1698

Taped at the Hoover Institution, this video is part of a series on congressional accountability and reform. Panelists include Peter Robinson (host), L. Sandy Maisel (moderator), Herbert Alexander, Randy Huwa, Thomas Edsall, and Daniel Lowenstein. The panel members discuss what should be done about the financing of political campaigns, make specific proposals for reform, evaluate the prospects for real change, and identify the potential effects of reform on Congress.

Vote for Me: Politics in America
Type: 1/2" videocassette (VHS format)
Length: 4 hours
Cost: $395
Date: 1996
Source: Vote For Me, CNAM Film Library
             22-D Hollywood Avenue
             Hohokus, NJ 07423

This is a four-part video. "The King of Retail" provides a portrait of how effective person-to-person campaigning can still be in the media age, focusing on Providence mayor Buddy Cianci as a master of this technique. "The Terminator" features commentary on negative political advertising and the use of this technique in a state supreme court race in Alabama. Negative political advertising is defended and criticized but also placed in a historical context going back to the 1800 campaign between John Adams and Thomas Jefferson. "Change Partners and Dance" discusses the effect of changing ethnic coalitions on Chicago politics, from the rainbow coalition formed by Harold Washington to the white-ethnic/Mexican American alliance of Mayor Richard M. Daley. The last part in the series, "The Political Education of Maggie Lauterer," illuminates what it really takes to run for office in

America, following first-time candidate from North Carolina Maggie Lauterer as she makes her bid for Congress. It depicts candidates asking for money, developing 30-second sound bites, and coping with negative attacks on their character. These stories are mixed with commentary from Mario Cuomo, Lyn Nofziger, Newt Gingrich, and other politicians. The video includes interviews with citizens and footage that captures American politicians in unguarded moments.

Vote Fraud in the '96 GOP Primaries
Type: Audiocassette
Length: 30 min.
Cost: Free on request
Date: 1996
Source: Cincinnatus
P.O. Box 11339
Cincinnati, OH 45211

James Condit of Citizens for a Fair Vote Count is a guest on Tom Valentine's "Radio Free America" program, where he presents charges of vote fraud. Condit holds that it is the responsibility of election officials to demonstrate to the public that there is no vote fraud.

Who Owns Our Government?
Type: 1/2" videocassette (VHS format)
Length: 60 min.
Cost: $89.95
Date: 1992
Source: Films for the Humanities and Sciences
P.O. Box 2053
Princeton, NJ 28543-2053

Bill Moyers hosts this examination of the effect political campaign contributions have on public policy. The report traces the relationship between campaign contributions to key committee members in Congress and the subsequent savings and loan debacle, identifies a loophole in the campaign finance law that subverts public financing of presidential campaigns, and reveals how special interest monies from the health care industry undermined health care reform.

Women in American Politics
Type: 1/2" videocassette (VHS)
Length: 60 min.
Cost: $89.95
Date: 1996
Source: Films for the Humanities and Sciences
            P.O. Box 2053
            Princeton, NJ 28543-2053

Congresswoman Pat Schroeder, former Secretary of Labor Lynn Martin, Senator Carol Moseley Braun, and other female politicians describe their experiences in the male-dominated field of politics. They discuss the importance of women's participation in U.S. politics and the contributions women can make to the governing process.

CD-ROMs and Videodiscs

American Government CD-ROM
Publisher: Films for the Humanities and Sciences
Distributor: Films for the Humanities and Sciences
               P.O. Box 2053
               Princeton, NJ 28543-2053
Price: $149 (for Windows and Macintosh)

An overview of the textbook *American Government* (6th edition) by James Q. Wilson and John J. DiIulio, this CD-ROM provides video footage of presidential debates, campaign commercials, and other subjects relevant to campaigns and elections. It includes multiple choice and true-false self-test questions along with glossaries of key terms.

The Presidency and the Congress
Publisher: Films for the Humanities and Sciences
Distributor: Films for the Humanities and Sciences
               P.O. Box 2053
               Princeton, NJ 28543-2053
Price: $159

This videodisc uses live-action video, still images, and charts to promote a better introduction to American government. The videodisc includes a segment on electing the president.

Databases

These databases can yield considerable information relevant to campaign finance and electoral reform.

Federal Election Commission
Information Division
999 E Street NW
Washington, DC 20463
(800) 424-9530
(202) 219-3420

The FEC has online computer access to federal campaign finance records, a combined federal/state disclosure directory, a summary of campaign finance law at the state and federal levels, and many other sources.

Internet Resources

Campaign Finance Reform

Abolish All Campaign Finance
Internet addresses: http://www.spectacle.org/195/spec2.html
http://www.tagsys.com/Spectacle/spec2.html

This is an Internet index of proposals to abolish all campaign finance.

All Politics/CNN Time: Campaign Reform
Internet address: http://allpolitics.com/issues/in.focus/reform/

This site provides a description of the current system of campaign finance at the federal level, a summary of campaign finance reform proposals, explanations of key terminology, and related stories and links.

All Politics/CNN Time: Follow the Money
Internet address: http://allpolitics.com/1997/gen/analysis/
follow.money/

This site specializes in providing links to news stories related to money and politics, campaign fund-raising scandals, and reform proposals under consideration in Congress.

American Association of Retired Persons—Position on Campaign Finance Reform
Internet address: http://www/aarp.org/whatnew/vote/
campfinreform.html

The American Association of Retired Persons examines the stances of various 1996 presidential candidates on campaign finance reform, providing a voter's guide for its members on this issue.

American Prospect
Internet address: http://epn.org/prospect/20/20~cnt.html

"Who Killed Campaign Finance Reform?" by Joan Claybrook and Ellen Miller (in *The American Prospect* 20 [Winter 1995], 16–19) can be found at this site.

Americans against Political Corruption
Internet address: http://www.essential.org/aapc/

The Americans against Political Corruption (AAPC) Web page represents this interest group's position on campaign finance reform. They provide their platform, stories, and quotes about money in politics, and an op-ed column.

The Association of Community Organizations for Reform
Internet address: http://www.acorn.org/community/

The Association of Community Organizations for Reform (ACORN) Web page explains the purpose of the organization, how to join, and what its members hope to accomplish. The group is affiliated with Americans against Political Corruption.

Brookings Working Group on Campaign Finance Reform
Internet address: http://www.brook.edu/gs/campaign/
home.htm

The Brookings Working Group on Campaign Finance Reform provides a lively discussion through several forums on how to improve the campaign finance reform debate and how to increase the likelihood of realistic, workable reform. It provides discussions of the implications of proposed reforms, their costs and benefits, and possible unintended consequences. The forums are moderated by Tom Mann of the Brookings Institution.

California Campaign Finance Reform Page
Internet address: http://www.cgl.ucsf.edui/sacs_home/cpr/

This Web site explains why the group's members believe campaign finance reform is necessary. This site is linked to United We Stand America. Direct e-mail questions to: mdgunn@itsa.ucsf.edu.

**Campaign Finance Reform Activist Theatre and
Town Hall Forum**
Internet address: http://www.amherst.edu/amherst/groups/
democrat/finance.html

This is an interactive presentation illustrating the role of money in today's electoral politics.

Campaign Finance Reform Alert
Internet address: http://www.2.eff.org/pub/Activism/
Cong_reform/campaign_finance_reform

Campaign Finance Reform Alert provides updates on congressional action related to campaign reform initiatives.

Campaign Finance Reform: Let the People Do the Talking
Internet address: http://www.newstalk.com/gpp/
edmonds.html

Thomas N. Edmonds, a Republican media consultant, argues that proposed campaign finance reforms would hinder free speech and therefore are unacceptable.

Campaign Finance Reform in Wisconsin
Internet address: http://www.execpc.com/~jlohman/

This site examines the role of money in politics and investigates reform proposals for Wisconsin and at the national level. It is also linked to United We Stand America.

Campaign for the Bipartisan Clean Congress Act
Internet address: http://www.emf.net/~cr/govreform/
claybrook-cfr

This Web site offers a discussion of the Bipartisan Clean Congress Act proposed by Public Citizen, a public interest group.

Campaign Reform—All Politics
Internet addresses: http://allpolitics.com/issues/in.focus/
reform/
http://allpolitics.com/issues/
counterpt/9611/25/

The first Web site provides an analysis of campaign reform. It examines the current system as well as reform proposals and provides key terms and related stories and links. The second Web site provides a point-counterpoint format, debating the desirability of limits on campaign spending.

Center for a New Democracy
Internet address: http://www.essential.org/orgs/CND/

The Center for a New Democracy, a nonprofit, tax-exempt group, offers facts on state campaign finance reforms as well as some publications and a newsletter.

The Center for Public Integrity
Internet address: http://www.essential.org/cpi/cpi.html

The Center for Public Integrity examines the 1996 presidential candidates and their campaign advisers. The CPI is especially concerned about the role of money in American politics. It offers data on campaign finance that can be downloaded.

Center for Voting and Democracy
Internet address: http://www.igc.apc.org/cvd/

The Center for Voting and Democracy is a nonprofit educational organization based in Washington, D.C. Its aim is to educate the public about the impact of voting systems on political representation, proportional representation, voter turnout, and the influence of money in elections.

Charlotte's Web Campaign Finance Reform Issues
Internet address: http://www/emf.net/~cr/finance.html

Providing many other electoral and campaign finance reform Web sites, this Web page alerts readers to campaign finance proposals, roll call votes in Congress that deal with campaign finance reform, full texts of legislation, and listings of related articles.

Citizen's Toolbox: Campaign Finance Reform
Internet address: http://www.usnews.com/usnews/wash/8camhigh.htm

At this site, U.S. News Online provides a databank and links to stories published in *U.S. News and World Report* on campaign finance.

Clean Elections, How to
Internet address: http://epn.org/prospect/30/f30mill.html

"Clean Elections, How to" is an article by Ellen S. Miller appearing in *The American Prospect* (January-February 1997). It provides an analysis of campaign finance reform proposals and links to related resources.

Committee on House Oversight
Internet address: http://www.house.gove/cho/welcome.htm

The Committee on House Oversight (the CHO Web site) furnishes access to publications on campaign finance reform hearings in 1995 and 1996.

**Common Cause Action Alert on Campaign
Finance Reform Legislation**

Internet address: http://www.tiac.net/users/~comcause/
alerts/h2566m.htm

This is Common Cause of Massachusetts's Web page, which focuses on legislative proposals to reform campaign finance procedures.

Common Cause's Issue Position on Campaign Finance Reform
Internet address: http://www.ccsi.com/~comcause/position/
pp_cfr.html

This is Common Cause of Texas's Web page, which provides information on campaign finance reform proposals.

Community News Project
Internet address: http://www.mcs.net/~commnews/
campaign.html

This Web site, sponsored by the Community News Project in Chicago, supplies information about campaign finance reform efforts under way at the state level.

Congressional Accountability Project (CAP)
Internet address: http://www.essential.org/orgs/CAP/
CAP.html

While focusing on congressional reforms, the CAP also examines campaign finance reform.

Congressional Voting Record Sampler
Internet address: http://www.vote-smart.org/congress/votes/

This site, affiliated with Project Vote Smart, provides the voting records of all members of the 104th Congress. Campaign finance reform is one of the issues that they include in their database.

Contract with America: Campaign Finance
Internet address: http://www.telusys.com:/contract/cf.html

This Web site presents proposals from the Republican party's Contract with America regarding electoral and campaign finance reform.

Cornell Law School's Legal Information Institute
Internet address: http://www.law.cornell.edu/syllabi?
campaign+finance

Cornell Law School's Legal Information Institute supplies a means to search for relevant U.S. Supreme Court rulings on campaign finance.

C-SPAN Online
Internet address: http://www.c-span.org/

This C-SPAN Web site offers access to C-SPAN and C-SPAN2 (both online and live audio). Its archives allow surfers to seek congressional debates on campaign finance reform and other electoral reform issues. It also provides access to the *Washington Journal*.

Current Laws for Campaign Finance
Internet address: http://ksgwww.harvard.edu/
third-party/fec.html

This site furnishes a description of current federal regulations on campaign finance and their effects.

Democracy Direct
Internet address: http://www.well.com/user/kr2/carl5.html

This government reform Web site calls for more direct citizen involvement in various political issues including campaign and electoral reform.

Election Law and Campaign Finance
Internet address: http://www.usia.gov/elects/fecpage.htm

This site provides access to documents with information on U.S. election law, fund-raising regulations, and campaign finance laws.

Election Sites across the Web
Internet address: http://www.pan.ci.seattle.wa.us/SEATTLE/
ETHICS/DISCLOS.HTM

This site supplies campaign finance and disclosure information from the states of Washington, Indiana, Florida, Alabama, Texas, and New Mexico.

FECInfo
Internet address: http://www.tray.com/fecinfo/

FECInfo supplies such information as the Federal Election Commission's data on PACs and contributions to candidates.

Federal Campaign Finance Menu: Florida
Internet address: http://members.gnn.com/users561582/ money/flhouse.htm

This Web page offers information on Florida's top contributors as well as financial summaries of Florida's delegation to the U.S. House of Representatives. It also has information on fund-raising activities by presidential candidates.

Frontline
Internet address: http://www.pbs.org/wgbh/pages/ frontline/president/

At this Web site there is a transcript of "So You Want to Buy a President," which aired on January 30, 1996. There is also a citizen guide with selected links and readings on campaign finance reform.

Government Expenses—Campaign Finance
Internet address: http://pathfinder.com/ @@q3ycTAUAx4e4hcju/reinventing/game2/ brfwl4tsl.html

Pathfinder provides a briefing on campaign finance and lists other sites that address campaign finance reform.

Grabbing Government's Gonads (Part I)
Internet address: http://www.boardwatch.com/mag/95/jul/ bwn54.htm

Columnist Jim Warren argues for local, state, and federal public disclosure of campaign income and expenditure data; of the personal economic interests of elected officials, incumbents, and senior officials; and of the registration of paid lobbyists and information on their activities.

Heritage Foundation Commentary on Campaign Finance
Internet address: http://www.townhall.com/heritage/
                       commentary/op-cc1.html

This is the Heritage Foundation's Web site, which contains commentary on campaign finance reform.

Hollywood Women's Political Committee
Internet address: http://www.hwpc.org/hwpc/look.html

The Web page for the Hollywood Women's Political Committee expresses the organization's political principles and candidate endorsements. The members support campaign finance reform and take stands on a variety of other issues.

Illinois Issues: Campaign Finance Reform Project
Internet address: http://www.uis.eud/~blee/cfp.html

At this Web site the Illinois Campaign Finance Reform Project is discussed as printed in the pages of *Illinois Issues,* the state's leading public affairs magazine.

Issue of the Week: Campaign Finance Reform
Internet address: http://policy.com/issuewk/
                       issuewk-111196.html

The policy.com Web site sponsors a weekly policy issue. On November 11, 1996, campaign finance reform became its focus. The analysis of campaign finance reform at this site is excellent, providing statistical information, public opinion polls on campaign finance, reform proposals, reports on activities at the state level, and links to other sources of information.

Just Because It's Called "Reform" Doesn't Mean It's Progress
Internet address: http://www.lead-inst.org/townhall/
                       columnists/

Written by Bruce Chapman of the Seattle-based Discovery Institute, this Web page argues that campaign finance reform might make matters worse, not better, by increasing the power of rich candidates and special interests while diminishing free speech.

League of Women Voters
Internet address: http://www.lwv.org/~lwvus/doing.html

This site explains what the League of Women Voters is doing to encourage campaign finance reform.

LEXIS-NEXIS—Election '96
Internet address: http://www.lexis-nexis.com/election96/

LEXIS-NEXIS provides online election information and includes such materials as federal and state campaign finance reports, congressional voting records and member background information, federal and state campaign news, debate and television transcripts, and a 24-hour Associated Press election day database covering congressional, gubernatorial, and local elections.

Mother Jones: MOJOWIRE
Internet address: http://www.mojones.com/

This Web site offers articles on campaign finance from the magazine *Mother Jones.*

National Public Radio (NPR)
Internet addresses: http://majorca.npr.org/hotnews/cf.html
http://majorca.npr.org/news/election96/cf.html

NPR's stories on campaign finance reform are compiled at these two Web sites.

National Resource Center for State and Local Campaign Finance Reform
Internet address: http://uwsa.com/uswa/issues/cfr/memoparty.html

This Web page, sponsored by the Center for Governmental Studies Project, examines the effects of the California Reform Initiative on political party organizations.

The Need for Campaign Finance Reform
Internet address: http://www.cnotes.com/telecom/pacs.html

At this Web site, Common Cause offers a brief explanation of campaign finance reform and why it is necessary.

The New Party
Internet address: http://www.newparty.org/

This is the Web site for the New party, which identifies itself as a progressive political party. Its stated goal is to break the stranglehold that corporate money and media have over the political process. It supports a living wage and campaign finance reform initiatives.

New Wave Campaign Finance Reform
Internet address: http://222.emf.net/~cr/govreform/
crp-on-cfr

This "new wave" site supplies information on the need for campaign finance reform in the states and offers a message from Ellen S. Miller, a representative of the Center for Responsive Politics.

New York State Board of Elections
Internet address: http://www.crisny.org/government/ny/
nysboe/index.html

The New York State Board of Elections furnishes voter information and campaign finance regulations.

North Carolina Alliance for Democracy
Internet address: http://www.rtpnet.org/~alliance/

This site provides information on the North Carolina Alliance for Democracy (NCAD) and on legislators and other public officials, as well as on candidates running for elective office in North Carolina. It presents options for reform and supports the Carolina Campaign for Fair Elections.

ONLINE FORUM—PBS NewsHour
Internet address: http://www1.pbs.org/newshour/forum/
june96/reform1.html

This forum from PBS's *NewsHour with Jim Lehrer* offers a discussion of the history of campaign finance. It includes a symposium on the power of PACs and the experience other countries have had with campaign finance reform.

Politics Now-Issues-Campaign Reform
Internet address: http://www.politicsnow.com/issues/creform/

This Web site examines campaign and electoral reforms, including campaign finance reform and term limits. The option of free television time is discussed in light of the presidential and congressional elections of 1996.

Proposition 212
Internet address: http://www.best.com.%7Emyk/fedup/text/

This CalPIRG site serves as an archive of information on Proposition 212, California's 1996 campaign finance reform initiative.

Public Broadcasting System (PBS) NewsHour: "Money Talks"
Internet address: http://www1.pbs/newshour/bb/election/president_money_2-12.html

"Money Talks" aired on PBS's *NewsHour with Jim Lehrer* (February 12, 1996). A panel of presidential historians look back on how the need to raise large amounts of money influences the political process. This site provides a full transcript of the interviews. Jim Lehrer talks with Doris Kearns Goodwin, Haynes Johnson, Michael Beschloss, and David Mason.

Public Broadcasting System (PBS) NewsHour: Shields and Gigot
Internet address: http://www1.pbs.org/newshour/shield&gigot/political_wrap.html

This Web page offers a discussion of the influence that money and fund-raising have on the political process ("Under the Influence," aired on PBS's *NewsHour with Jim Lehrer,* August 30, 1996). Another segment is devoted to reasons for the failure of campaign finance reform ("The Wreck in Politics," aired on PBS's *NewsHour with Jim Lehrer,* June 28, 1996).

Public Citizen
Internet address: http://www.citizen.org/

Founded by Ralph Nader in 1971, Public Citizen, a consumer and government watchdog organization, provides access to information about its activities. Congress Watch, an arm of the organization, exposes campaign finance abuses and seeks to bring the democratic process back to the people.

Public Interest Research Groups (PIRGs)
Internet address: http://www.pirg.org/pirg/

An index of state Public Interest Research Groups (PIRGs) as well as information on the national Public Interest Research Group is provided. This site makes available recommendations for taking back government from special interests through campaign finance and electoral reform.

San Francisco Online Voter Guide
Internet address: http://sf95.election.digital.com/

The San Francisco Online Voter Guide furnishes information on candidates and propositions as well as campaign finance data.

U.S. News and World Report
Internet address: http://agtnet.com/usnews/issue/
                      buxmore.htm

The *U.S. News and World Report* site offers access to campaign finance reform articles and links to other reform sites.

Vote Smart Web/Project Vote Smart
Internet address: http://www.vote-smart.org/

With extensive information on candidates and campaigns, this online political news source is very useful. It provides research and data, including campaign finance information on congressional candidates, and examines a variety of issues related to campaign finance reform.

White House Publications
Internet address: gopher://info.tamu.edu:70/77/.dir/
                      president.dir/.index/pres95?campaignfinance

Texas A&M supplies online speech texts, press briefings, and other White House publications dealing with campaign finance reform.

Wisconsin Campaign Reform
Internet address: http://www.execpc.com/~jlohman/
                     difts.html

This site discusses campaign reform efforts in Wisconsin.

Electoral Reform

Approaches to Electoral Reform
Internet addresses: http://www.constitution.org/
                     http://www.constitution.org/cs_elect.htm
                     http://www.constitution.org/elect000.htm

From the home page of the Constitution Society, these Internet addresses offer proposals for public funding of elections, abolition of winner-take-all elections, opening the two-party system, and increasing party competition. The society wishes to make information on candidates more accessible via the Internet and World Wide Web.

Campaign Central
Internet address: http://www.clark.net/ccentral/

Campaign Central (sponsored by the Accountability Group [TAG]) provides information on political parties, issues, and campaigns.

Campaign '96
Internet address: http://campaign.96.com/

Providing a comprehensive guide to presidential and congressional campaigns on a state-by-state basis, this is a valuable resource. There is also online public opinion polling and a chat room.

Center for Voting and Democracy
Internet address: http://www.igc.apc.org/cvd/

The Center for Voting and Democracy is a nonprofit educational organization based in Washington, D.C. Its aim is to educate the public about the impact of representation systems including proportional representation, voter turnout, and the use of campaign money in elections.

Congressional Research Service Documents on Elections
Internet address: http://www.clark.net/pub/pennyhill/
                      election.html

For a comprehensive listing of Congressional Research Service documents on elections dealing with campaign finance reform, reapportionment, presidential primaries, and the nominating process, consult this site constructed by Penny Hill Press. Titles and order numbers are provided.

Democracy and Electoral Reform
Internet address: http://www.greens.org/california/
                      pl_democ.html

Sponsored by the Green party, this Web site reviews electoral reform efforts in California (including the initiative, referendum, and recall) and the need for campaign finance reform.

Electoral Reform Newsgroup
E-mail address: majordomo@igc.apc.org

For those who would like to join in a newsgroup discussion of electoral reform issues, this e-mail address offers an opportunity for exchange of ideas.

Grolier Online: The American Presidency
Internet address: http://www.grolier.com/presidents/ea/
                      side/elecollg.html

Grolier Online supplies in-depth information on the electoral college, its operation, and its historical development. This site also issues reform proposals and suggests readings.

New Democracy's List of Election Reforms
Internet address: http://www.mich.com/~donald/
                      reassign.html

This Web site offers reasons for eliminating single-seat districts and at-large pluralities and discusses other electoral reforms.

1996 Presidential Campaign in the U.S.
Internet address: http://www.lsu.edu/guests/poli/
                            public_html/1996camp.html

This link provides several Web sites as well as 1996 election materials including public opinion polls, information on the candidates, the operation of the electoral college, and campaign finance.

The 1996 Presidential Election
Internet address: http://www.trinity.edu:80/~mkearl/
                            electn96.html

This Web site furnishes a spectrum of other Web linkages for readers, including sites that deal with past elections, voting behavior, opinion polling, political party headquarters, congressional records, and state electoral campaigns.

The Pew Research Center: For the People and the Press
Internet address: http://www.people-press.orf/postrpt.htm

The Pew Research Center conducts surveys of public opinion on campaigns and elections. The Web site offers access to their findings.

Proportional Representation
Internet address: http://www.ziplink.net:80/~ewl/
                            proprep.html

As the title suggests, this site advocates proportional voting systems as a means for building a stronger democracy. Links to other sites that advocate proportional representation are also provided.

**Proportional Representation vs. Single-Member
Districts in the States**
Internet address: http://www.mtholyoke.edu:80/acad/polit/
                            damy/lijphart.htm

Arend Lijphart, a prominent political scientist, addresses the California State Legislature, which is holding hearings on a proposal to amend the state constitution. Lijphart testifies that adding a provision to elect legislators by proportional representation would greatly improve the system.

Real Choices/New Voices
Internet address: http://www.mtholyoke.edu/acad/polit/
damy/bookhtml.htm

Offering excerpts from the book *Real Choices/New Voices: The Case for Proportional Elections in the U.S.*, Douglas J. Amy presents the case for proportional representation.

Reform Party
Internet address: http://www.reformparty.org/

This official Web site of the Reform party, founded by Ross Perot, discusses its electoral reform initiatives and supplies a listing of news releases about the organization's activities.

Ten Election Reforms According to New Democracy
Internet address: http://www.mich.com:80/~donald/
reassign.html

Donald Eric Davison has assembled a list of New Democracy's ten election reforms. The more prominent reforms include outlawing single-member districts, reforming the electoral college, and instituting preference voting. Each suggested reform is described and analyzed.

We the People: Platform in Progress
Internet address: http://www.wtp.org/pip-toc.html

Containing planks on political reform, We the People seeks broad, sweeping changes in American political practices.

Political Participation

American Voter Coalition
Internet address: http://www.avc.org/

The American Voter Coalition (AVC) home page is devoted to voter education and registration. The AVC is a nonprofit, nonpartisan organization that advocates ending negative campaign advertisements, establishing a National Voter Registration Day, posting positions of candidates for public office in post offices, and establishing online voter registration and databases with election news and statistics.

Campaign Central
Internet address: http://www.clark.net/ccentral/

For news and facts on elections, Campaign Central (sponsored by the Accountability Group [TAG]) provides information on political parties, issues, and campaigns.

Campaign '96
Internet address: http://campaign.96.com/

As a comprehensive guide to presidential and congressional campaigns on a state-by-state basis, this is a valuable resource. There is also online public opinion polling and a chat room.

Center for Living Democracy
Internet address: http://www.irsociety.com/dodem4.htm

The Center for Living Democracy Web site seeks to encourage everyday citizens to become involved in solving America's toughest problems. They create and disseminate information on effective democratic action and offer workshops and seminars on creating an effective, democratic culture.

Center for National Policy by Strategic Frameworking, Inc.
Internet address: http://www/access.digex.net/~cnp/ voterd.html

In this article on "Diagnosing Voter Discontent," the Center for National Policy explores reasons for increased voter discontent and cynicism and examines ways to improve the political dialogue for more meaningful elections. This Web site has a general Elections '96 click-on.

Civic Participation Page
Internet address: http://epn.org/idea/civic.html

This site provides linkages to other Web sites that deal with reforming the electoral process. It also provides reports on state experimentation with ways to make the democratic system more effective and participatory.

Community Networking and Political Participation
Internet address: http://ezinfo.ucs.indiana.edu/~kgregson/
teledemocracy.html

This home page contains online print resources on community networks and ways they can be used to increase political participation.

Democracy Network
Internet address: http://www.democracynet.org/

This futuristic interactive political Web site allows net surfers to discuss politics online and to post their views on bulletin boards. It is a national system of political participation on which candidates upload and update their issue positions.

Democracy Place USA
Internet address: http://soundprint.org/~democracy/

This site provides a forum for civic journalism and citizen participation in public policy debates.

Democratic Leadership Council and Progressive
Policy Institute
Internet address: http://www.dlcppi.org/

This site covers a host of issues including explanations of voting behavior (for instance, the gender gap) and the impact of redistricting and other electoral reforms.

EMILY's List
Internet address: http://www.emilyslist.org/home.htm

EMILY's List compiles facts about the role women voters play in the electoral process and also supports women candidates for political office. This site provides information on their activities.

GOPAC
Internet address: http://gopac.com/

GOPAC, a Republican organization that recruits conservative Republican candidates and offers them training in effective campaign tactics, is online at this site. Currently GOPAC is under investigation for questionable campaign practices.

Government by the People
Internet address: http://www.vote.org/

This Web site, formerly the Voting by Phone Foundation, advocates voting by phone or Internet in regular elections, encourages more citizen initiated legislation, and supports numerous other reforms.

International Association of Public Participation Practitioners
Internet address: http/www.pin.org/iap2.htm

The International Association of Public Participation Practitioners, established in 1990, is a nonprofit corporation dedicated to serving political activists around the world who wish to conduct public involvement programs.

The National Committee for an Effective Congress
Internet address: http://www.ncec.org/

The National Committee for an Effective Congress seeks to pool the resources of small contributors around the country and use those funds to elect progressive U.S. House and Senate candidates.

Neighborhoods Online: National
Internet address: http://libertynet.org/community/phila/
natl.html

As part of a joint project of the Institute for the Study of Civic Values and LibertyNet, Neighborhoods Online is aimed at helping neighborhood activists and organizations gain information and resources for community problem solving.

NetAction
Internet address: http://www.netaction.org/

The mission of NetAction, a national, nonprofit organization, is to promote effective grassroots citizen action by building coalitions that link online activists to grassroots organizations, offering training in organizational skills and strategies to online activists, and educating the public and policy makers about technology-based social and political issues.

New Politics: The Non-Partisan U.S. Political Participation Resource
Internet address: http://www.newpolitics.com/

New Politics is a successor to Countdown '96 and seeks to assist in and encourage participation in the American political process. This site provides linkages to information sources, including polls, think tanks, election results, and campaign finance Web sites for national, state, and local organizations that are interested in sponsoring greater participation.

Oregon's Vote by Mail Program
Internet address: http://www.sos.state.or.us/executive/ vbmq&ac.htm

This site allows an exploration of the all-mail-ballot idea and welcomes questions about the process.

Project Democracy
Internet address: http://www.pin.org.projdemo.htm

Created in 1992, Project Democracy was established by the National Association of Secretaries of State to identify ways to reconnect citizens and the political process. The organization identifies promising ways to involve people and disseminates lessons and insights about the political process.

Reasons for an Open Primary
Internet address: http://www.prop198.org./reasons.html

As implied by its Internet address and title, this site examines Proposition 198 and the reasons why there should be open primaries.

Report of the Growe Commission on Electoral Reform
Internet address: http://wwwstate.ma.us/ebranch.sos/ growerpt.html

Seventeen citizens, convened by Minnesota's secretary of state, met to suggest ways to open up political participation in Minnesota. The results of their inquiry are reported on this Web site.

Scampaign '96
Internet address: http://www.comedyusa.com/home.html

This site provides a satirical look at presidential candidates and provides humorous insight into American politics. It gives Web site visitors an opportunity to vote for the politician most skilled at lying to the American public.

Votelink Home Page
Internet address: http://www.votelink.com/

This home page allows free online voting and forums for discussing world and political events.

Voter Participation
Internet address: http://Policy.com/issuewk/
issuewk-102896.html

Analysis offered by the Policy.com Web site is insightful and provides linkages to reports and statistics on voter participation, including voting reform measures, voters' guides, and other resources.

The Women's Campaign School
Internet address: http://www.yale.edu/wcsyale/index.html

Based at Yale University, the Women's Campaign School, sponsored by Yale Law School and the women's studies program, educates women in political campaign skills and strategies.

Youth Vote Project
Internet address: http://www.tedmondale.org/yvproject.html

The Youth Vote Project site offers findings from an instant audience reaction polling technique and focus groups, which are used to gauge why younger voters are turning away from political parties and to determine what issues are of importance to them.

Racial Gerrymandering and Redistricting

Breaking News: Gerrymandering
Internet address: http://www.usnews.com/usnews/news/
gerrym.htm

This site provides Associated Press news reports on redistricting.

California Reapportionment and Redistricting
Internet address: http://orpheus.ucsd.edu/av/FVL/catalog/
california_reapportionment_and_
redistricting.html

This site describes a VHS tape of California reapportionment and redistricting.

Citizens Guide to the U.S. Constitution
Internet address: http://www.world.std.com/~weezer/co/
coixsu26.html

This Web site furnishes annotated analyses of the U.S. Constitution regarding gerrymandering and reapportionment issues.

Common Cause Issue: Reapportionment and Redistricting
Internet address: http://www.ccsi.com/~comcause/position/
pp_rr.html

Common Cause supports the establishment of an independent Redistricting Commission to draw congressional and state legislative districts. Rationales for this proposal are presented in this Web site.

Disenfranchisement of Minority Vote
Internet address: http://www.afrinet.net:8080/~hallh/
afrotalk/afrojun95/1122.html

This Web site is a message line for those interested in redistricting, gerrymandering, and U.S. Supreme Court decisions that challenge majority-minority districts.

Legal Information Institute and Project Hermes
Internet address: http://supct.law.cornell.edu:80/supct/html

This site provides access to redistricting, reapportionment, and gerrymandering decisions issued by the U.S. Supreme Court. Syllabi of cases are also available along with dissenting, concurring, and majority opinions.

Problems with Political Redistricting
Internet address: http://www.geog.buffalo.edu:80/ucgis/
UTopic_redistrict.html

Based at the University of Buffalo, this site examines redistricting issues and discusses the way in which new computational tools and specialized software may facilitate more equitable drawing of electoral districts.

Race and Redistricting: A Recent History
Internet address: http://www.politicsnow/news/June96/17/
pn0617line/

This site provides a chronology of events since 1965 concerning the race and redistricting controversy.

Redistricting Rulings
Internet address: http://www.nando.net/insider/redistrict/
redistrict.html

Offered through "The Insider: N.C. State Government News Service," this site offers a summary of recent U.S. Supreme Court rulings on redistricting—with majority, plurality, concurring, and dissenting opinions for each case.

Supreme Court Alert
Internet addresses: http://www.ncsl.org/programs/legman/
elect/elecrpt.htm
http://www.law.cornell.edu/supct/
supct.june.1996.html

Sponsored by the National Conference of State Legislatures, the Supreme Court Alert sites examine redistricting case law since the 1965 Voting Rights Act.

TMG's Voter Redistricting Projects
Internet address: http://www.gnofn.org/~mumphrey/
vot2.htm

The Mumphrey Group, which engages in redistricting consulting, maintains this home page.

The Virtual Realist
Internet address: http://www.gwarbco.com:80/vrealist/
                       issue02.html

This Web site provides access to articles that address congressional reform and explores in particular whether congressional district reform is desirable.

Term Limits

All Politics/CNN Time: Counterpoint
Internet address: http://allpolitics.com/1997/02/11/
                       counterpoint/jacob.html

Counterpoint on the All Politics/CNN Time Web site presents a point-counterpoint discussion of term limits between Paul Jacob (who supports term limits) and Representative Henry Hyde (who opposes term limits).

Americans for Term Limits
Internet address: http://www.termlimits.org/ustl.shtml

The Americans for Term Limits home page offers access to research, public opinion, and legal issues surrounding term limits.

Congressional Votes on Term Limits
Internet address: http://www.pathfinder.com/
                       @@OgBjuwYA7d0toD3b/cgi-bin/
                       congress-votes

This Web site allows readers to discover how members of Congress voted on term limits.

Term Limits Home Page
Internet address: http://www.termlimits.org/

This home page explores congressional and state term limit efforts and recommends amending the U.S. Constitution to accommodate term limits for members of Congress. It provides a list of advocacy organizations affiliated with the term limit movement at the state and national levels plus editorials on term limits.

Term Limits Leadership Council
Internet Address: http://www.termlimits.org/
                       tllc.shtml

Sponsored by the Chair of the Term Limits Leadership Council, Scott W. Rasmussen, this site allows readers to offer their opinions on term limits.

Glossary

absentee ballot   See **absentee voting.**

absentee voting   A system that allows qualified voters to cast their votes without going to the polls on election day. If voters anticipate that they will be unable to cast their ballots at the polls on election day, they may obtain a ballot within a specified time period leading up to the election, mark it, have it notarized or witnessed, and return the sealed ballot to the proper authority. State laws or provisions in state constitutions enable this practice. First used during the Civil War to allow Union troops to vote, such provisions also allow American citizens residing overseas to vote.

add-on voting   See **cumulative voting.**

advisory primary   A primary that is nonbinding and merely registers voter preferences.

affirmative gerrymandering   This variation of gerrymandering involves the drawing of district lines to help a minority group candidate consolidate minority votes to win representation. See also **gerrymandering.**

alienation   Results when individuals experience a sense of helplessness when confronted with the political process, believing that their votes do not count or that their government is not responsive to their needs. Distrust, cynicism, or outright rejection of the political system are associated with alienation.

all-mail-ballot election   A system in which registered voters in a voting jurisdiction receive a ballot through the mail instead of going to a polling place on election day. Voters then return the completed ballot by mail or drop it off at a designated site before a specified date. Most often used in nonpartisan and referendum voting, some states, most notably Oregon, use mailed ballots to elect public officials in partisan elections.

apportionment   The allocation of seats in state legislatures, Congress, and other representative bodies. District lines are drawn so as to provide roughly equal representation to all citizens.

approval voting   An electoral process in which voters can vote for (approve of) as many of the candidates as they desire but cannot cast more than one vote for each candidate. Voters do not rank candidates, and the candidate with the greatest number of votes wins. This system has been rarely used.

at-large election   An election in which one or more candidates for a representative body are chosen by all of the voters in a jurisdiction (a large geographical area) rather than from smaller subdivisions or districts. Voters select several candidates to represent them rather than only one. While proponents of this system claim that representatives elected tend to serve the interests of the whole community, some argue that at-large elections disadvantage minority candidates and hence fail to represent minority interests adequately.

Australian ballot   A secret ballot which is printed, distributed, and tabulated by government officials. This reform, which replaced party ballots and oral voting, was instituted in the United States to protect voters from coercion at the polls.

ballot box stuffing   Fraudulent practice in which corrupt election officials mark ballots illegally and place them in ballot boxes in order to assist a favored candidate or political party.

ballot propositions   Issues placed on the ballot for a vote during a primary or general election.

beauty contest primary   A type of primary that occurs during the presidential primary election season in which voters register their preference for a favored candidate in party primaries, caucuses, or state conventions without selecting delegates to the national nominating convention.

blanket primary   Sometimes called a wide-open primary, this is a system of nomination that allows voters, regardless of their party label, to participate in nominating candidates from more than one party. Participants are limited only in that they may not vote for more than one candidate for the same office.

Buckley v. Valeo **424 U.S. 1 (1976)**   In this case, the U.S. Supreme Court upheld the constitutionality of the Federal Election Campaign Act but disallowed provisions that would have limited campaign spending and resources a candidate could devote to his or her campaign. The Court held that such provisions violated the First Amendment, stating that government cannot have ultimate power over campaign spending because an individual's financial resources can be an important ingredient in promoting political views. People must retain ultimate control over the quantity and scope of political debate.

bullet voting   A voting strategy likely to occur when there are several seats open for the same office, such as city council or board of education, and voters have multiple votes. A group of people engage in bullet voting when they cast all or most of their votes for a favored candidate, thus increasing the probability that this person will be elected. A minority party or group has a greater chance of winning representation under a system that allows bullet voting. See also **cumulative voting.**

bundling   Combining several small donations into one large contribution. Federal law prohibits individuals from giving more than $1,000 to a presidential or congressional candidate per election. To circumvent this limit, fund-raisers use "bundling." Several $1,000-maximum contributions are solicited from, for instance, a corporation's executives and their families, and the checks are sent together to a candidate. While no one has given more than the law allows, a significant amount of money has in fact come from one source.

canvassing board   A state or local government unit that receives vote counts from election precincts, tabulates the votes, and certifies winners.

cemetery vote   Occurs when people who reside in the local cemetery appear to rise from the dead long enough to vote. This form of vote fraud is possible because voter registration lists are not adequately monitored and therefore the names of individuals who have died are not purged from the voting rolls.

checkoff   See **IRS checkoff.**

civic duty   The responsibility of citizens to vote. Those with higher socioeconomic status tend to have a greater sense of civic duty, thus helping explain their higher voter turnout rates relative to the less well-to-do.

closed primary   A primary in which voters must declare their party affiliation and vote on that party's primary ballot only.

compulsory union dues   Assessments on members of labor organizations that must be paid in order to maintain membership and possibly employment. As a part of campaign finance reform in the 1990s, some seek to prohibit unions from spending workers' required dues on political activities. They argue that union leaders may contribute workers' resources to candidates that the rank-and-file members do not support.

compulsory voting   The practice of legally requiring eligible voters to cast a ballot on election day. In the United States this practice was held unconstitutional in a 1939 U.S. Supreme Court decision, *Lane v. Wilson,* which stated that penalties for not voting are invalid and in violation of the Fifteenth Amendment. However, other countries have instituted systems of compulsory voting.

concentration gerrymandering   The grouping together of identifiable populations in one or a few "safe" districts so that these seats are won by huge margins. This tactic can be a way of limiting the influence of a particular political or racial group and is also used to protect incumbents.

conflict of interest   A situation in which the personal or financial interests of officeholders influence or is likely to affect their public-policy decisions. A suggested campaign reform proposal would require candidates to reveal any conflict between personal interests and the performance of public duties.

congressional and senatorial campaign committees   Committees established by members of the two major political parties in Congress to raise money for congressional and senatorial campaigns. They may also establish linkages with efforts sponsored by the state and local committees of their respective parties.

constitutional initiative   A type of initiative that presents proposals aimed at amending a state constitution. In states that have enacted this provision, citizens rather than state legislators propose by petition and ratify by election any amendments to the state constitution.

contested election   An election in which more than one candidate for the office claims to have won. This may lead to a recount or, if left unresolved, the dispute could be decided in court.

contribution limits   At the federal level, the Federal Election Campaign Act has set limits on contributions to candidates for federal office. For example, an individual can give a candidate a maximum of $1,000 during the primary season and another $1,000 for the general election. Political action committees may give no more than $5,000 for the primaries and another $5,000 for the general election. Corporations, labor unions, and foreign nationals may not contribute at all. There are a number of loopholes, however, that make it possible to give far more than these prescribed limits.

Corrupt Practices Acts   Federal legislation, beginning with the Federal Corrupt Practices Act of 1925, that seeks to regulate sources of campaign contributions and expenditures in federal elections. These measures include the Political Activities Act of 1939, the Federal Election Campaign Acts of 1972 and 1974, and the 1971 Revenue Act.

corruption Unlawful or unethical behavior in campaigning, the conduct of elections, or governing once in office. It may also refer to the unauthorized use of public office for private benefit.

cracking See **dispersal gerrymandering.**

critical election An election that indicates a long-term shift in partisan identification among the electorate and results in the ascendancy of a new political majority at the state and national levels. V. O. Key in "A Theory of Critical Elections" proposed this concept.

cross filing A practice, allowed in some states, that permits a candidate to file for elective office in the primary elections of more than one political party.

crossover voting A practice in open primaries in which voters cast a vote for a candidate of the opposition party with which they are not normally affiliated in order to help that party's weakest candidate gain the nomination or to support the least objectionable candidate. Some crossover voters sincerely support a favored candidate who happens to belong to another party.

cumulative voting A voting system in which voters cast more than one vote in the simultaneous election of several candidates for political office. Each individual can give two or more votes to a single candidate or may distribute them among several. This voting procedure may be used to obtain greater representation for third parties or for minority groups. See also **bullet voting.**

direct initiative An initiative that must be submitted directly to voters in a special or general election to approve or reject legislative proposals and requires no action by the legislature.

direct primary A primary that allows voters to select the political party nominees by ballot without any intervening decision by the party organization, as in a convention.

disfranchisement The loss of voting privileges. Convicted felons, those who fail to register during specified time periods, and those who lose their citizenship are examples of people who may be disfranchised. Citizens may be illegally disfranchised, as when African Americans were denied the right to vote in the South following Reconstruction.

dispersal gerrymandering Divides members of an identifiable group into two or more districts so that their votes can no longer determine the outcome of an election. See also **vote dilution.**

donor fatigue   The feeling by many campaign contributors of being co-erced into giving ever-larger sums of money to political campaigns in order to be assured of access to government officials and their conclu-sion that the system is in need of reform in order to protect them from such pressures.

***Dunn v. Blumstein* 405 U.S. 330 (1972)**   In this U.S. Supreme Court case, "durational" (or unusually long) residency requirements for purposes of voting were declared unconstitutional. However, the Court recognized that closing voter registration rolls 30 to 60 days prior to an election could be considered a practical necessity.

Duverger's Law   This "law," drawn from the writings of Maurice Du-verger, holds that the single-member district plurality electoral system favors a strong two-party system such as that in the United States. A more general conclusion is that electoral rules are not necessarily neutral but, rather, may favor a particular outcome.

early money   Contributions made early in a political contest, valued because it allows candidates to build their campaign organizations and gain early media exposure.

early voting   In some states, voters may cast their ballots at designated sites, such as supermarkets and shopping malls, during a period of time prior to election day. Any qualified voter has the option of early voting.

electoral college   The 538 electors who gather in their respective state capitals to cast their vote for president on the first Monday after the sec-ond Wednesday in December of a presidential election year. They offi-cially elect the president and vice president. Every state but Maine and Nebraska follow the unit rule, whereby the candidate who receives the most popular votes in a state wins all that state's electoral votes. Each state has a number of electors equal to the total number of senators and representatives it has in Congress. Each political party nominates a prospective slate of electors, and the slate pledged to the candidate who wins the most popular votes is selected to vote for president and vice president.

electoral vote   See **electoral college.**

equal time rule   A rule stipulating that candidates for public office should be given equal access to free or paid use of television. It was es-tablished and is enforced by the Federal Communications Commission (FCC). If a radio or television broadcast sells time to one political candi-date, the broadcaster must also be willing to sell equal time to opposing candidates.

ethanol tax break   One of several famous (or notorious) tax loopholes, this one was extended by Congress in 1996. It is a subsidy that costs consumers approximately $770 million a year and is particularly beneficial to the Archer-Daniels-Midland agribusiness giant. This company alone contributed almost $750,000 in political action committee money and soft money contributions in 1996.

Ethics in Government Act of 1978   This act requires financial disclosure by senior federal government officials and their families and restricts their outside earned income to 15 percent of their salaries. The act also limits the activities of public officials as representatives before government agencies.

Ethics Reform Act of 1989   This act requires personal financial disclosures from federal candidates.

exit polls   Interviews, often carried out by pollsters and news organizations, of voters immediately after they have finished voting and are leaving the polling place. These exit polls are used to make projections about who will win an election. Sometimes winners of presidential contests have been projected before all the polls close on the West Coast, creating controversy about the practice of exit polling. In order to avoid this problem, some have recommended uniform poll hours across the nation.

fail-safe voting   The practice of allowing individuals to cast a ballot even though their registration status is in question. After an investigation, the ballot will be verified and counted, or invalidated. Critics argue that this practice has led to considerable vote fraud.

faithless elector   An elector in the electoral college who refuses to follow the will expressed by the presidential popular vote and instead casts an electoral vote for another candidate. Most states legally require electors to vote for the candidate to whom they were pledged, although the U.S. Constitution allows them discretion.

fat cat   Term typically used to describe big political contributors who seek political influence or favors in exchange for money. According to *Safire's Political Dictionary,* the expression goes back to the late 1880s, when the use of high-pressure tactics on contributors was called "fat-frying." A leading Republican fund-raiser during that era wrote a letter urging his colleagues to "fry the fat out of the manufacturers."

Federal Election Campaign Act   This 1972 law created contemporary campaign finance rules. The act replaced the old—and widely ignored—Federal Corrupt Practices Act of 1925.

Federal Election Campaign Act of 1974   This amendment to the Federal Election Campaign Act enacted campaign contribution limits on individuals and political action committees as well as expenditure limits on presidential candidates who accepted public financing.

Federal Election Commission (FEC) Created by Congress in the 1974 Federal Election Campaign Act, the FEC monitors compliance with federal election laws. Its authority was limited by *Buckley v. Valeo* in 1976. Campaign organizations and political action committees are required to disclose their contributions and expenditures to the FEC. Those records are public documents that are open to public scrutiny.

federal political committee Any organization or group that makes federal contributions or expenditures (or a combination of both) exceeding $1,000 per year; federal political committees must register with the Federal Election Commission.

Fifteenth Amendment This amendment to the U.S. Constitution, ratified in 1870, officially granted the right to vote to black males.

filing A prospective candidate's legal declaration of his or her intention to run for public office. Many states limit the number of candidate filings by requiring that candidacy petitions be signed by a specified number of registered voters. The prospective candidate must present the petitions and files to an appropriate official (for instance, the secretary of state or county clerk). In some states, individuals may seek candidacy for local office simply by declaring their intentions before a designated official. In other states, a sum of money must also be deposited along with petitions.

foreign national Foreign governments, political parties, corporations, associations, and partnerships; individuals with foreign citizenship; and immigrants not possessing a green card. Foreign nationals are prohibited from making contributions or expenditures to any American election (federal, state, or local), either directly or through another person. The acceptance of contributions from foreign nationals is also prohibited.

franchise The right to vote.

front loading The practice by some states or regions of scheduling their caucuses and presidential primaries early in the season. This practice burdens candidates, forcing them to run in several states at the same time, and it also favors candidates with name recognition and well-financed campaign organizations.

full disclosure A proposed campaign finance reform that would require all candidates to disclose publicly the sources and amounts of all their campaign contributions.

gerrymandering A process by which electoral district boundaries are drawn to enhance the fortunes of a political party or group or to protect incumbents.

grandfather clause A practice used by some southern states following the Reconstruction era, written into state constitutions, bestowing the right to vote or granting immunity from suffrage requirements to those whose ancestors had voted prior to 1867. A major intent of grandfather clauses was to disfranchise black citizens.

hard money   Individual campaign contributions that fall under Federal Election Commission limits. The maximum limit for such hard contributions is $1,000 for an individual per election up to $25,000 per year for all candidates.

Hare system   See **preferential voting** and **single transferable vote.**

Hatch Act   See **Political Activities Act of 1939.**

hatched   A term used to describe those federal government employees whose opportunities for political activity have been limited by the Hatch Act.

inaugural committee   Committee established to raise funds to pay for a president elect's inaugural. Although campaign contributions are regulated by the Federal Election Commission, donations to pay for an inaugural are not. Consequently, inaugural committees are not required to publicly identify contributors. President Clinton's 1992 inaugural committee raised large sums from corporate sponsors. Anheuser-Busch, for example, donated products to the event and contributed $100,000. In fact, this $32 million inaugural was such a success that $9.7 million remained after expenses were paid.

incumbency effect   The inclination of voters generally to support public officials running for reelection, thereby giving incumbents an advantage over challengers. This incumbency effect has many explanations, including the tendency of political action committees to focus contributions on incumbents and the ability of incumbents to use perquisites of office, such as the franking privilege, in their campaigns.

independent expenditures   Expenditures for a candidate by individuals or groups that are not officially coordinated with the candidate's campaign; there is no limit on these expenditures. In 1988 a television ad that attacked Democratic presidential nominee Michael Dukakis by linking him to the parole of convicted murderer and rapist Willie Horton was financed by an $8.5 million independent expenditure garnered by a group of Republican consultants. See also **soft money.**

indirect initiative   An initiative that, after the required number of citizen signatures have been acquired in a petition, goes first to the state legislature for approval and is submitted to voters if the legislature rejects it or suggests a substitute measure.

initiative   A process by which citizens may propose a new law and have it placed on the ballot by petition, which requires signatures of from 5 to 15 percent of the registered voters.

Iowa caucus   This caucus, in which delegates to the national political party nominating convention are selected, is held in February and is the earliest in the presidential election season. A presidential candidate who does well in Iowa is taken more seriously than those who fail there. Some reformers argue that the presidential primary and caucus system should be altered so that less-populous states like Iowa do not have inordinate influence on the nomination process.

IRS checkoff   The box on the federal income tax return that taxpayers may mark if they wish to have three dollars of their tax obligation contributed to the Presidential Election Campaign Fund. Checking the box neither increases any tax due nor reduces any refund due. Public funding of presidential elections has occurred since 1976. Originally the voluntary contribution was one dollar, but it was raised to three dollars in 1994. The checkoff has never been very popular with the public, and consequently the fund has been unable on occasion to provide full payments of matching funds to candidates in presidential primaries.

issue advocacy ads   Ads, run by numerous groups and both political parties, that are outside the U.S. Supreme Court's narrow definition of a political ad as one that explicitly advocates the election or defeat of a political candidate and that consequently may be financed by unlimited and unregulated independent expenditures. Many so-called issue advocacy ads are thinly veiled attacks on specific candidates.

late money   Money that is contributed in the final days or weeks of a campaign; late money may serve as an indicator of candidate momentum in the final days.

leadership PACs   Political action committees (PACs), termed "independent" PACs, that are organized by politicians. They can serve as fronts for a candidate's own campaign fund-raising. For instance, Senator Bob Dole in 1995 disbanded his Better America Foundation, which critics claimed was used to free donors from Federal Election Commission limits or reporting regulations.

limited voting   Employed in voting systems with multimember districts, limited voting is a system in which each voter has at least one vote fewer than the number of positions to be filled. This voting procedure is used in several cities, including Boston, New York, and Philadelphia. Supporters of this voting system claim that it assists members of minority parties or groups to win elections.

literacy test   Supposedly a method to determine an individual's fitness as a voter, literacy tests were used primarily to disfranchise black voters in several states. Prospective voters had to answer a set of questions or interpret constitutional passages to the satisfaction of white voter registration officials. Congress suspended literacy tests in the Voting Rights Act of 1965 and prohibited them in subsequent legislation.

long ballot   A ballot that is literally long because a large number of offices are subject to election. Instituted in some states ostensibly to enhance democratic government, these ballots may cause confusion among voters and lead to uninformed choices.

macing   The practice of levying assessments on public officials' salaries as contributions to campaigns. Prior to reform legislation, political parties would routinely engage in this practice.

majority-minority district   A legislative district that is drawn to enhance opportunities for citizens of a racial or ethnic minority to elect representatives.

malapportionment   The result of a state legislature's drawing of electoral districts so that district populations are very unequal or of failing to redraw district lines when significant population shifts have occurred.

matching funds   Funds that provide public financing of candidates in presidential primaries on an optional basis. The federal government will "match" the first $250 of each contribution to a campaign if candidates observe spending limits imposed by the Federal Election Commission and raise $5,000 in donations of $250 or less in 20 states. Candidates who refuse matching funds, such as billionaire Ross Perot in 1992 and former Texas governor John Connelly in 1976, may spend as much as they like.

McCain-Feingold bill   Campaign finance reform proposed by Senators John McCain and Russell Feingold in the 104th Congress that calls for a ban on soft money and political action committees, closer monitoring of independent expenditures, a prohibition on most bundling, incentives to limit campaign spending such as offering candidates 30 minutes of free broadcast time, raising contribution limits, and banning the use of postal franking privileges for mass mailings by senators and representatives during reelection seasons.

Missouri plan   Originated in Missouri in 1940, this plan, also referred to as merit selection, is a method of selecting state court judges that may take several forms. The most common form is the selection by a nonpartisan nominating commission (usually appointed by the governor and composed of laypersons and persons with legal expertise) of three or more candidates to fill a vacancy on the bench. The governor appoints one of the candidates, who serves for a period of at least one year. After this initial term is served the judicial candidate runs unopposed in a retention election and then serves a normal term of office.

motor-voter bill   See **National Voter Registration Act.**

multimember district   Type of electoral district in which voters elect more than one member to a legislative body.

National Voter Registration Act   Act passed by Congress in 1993, popularly called the motor-voter bill, that facilitates voter registration. The law went into effect in 1995 and requires states to allow voter registration by mail or in person when an eligible citizen applies for a driver's license. Voter registration may also occur at state offices that serve the poor or the disabled.

negative advertising   Advertisements used by candidates to define their opponents, primarily portraying them in a negative light. Negative advertisements not only define an opponent but may also expose weaknesses in an opponent's record. Often opponents respond to negative ads by charging their attackers with mudslinging. Negative advertising has been blamed for increased voter cynicism and low voter turnout.

New Hampshire primary   The first primary election in the presidential election year. Because it is first the New Hampshire primary has become crucial to candidates as they seek political and financial support and momentum. Some reformers see the inflated importance of one state's primary as good reason for changing the presidential primary system.

Nineteenth Amendment   This amendment to the U.S. Constitution, ratified in 1920, granted women the right to vote.

nonpartisan election   An election that occurs at the local level (for instance, for judges, members of a board of education, or positions on a city council) and allows a candidate to run for office without indicating a political party affiliation.

office block ballot   A general election ballot that groups all the candidates under the office for which they are running. It places more emphasis on the office and may discourage straight ticket voting. Those who oppose party voting (or straight ticket voting) consider the office block ballot a desirable election reform.

one person, one vote   The principle that when legislative reapportionment occurs the districts must be apportioned on the basis of population—no one district should be much larger than another in population—therefore ensuring that no person's vote counts more than anyone else's. This principle was enunciated in *Reynolds v. Sims* 377 U.S. 533 (1964).

open primary   A type of primary in which voters may determine on election day in which political party's nominating election they will participate.

opportunity district   In an argument before the U.S. Supreme Court in 1995, an attorney who favored majority-minority districts referred to them as "opportunity districts." Justice Antonin Scalia found the phrase objectionable. Scalia stated that the term was emotionally loaded and that he much preferred the phrase "majority-minority district."

packing   See **concentration gerrymandering.**

participatory democracy   A type of democracy in which individuals and groups are directly involved in political decision making. Citizens formulate policy without representatives serving as buffers between them and the political system, such as in New England town meetings.

party boss   A political leader who has an extraordinary amount of control over a state or local party organization and retains power through patronage, graft, and the manipulation of election procedures and voting behavior. The direct primary, civil service reform, and a more literate electorate have diminished bossism.

party column ballot   This general election ballot lists all candidates for elective office under their party label and symbol, thereby making it easier for voters to select a straight ticket or to vote for all candidates from one party by pulling a single lever on the voting machine.

Pendleton Act (Civil Service Reform Act of 1883)   This act created the Civil Service Commission and introduced considerations of merit into federal hiring and firing policies, thus limiting the patronage the political parties could award to faithful campaign workers.

plurality system   An electoral procedure in which a candidate for public office can win an election by receiving more votes than any other candidate without necessarily securing a majority of votes cast. The plurality winner may not receive a majority of votes if more than two candidates are competing for the position. Those supporting greater minority representation advocate a plurality rather than a majority requirement in primary elections.

political action committees (PACs)   PACs collect money from their membership and donate it to political candidates and parties. Although not officially recognized until the 1974 Federal Election Campaign Act, PACs have existed since 1943 when the Congress of Industrial Organizations formed a separate committee to avoid the ban on contributions from labor unions. Under current federal law, a PAC may give up to $5,000 to a federal candidate during the primaries and another $5,000 during the general election.

Political Activities Act of 1939   Also known as the Hatch Act, this legislation forbade political activity by federal employees, limited individual contributions to a political committee to $5,000, and made it illegal for a political action committee to spend more than $3 million in any campaign.

political apathy   By failing to vote or take an interest in public affairs, a person might be labeled apathetic. Political apathy may indicate satisfaction with the political process or it may represent alienation and despair.

Some point to political apathy as a reason for reforming the electoral system and using "get out the vote" drives and other mobilization techniques to increase interest and participation.

political editorializing rule Federal Communication Commission requirement that if a broadcaster endorses a political candidate, the broadcaster must give the opposing candidate the right to reply. This is not the same as the fairness doctrine policy, now abandoned, which required radio and television broadcasters to allow all sides on public issues equal access to public airwaves.

political machine A local or state political party organization that is characterized by highly centralized leadership control over member activity. The organization recruits members through patronage and dispensing of favors. One of the objectives of reform crusades such as the Progressive movement was to minimize the influence of political machines.

poll tax A tax once required of citizens, mostly in southern states, who wished to register to vote; ostensibly instituted to pay election costs, it was intended to discourage blacks and poor whites from voting. Although the sum of the poll tax was relatively small, the states that used it could up the ante by requiring an individual to pay back taxes for past elections in which they had not voted—thereby increasing the taxes due. In 1964 the Twenty-fourth Amendment prohibited poll taxes in federal elections. Poll taxes were declared unconstitutional in all elections, federal and state, by the 1966 Supreme Court decision *Harper v. Virginia State Board of Elections.*

poll watcher Poll watchers observe voting practices and procedures during elections, usually on behalf of a political party or candidate. They attempt to foster proper behavior and may report irregularities.

precinct The smallest subdivision used for organizing the vote in elections. Most precincts contain fewer than 1,000 voters and serve as the basic unit for building political party organizations. The introduction of at-large elections lessened the importance of precincts.

preclearance See **Voting Rights Acts.**

preference primary See **advisory primary.**

preferential ballot A ballot that is not binding and may be used in an advisory capacity. For example, in a presidential primary of this type, the voters inform the delegates to the national nominating conventions of their nonbinding preferences.

preferential voting In a preferential voting system, electors rank candidates from first choice to last. The system is employed in a version of proportional representation. The candidate with the least number of first-place votes is declared defeated and those who designated him or her as their first choice will have their second-choice votes distributed among the remaining candidates. This process continues until all seats have been filled.

presidential primaries Statewide elections that give rank-and-file party members an opportunity to select the delegates to their party's national nominating convention. In the last 30 years these primaries have become increasingly important to the ultimate selection of party candidates. The large financial resources and the time and energy presidential hopefuls must devote to primaries that are conducted by individual states from February through June of presidential election years has led to proposals for reforms such as holding a few regional presidential primaries.

primary election An election held before the general election to nominate a political party's candidates for office. Primary elections are held for state and federal offices.

Progressive movement A movement in American politics that reached its peak in the early twentieth century with the creation of the Progressive party in 1911. The Progressives believed that governing institutions could "progress" if science were applied to public problems. They were a disparate group of reformers who advocated a number of successful reforms, including the civil service system; the direct primary; the initiative, referendum, and recall; and nonpartisan municipal elections.

proportional representation In proportional representation (PR) systems seats to the legislature are allocated according to each party or group's popular voting strength. For example, a minor party that receives 10 percent of the popular vote will win roughly 10 percent of the legislative seats. PR has taken many forms, although there are two major types: the list system, in which political parties receive legislative seats in proportion to their popular vote, and the single transferable vote, which employs preferential voting.

public financing (general election funding) The presidential nominees of each major party are eligible for a public grant, the amount of which is determined by a cost-of-living adjustment, if they limit their spending to the amount of the grant and do not accept private contributions for the campaign (with the exception of paying for legal expenses or spending up to $50,000 of their own personal funds). Minor party candidates may qualify for partial public funding if they receive 5 percent or more of the popular vote in the election. This reform measure applies only to presidential elections. So far Congress has failed to establish a public financing system for elections to the U.S. House of Representatives and Senate. However, some states have instituted public financing for selected political offices, such as governor, other executive branch offices, and state legislative seats.

push-polling   Considered by many an unethical practice, push-polling occurs when pollsters call potential voters in the guise of a legitimate public opinion survey but with the actual intent of persuading people to support a particular candidate.

reapportionment   The new apportionment (or reapportionment) of congressional seats that occurs every ten years. Each state is assigned a new number of congressional seats based on U.S. Census data on changes in state population. Reapportionment results in redistricting, which is the redrawing of congressional district boundaries. Periodic reapportionment is also required of representative bodies such as state legislatures and county commissions.

recall   An election, allowed in some states, for removing elected officials from office before their terms expire. Typically at least 25 percent of voters in the previous election must sign a petition indicating their desire to remove the official.

redistricting   Under redistricting, state legislatures must redraw congressional district boundaries in response to a reapportionment of congressional seats among the states. See also **malapportionment** and **reapportionment.**

referendum   A procedure by which a law or constitutional amendment proposed by the legislature is submitted directly to the voters for approval.

regional primary   During the presidential primary season, a geographically contiguous group of states hold their primary elections on the same day. Some reformers have recommended a system of regional primaries organized at the national level in order to shorten the primary season and lessen the influence of primaries held in less-populous states early in the season.

repeat voting   See **repeating.**

repeating   The illegal practice of voting more than once in the same election. It was used extensively during the era of urban political machines. Accusations occasionally surface today that repeat voting occurs to assist a candidate in winning an election.

residence voting   A voting qualification based on where a citizen resides. Lengthy residency requirements were declared unconstitutional by the U.S. Supreme Court in 1972. The Voting Rights Act of 1970 specified that states could require no more than 30 days' residence for citizens to be eligible and vote in presidential elections.

responsible party government Responsible party government places emphasis on party discipline and accountability of political parties to voters. In a responsible party government, political parties give their support to party objectives and platforms and offer voters "a choice, not an echo." Some reformers argue that significant improvement in the American electoral process requires implementation of this model.

results test A part of 1982 revisions to the Voting Rights Act, the results test emphasizes the potential discriminatory outcomes of electoral arrangements, rather than the intent of lawmakers, in determining the acceptability of changes in voting rules.

retrogression A decline in minority representation, a phenomenon that, under the Voting Rights Act, should not occur.

Revenue Act of 1971 This act authorized a voluntary one-dollar check-off on federal income tax returns in an effort to create public financing of major political party candidates for president.

runoff election Election required by some states, particularly in primaries, if no one candidate receives a majority of votes. Minority candidates and interest group representatives have criticized runoff elections, arguing that minority candidates who may be successful in achieving a plurality in the first election cannot win the runoff election.

short ballot A ballot containing only a small number of elective offices for voters to fill. Short ballots are advocated as a means to simplify elections and allow voters to make more intelligent choices.

short counting A type of vote fraud, available to dishonest election judges or tellers, in which vote totals are intentionally misreported in order to benefit a favored candidate. The appointment of poll watchers to oversee the ballot-counting process can discourage short counting.

single-member district Any electoral district that elects only one candidate, based on a plurality of votes, to an office. Voter choices are more restricted compared to a multimember district. However, if a system of proportional representation is not used with multimember districts, the single-member district provides greater opportunities for minority representation.

single transferable vote A type of proportional representation that employs preferential voting and the transfer of second-choice votes from a losing candidate to the remaining contenders.

Smith v. Allwright **321 U.S. 649 (1944)** In this case the U.S. Supreme Court ruled that white primaries violated the Fifteenth Amendment. Previously the Court had ruled that political parties or private organizations could exclude anyone they wished, including blacks, from membership. In this case the Court ruled that parties were performing a state function and hence could not exclude anyone from membership.

smoke-filled room   When political bosses reigned supreme, the smoke-filled room became the stereotypical image of any place where political bargaining and deal making occurred. In days gone by, the bosses would decide who to nominate to run as candidates under the party label. The phrase definitely carries a sinister, undemocratic connotation.

soft money   Contributions that are not subject to Federal Election Commission limits. These funds may be used for such activities as "get out the vote" and voter registration campaigns and party-building efforts. Soft money includes funds that are not spent on behalf of a specific candidate for federal office. Considered a loophole in federal election law, soft money enables parties to raise huge amounts of money through contributions to state party committees and the "nonfederal" bank accounts of the Democratic and Republican National Committees.

solid South   Phrase used by V. O. Key, Jr., referring to the fact that at one time the South voted consistently and uniformly Democratic. Voters in the solid South were overwhelmingly white because discriminatory registration laws and intimidation tactics were used to discourage blacks from voting. The Democratic party's advocacy of equal rights for blacks is cited as one of the pivotal explanations for why the South is no longer "solid."

special election   An election held to fill an office that an incumbent has vacated before the term expires.

straight ticket voting   Voting only for candidates of the same political party. The party column facilitates, and the office block ballot discourages, straight ticket voting.

targeting   A technique, used by political action committees, of identifying particular members of the U.S. Congress for defeat and channeling campaign funds to their opponents.

Tasmanian dodge   A form of illegal voting, also called the endless chain, in which a bribed voter returns a blank paper ballot to a candidate's worker, who marks the ballot appropriately and gives it to another voter who agrees to cast it and return with the blank ballot he received at the polls. In this way, unscrupulous politicians can assure that bribed voters vote as promised.

term limits   Restrictions on the number of terms a public official may serve consecutively in office. The Twenty-second Amendment, ratified in 1951, limited presidents to two terms or no more than ten years of service. More recently many Americans have supported term limits for members of Congress and state legislatures. The term limits movement, which gained momentum in the late 1980s and early 1990s, has lobbied strongly for such limits.

Twelfth Amendment   This amendment to the U.S. Constitution, ratified in 1804, requires that electors vote separately for president and vice president. The development of political parties after 1787 led to this change in the original system of electing the president.

Twenty-fourth Amendment   This amendment to the U.S. Constitution, ratified in 1964, eliminated the use of poll taxes in federal elections.

Twenty-sixth Amendment   This amendment to the U.S. Constitution, ratified in 1971, extended the right to vote to citizens between the ages of 18 and 20. Prior to this amendment, 21 was the legal voting age in most states.

Twenty-third Amendment   This amendment to the U.S. Constitution, ratified in 1961, gave residents of the District of Columbia the right to vote in presidential elections.

two-party system   A system in which two parties dominate the electoral process. Because candidates in the United States generally run in single-member districts with a plurality vote required for victory, a two-party system is reinforced. Third parties are discouraged under such electoral arrangements because voters tend to conclude that their votes will be wasted if they vote for candidates who have little chance of winning a plurality of the popular vote.

vote dilution   The result of efforts to limit a group's voting strength by reducing its ability to influence or elect public officials of their choice. The dispersal gerrymander is an obvious way to dilute a group's vote strength.

voter fatigue   See **voter roll-off.**

voter registration   A procedure required of prospective voters and used to establish their identity and place of residence prior to an election so that they are certified as eligible to vote in a precinct. The purpose of voter registration is to diminish opportunities for election-day vote fraud. However, some reformers argue that the registration requirement significantly decreases voter turnout when otherwise eligible citizens fail to register.

voter roll-off   Voter roll-off, or ballot roll-off, is the failure of voters to make selections for offices beyond the more prominent offices at the top of the ticket. For example, they vote for president, U.S. Senator, and governor but may fail to vote for lesser offices such as judges, school board officials, and county commissioners. Long ballots may induce voter roll-off.

Voting Rights Acts The original Voting Rights Act of 1965 was amended in 1970, 1975, and 1982. The Voting Rights Act and subsequent revisions and amendments require preclearance of all proposed changes in voting laws by the attorney general or the federal District Court of the District of Columbia if a jurisdiction has a history of low minority electoral participation. The act and subsequent amendments banned literacy tests nationwide and required bilingual voting ballots in 24 states.

Watergate Term referring to the break-in at the Democratic national party headquarters in the Watergate building complex in Washington, D.C., by individuals affiliated with the Committee to Reelect the President and the subsequent cover-up efforts of Richard Nixon's administration. Other acts associated with the Watergate scandal included illegal use of the Central Intelligence Agency, the Federal Bureau of Investigation, the Internal Revenue Service, and other governmental agencies for partisan purposes; employment of dirty tricks during the 1972 election campaign; and receipt of illegal campaign contributions and their use for purposes unrelated to the campaign. Watergate is partially responsible for triggering campaign finance reform in 1974.

white primary Primaries instituted in southern states in the early twentieth century that either forbade or discouraged black participation in primary elections. Because the Democratic party dominated southern politics at that time, excluding blacks from the party primary amounted to disfranchisement. Also see *Smith v. Allwright.*

Index

Glenn H. Utter, professor and chair of the Political Science Department at Lamar University, was educated at Binghamton University, the University of Buffalo, and the University of London. Utter specializes in modern political theory and American political thought. He coedited *American Political Scientists: A Dictionary* (1993), coauthored *The Religious Right* (1995), another book in the Contemporary World Issues series, and has written a number of articles for political science journals.

Ruth Ann Strickland, associate professor of political science at Appalachian State University, received her Ph.D. from the University of South Carolina. She coauthored *The Constitution under Pressure* (1987) and has written several articles for political science journals.